D1186983

KEEPERS OF THE
KINGDOM

KEEPERS OF THE KINGDOM

THE ANCIENT OFFICES OF BRITAIN

ALASTAIR BRUCE

PHOTOGRAPHS BY
JULIAN CALDER
AND MARK CATOR

WEIDENFELD & NICOLSON

'One should appreciate, after all, the advantages of one's origins. Its worth lies in the power it gives one to detach oneself from the present moment.'

ALBERT CAMUS

706652
MORAY COUNCIL
Department of Technical
& Leisure Services
394·4

First published in the United Kingdom in 1999 by Weidenfeld & Nicolson

Text copyright © Alastair Bruce, 1999
Photographs copyright © Julian Calder and Mark Cator, 1999
Design and layout copyright © Weidenfeld & Nicolson, 1999

The moral right of Alastair Bruce to be identified as the author of this work has been asserted in accordance with the Copyright, Designs and Patents Act of 1988

All rights reserved. No part of this publication may be reproduced in any material form (including photocopying or storing it in any medium by electronic means and whether or not transiently or incidentally to some other use of this publication) without the written permission of the copyright owner, except in accordance with the provisions of the Copyright, Designs and Patents Act 1988 or under the terms of a licence issued by the Copyright Licensing Agency, 90 Tottenham Court Road, London W1P 9HE. Applications for the copyright owner's written permission to reproduce any part of this publication should be addressed to the publisher.

The picture acknowledgements on p. 220 constitute an extension to this copyright page

A CIP catalogue record for this book is available from the British Library
ISBN 0 297 82456 2

Art Direction by David Rowley
Designed by Nigel Soper
Typeset in Perpetua
Printed and bound in Italy

Weidenfeld & Nicolson
Illustrated Division
The Orion Publishing Group
Wellington House
125 Strand
London WC2R 0BB

Previous page left: **Page of Honour to the Queen**. Originally a position of cadetship for those destined for powerful positions within the court.

Previous page right: The **Earl Marshal** and hereditary Marshal of England is the nation's master of ceremonies. State Occasions are his remit, and pageantry his 'bread and butter'. Once he would have helped command troops in battle; today his baton is wielded to choreograph the State's greatest occasions.

Right: The tiny Thistle Chapel in St Giles's Cathedral, Edinburgh, has just enough room for the sixteen **Knight Brothers of the Thistle** to meet in conclave with the Sovereign and officers of the Order and is full of heraldic symbolism. The star is based on St Andrew's cross, which legend says appeared in a vision to the Scots and Picts before they inflicted defeat on the West Saxons. St Andrew holding his cross is appended from the collar, made of golden thistles and rue sprigs.

Next page: Scotland's **Historiographer Royal** in the Scottish Record Office.

CONTENTS

INTRODUCTION
unwrapping the clues

HISTORY HAS LEFT ITS MARK all around Britain. The story of these islands can be read in scars that mark the landscape, in buildings, in institutions, in documents, books and pictures, and in the wealth of archives. But it is also brought to life, uniquely, in the people who hold titles, names and appointments: jobs that were created over fifteen hundred years in response to the changing needs of the islands and their inhabitants.

This unique collection of clues vested in living people encouraged us to compile this book. We found them primarily through conversation – sometimes dismissive, sometimes admiring, often uncomprehending – and through newspaper articles and obituaries, that told stories of people who hold appointments that offer a clue to Britain's past. Often these holders had no idea themselves about the beginnings of the chain in which they are the most recent link. Time has changed the profile and purpose of most of these jobs, but in each case there was once an indisputable utilitarian need for their foundation and it is in that discovery that the true value of each can be found. Just as today the government have decided to appoint a Children's Laureate and an Inspector of Her Majesty's Prisons in order to meet needs, so Odo Earl of Kent was appointed by his half-brother William the Conqueror to run England's finances as Treasurer. The Treasurer's post has evolved into First Lord of the Treasury, and is held today by the Prime Minister.

This living collection of odd titles, names and appointments acts like stepping stones into the nation's history. Each tells a story from the post-Roman invasions, through the evolution of nations, their union and their shared empire that grew around the world before shrinking back. Most no longer have any power but they have survived as vestiges of the past because there has been no need to destroy them.

One reason for this is that since 1066 Britain has never suffered invasion and no revolution has ever completely swept the old order aside. Even Cromwell's Commonwealth was followed by a Restoration of much that had been swept away: not least the monarchy, which has run as a continuous thread through the story of the kingdom. As a result, a rare group of men and women still carry the relay batons of a living history among us today. Much survives because monarchy survives. Just as there is still a Chancellor of the Exchequer, there is also a Lord High Admiral of the Wash. While the Chancellor performs a clear utilitarian role within the constitution, the Lord High Admiral no longer has any purpose; however, as with most of the surviving titles, his work was once vital to the needs of England. His responsibility was to keep the coastline safe from invasion when this shore was vulnerable. In the sixteenth century, reassessment of the situation indicated that the Admiral's duties were no longer relevant: those requirements are now met by an RAF AWACS aeroplane. However, the Admiral's family were never told the job was off. There was no need. And nor was there a revolution that demanded a cultural cleansing of the past; instead, succeeding events have concealed history as weeds gradually grow over a deserted building. Rediscovering clues such as these offers a chance to recall the testing path taken by our ancestors to wrest power from kings, to place it in parliament and, eventually, in parliamentary democracy.

Today's Admiral has no illusions of grandeur about his historic appointment: far from it. But he does not forget that the land he works was given by a medieval king to his ancestors, along with the vital task of keeping watch from the cliffs. Should this provenance slip his memory, the local church is filled with tombs which are silent witnesses to his inheritance. Without proactive legislation to the contrary, it would seem that this Admiralty, a piece of interesting historical detritus, will survive: an interesting, cost-free and living clue to part of our history and culture.

While Britain is reflecting upon its own identity – a process which may lead ultimately to its dissolution into separate historic states within a European federation – reaction to these clues from the past are mixed. To some, the sight of men and women in ceremonial costume or fulfilling some odd ritual provokes a negative reaction. Such things are laughable because they seem irrelevant, or worse: they are seen to demonstrate that Britain is backward looking, arcane and obsessed with the fripperies of snobs in bobs. The media is often quick to fuel this derision and, at a time when post-imperial Britain has lost some of her confidence, these things are ripe as grist to the approaching millennium's mill of reassessment.

Titles are an easy target. Without them the nation will rise refreshed from the burden of its class history. By simplifying and modernizing appointments and eradicating symbols Britain will be a better place, more at ease, and equipped for tomorrow. It would be better if the Chancellor of the Exchequer were relabelled simply as Finance Minister, the First Sea Lord's archaic name were dropped in favour of the true title Chief of Staff (Navy). The Queen's Champion has no contemporary relevance and so should not be referred to any more, and the Court Leet of Alcester (whose historic powers are now vested in the hands of locally elected representatives) should no longer meet as it is redundant and anachronistic.

Not everyone accepts that these changes would enable Britain to operate more effectively or even that they would offer any benefit at all. Arguably, if power is where the democratic wishes of the country require it to be then, if there is still confidence, there can be no possible harm in the survival of traditions that enable us to understand our past. Such vestiges would be valued and urgently preserved if threatened in another part of the world. In revolutions, statues are torn down along with everything else, but later a time comes to raise them again because it was not the statues that created the need for change: instead their relevance grows as a reminder of the history that caused rebellion.

Britain possesses something that many other countries envy. Even in places which celebrate cultures far older, it is understood that preserving history within an evolving and competitive structure provides a valuable living fingerprint: one which has touched more than most people realize. This print survives because, so far, the country has modernized and evolved without feeling the need to rid itself of the past: it may often dislike that past, even detest it, but confidence in the present and future are best measured by a country's ability to live both, while at ease with its history. So we have an intricate pattern which has been formed by generations from which we all descend. To destroy it would be painful, leave a mess and improve little. China's revolution wrought such an upheaval: overnight, centuries of history and culture were destroyed. Those can never be revived, any more than the dead can be restored to life. In the ideological revolution the lessons of the past were lost; China is struggling to recreate itself, and few Chinese will ever know and understand their provenance or the rich culture from which they descend. The nations that formed Britain wisely maintained their individual identities at the time of their respective unions; these remain available to be recollected.

People generally enjoy a good story. While some traditions, and historical appointments, often appear utterly bizarre, if they are explained and the anecdotes associated with their evolution are recounted, people usually find sympathy with and accept them. This is particularly true when most of these appointments have either evolved into very different full-time roles today, or survive at no pecuniary cost. However, over the past fifty years, as the wider public have become increasingly well informed and the means of communication have improved, little has been done to share these stories or to explain why things happen. In fact, the opposite has often been the case. Some events, which are enactments of the difficult evolution of the constitution, remain closed to the wider community. The participants seem to forget that their privilege involves a responsibility to explain and share openly the significance of their roles and the ceremonies themselves. Sensing opposition, institutions have tended to close their doors. This closing of ranks, which seems like keeping sweets for the few, has rightly earned the indignation of an excluded public. This is particularly the case when it appears that great moments in the life of the State, which is us all, remain exclusive and inaccessible: they are no longer the collective preserve of the nation but the privileged indulgence of the few. If these events fail to communicate to all of us they lose their purpose, and then the history that they symbolize becomes alienated from the people whose inheritance it is.

Perhaps because of recent trends towards populist politics, the monarchy, which derives its authority both from popular will and from the same history that gave life to the other appointments in this book, does not seem to understand and cherish historic titles: they do not fit into its current strategy. While many within its wider structure encouraged the aims of this work, those responsible for image refused access, stressing that 'current presentation of the Royal Household's work is focused on the present and the future'. As a result, a number who hold fascinating honorary appointments with history to share were discouraged from becoming involved with this book.

Every title-holder who trusted in the value of the past as an illuminator of the present and stepped into the theatre of these pages has overcome this reserve and taken on the responsibility of sharing the history that, for their lifetime, it is their privilege to carry. It was not always an easy decision for people to make. Theirs is the story of the nations and communities that presently form the United Kingdom of Great Britain and Northern Ireland. It is our story, and through its telling we can understand our own past.

1
FIRST STEPS
from the first beginnings to AD 1150

BRITAIN'S CIVILIZATION developed from seeds that germinated in the disorder left by Rome's withdrawal at the onset of the fifth century. This disintegration of unity with its tribal power struggles was further stirred by the arrival of barbarian immigrants from the continent. These included Angles, Jutes and Saxons, all of whom landed in pioneering warlike bands driven by territorial ambitions and a similar determination to survive. With them came diverse religious cultures that collided and combined with those of the indigenous Celts and Britons. Consequently, by the century's close, Scotland, Ireland, Wales and England were all subdivided into armed camps. Just as the survival instinct had driven migration and expansion, so it came to seek the return to order. Thus the evolution from anarchy to structure began; through force of power these tribal kingdoms were united, religions struggled for supremacy and administration was reintroduced.

Power was the key to forming unity from anarchy. The leaders who emerged were mostly proven warriors who held sway for as long as they were victorious. This changed in the four centuries that followed as brawn gave way to statecraft and a structure of kingdoms developed known as the Heptarchy. Each king demonstrated his power by patronage, granting wealth and privilege as a reward for good work, crudely but efficiently forming a loyal administration founded on the understanding that what was given could be taken away. The Heptarchic kingdoms developed systems for passing power from generation to generation. Religion justified heredity, and the patronage distributed was granted with similar rights of inheritance.

'Reeves' (administrators of land for the owner) were the most successful of those appointed by the Saxon kings to enforce their rule. Among them were shire reeves (sheriffs), who enforced the law, gathered revenues and made a profit for themselves. A structure of devolved responsibility enabled the increase of wealth and land among the most successful, and it also formed a more cohesive society based on a balance of responsibility in which all participated.

The *Anglo Saxon Chronicle* records regular invasions of Viking warriors, who settled wherever they could land, particularly among the islands of Scotland and north-west England. The Isle of Man was one such strategic location, providing easy raiding access to the wealthy shores of England and Ireland.

With the end of the time of chaos went the beliefs of the ancients. However, evidence of pre-pagan rituals, particularly those of Druidism, survive in enigmatic monuments such as Stonehenge, and the movement has been revived to celebrate that lost culture. The archbishops of Canterbury and York carry with their appointments the history of the missionaries who brought Christianity to the Saxon courts. In Scotland, Ireland and Wales, Saints Columba, Patrick and David have also placed their indelible print upon offices that follow.

The Heptarchy that had ultimately unified under the kings of Wessex enshrined a democracy, albeit limited, in the Witenagemot that surrounded the king with counsellors. St Dunstan, in a design of supreme balance, devised a coronation ceremony that placed the king's authority subject to God, granted only with the Witen's will. The Church thrived, as did the sheriffs. The influence of feudal government touched everything. It was this, and England's agrarian riches, that the Duke of Normandy won by conquest in 1066, although he ensured that the Witen approved his claim and was careful that Dunstan's ritual was used at his coronation.

William the Conqueror then used his power to dominate a defeated people. Ultimate feudal authority was his because the country belonged to him alone. All land was held subject to his will and terms. Successful Norman knights were rewarded with manors and acreage, and in return, they became responsible for enforcing William's laws, gathering his dues and providing whatever services he might demand. This duty was called sergeanty.

Government with reference to a council continued under Norman kings, though the Saxon magnates were soon 'cleansed' from the Witen and Normans formed a new *Curia Regis*. The Byzantines had developed a feudal system of government distributing royal authority to great officers of State. William I adopted this system. The Great Officers of State are still part of the constitutional arrangements in both England and Scotland. The Steward's power became so great that, since the fourteenth century, it is only vested for the day of coronation in each reign; the Lord High Chancellor, a secretary in Norman times, came to be the executive's principal representative in Parliament: this remains the most senior of the Great Officers. The Marshal, originally right-hand man to the Constable in handling military matters, is now Earl Marshal and remains the architect for England's greatest State occasions. The Chamberlain looked after personal administration, and the Almoner maintained the monarch's obligation to pass on largesse, reflecting Christian duties of charity. All these roles have survived, though it is only at coronations that all of them are gathered together to perform a role: they ensure that the monarch to be crowned is the selection of the country, according to law, and then, after the crowning, they 'lift' the Sovereign into the Chair of Estate. This is the symbolic moment when possession is taken of the kingdom.

The Crusades launched Christianity as a militarily potent political force in Europe. The pope's call to arms was answered by Norman England, and the Templar and Hospitaller orders established themselves while other religious institutions, founded for the more traditional purposes of caring for the elderly, such as the Hospital of St Cross, continued to distribute alms from the Church's wealth.

Forests, common ground under the Saxons, became private playgrounds for the king, and at both Savernake and the New Forest wardens were appointed to enforce unique Forest Laws. While the king was hunting, Norman knights took their leisure colonizing further territory; when the treaty with Wales expired, the small, mountainous principality was ripe for conquest. The king supported the Marcher Barons in their quest to seize power and wealth in new territory and became one as well. As with England's Heptarchy, the gathering of so many independents spelled danger; not until Edward I was Wales to be united under royal authority.

Roman order dissolved into chaos and leaders emerged to territorially and spiritually unify the land under one system of effective royal government. The Saxons and Normans in these first steps established appointments to develop and administer the land. As the structure was feudal the appointments were broadly territorial and derived their authority and their titular names from the land. Agricultural revenue was administered so that it passed in feu from the peasant farmer up through the chain of tenants to the king. In time of crisis the king could demand soldiers as well.

The Conqueror's feudalism, based on the Byzantine Court, used great officers to govern the kingdom. This was mirrored with a similar grouping of officers at every level down to the Manor: a system for devolving power effectively at both national and local level that was to be the norm for seven centuries.

The evolution of power from the hands of many leaders into those of a single king followed a predictable path. Supremacy was attained gradually by treaty, defeat and consent. It depended upon loyalty, and rested upon the need for legitimate status and heritable continuity. This right to wield power and patronage was ultimately legitimized by God; and the Queen's motto *Dieu et mon Droit*, 'God and my right', still echoes this idea today.

Druids at Stonehenge.

The Sovereign

BRITAIN'S MONARCHY sparked from the smouldering ruins of Rome's empire, which reached into the British Isles but never conquered them all. During its decline opportunities were seized by barbarian tribes from the German plains. Unable to hold back these warrior hordes, Rome retreated, withdrawing its legions, its governors and its reputation to the comforts of its doomed civilization. Britain was left in 409 to be picked over by an unending stream of invaders, including Picts, Scots, Attacotti, Franks, Jutes and Saxons.

One such invasion force, a group of Saxons led by Cerdic, landed on Hampshire's coast in 495. Cerdic founded the kingdom of the West Saxons (Wessex) in 519, and his direct descendant, Elizabeth II, continues the unbroken line of succession that he established, which follows the evolution of kingship from warrior chief to constitutional figurehead.

Cerdic, like many rulers from the continent, claimed his own legitimacy by descent from the God-king Woden, his eight times great grandfather. Without this genealogy, pagan society would have had little reason to respect one man in preference over another. It was a period of warfare when communities survived according to their combined strength and successful leadership. The order of precedence in this anarchy was hammered out by brawn and military prowess.

For most of the second half of the first millennium AD, a mass of small kingdoms, known as the Heptarchy, divided Angle Land (or England). When early Christian missionaries came to convert these dispersed monarchs, they recognized that credible authority was vital if they were to oust the legitimacy which Woden's ancestry already gave kings in this pagan world. To elevate and separate kings, the new Church offered a cocktail mixed from pagan practice and Biblical text: the sacrament of God's unction. With Holy Oil, the Sovereign, or supreme leader, was anointed as God's vicegerent on earth, just as

Zadok and Nathan had anointed Solomon. This conversion was further justified by a genealogical table in the *Anglo Saxon Chronicle*, written around 840, which extends a further fifteen generations beyond Woden to Sceaf, the son of Noah and thence to 'Adam the first man and our Father, that is Christ, Amen'.

Offa, king of the Mercians in the eighth century, was the first ruler to claim all England under his rule, as *Rex Totius Anglorum Patriae*. But Wessex was flourishing, and in 973, when St Dunstan crowned Edgar the Peaceable according to rites observed nearly one thousand years later for the Queen, he was recognized as Emperor of Britain. As a mark of fealty, he was symbolically rowed on the River Dee by the eight Tributary Princes, including Kenneth of Scotland, Malcolm of Cumberland, M'Orvie of Anglesea and the Isles, Jukil of Westmorland, Iago of Galloway, and Howel, Dyfnwel and Griffith, the Princes of Wales. Edgar assumed the tiller and said, 'When my successors can command the service of the like number of Princes, let them consider themselves Kings.'

The Normans cleverly grasped the rituals of Saxon kingship to bring legitimacy to their coup. The Conqueror styled himself *Willelmus Rex Anglorum*, his son prefixing this for the first time with *Dei Gratia*, which spelled out a claim to God's specific patronage. Variously the title is added to with dukedoms of Normandy and Aquitaine; lordship over Ireland is claimed by John; and Edward III claims France through his mother, as *Rex Angliae et Franciae*. A well-written book earned Henry VIII the suffix *Fidei Defensor* (Defender of the Faith) from the pope; however, statesmanship and marital policy saw his title inflate to include 'of the Church of England on Earth Supreme Head'. He was also the first sovereign to be styled as 'Majesty'.

Elizabeth I included Ireland as a kingdom. The list of kingdoms was completed in 1603 with Scotland, when James VI came south to claim his Tudor cousin's titles.

'The Sovereign is first in honour, dignity, and in power — and the seat and fountain of all three.'

DEBRETTS PEERAGE

For the first time since Edgar the Peaceable, the Act of Union in 1707 confirmed Great Britain back into the title. Claims to France and Aquitaine were dropped in 1801, and in 1837, when Victoria became queen, the Hanoverian monarchy slipped away under Salic Law. However, the growing Empire brought its rewards in 1877, with the imperial title of India, and in 1927, 'the British Dominions beyond the Seas' embraced an empire over which the sun never set.

Today, as each coin in England, Wales and Northern Ireland still shows, Cerdic's direct successor is styled Elizabeth the Second, by the grace of God of the United Kingdom of Great Britain and Northern Ireland, Queen, Head of the Commonwealth, Defender of the Faith, *D·G·REG·F·D·* (*dei gratia regina fidei defensor*). In Scotland she is shown only as Elizabeth, as Elizabeth I did not reign over that kingdom.

The Sovereign in Parliament. Monarchs have ruled through councils since Saxon times. Gatherered around the throne are the Great Officers of State, Law Lords, Peers of the Realm, members of the Court of St James and Members of the House of Commons. Parliaments have always been summoned for a reason. As Elizabeth II now rules as a constitutional monarch the agenda is drafted by Her government.

'Here Edgar was (of Angles wielder!) with mickle pomp to king yhallowed in the old borough Acheman's-chester, but those that dwell there in other word Bath name it. There was bliss mickle on that happy day caused to all which sons of men name and call Pentecost-day. There was of priests a heap, of monks much crowd, I understand, of wise ones gathered. And then was gone ten hundred winters told of rime (number) from the birth-tide of the illustrious king, the Lord of Light, but that there left then yet was of winter-tale, as writings say, seven and twenty; so nigh then was of the Lord of Glory a thousand run when this befell. And Edmund's son had nine and twenty (brave man of deeds!) winters in world when this took place: and in the thirtieth was hallowed king.'

ANGLO SAXON CHRONICLE

High Sheriff of the Bailiwick of Norfolk

ROBIN HOOD WAS THE FIRST great folk hero whom the people of England took to their hearts. Not by accident was his struggle with the Sheriff of Nottingham, for that was where power was vested in medieval times, but it was also where it was most frequently corrupted. The king's power within each shire rested almost without check in the sheriff's hands; he had responsibility to preside over the shire court in the absence of the earl, preserve the king's peace by means of powers to arrest and imprison criminals, collect taxes and fines, raise and lead the local fighting force (*posse comitates*) and enforce regulations as to trade, currency, weights and measures, fairs and markets. To the simple yeoman, he was the embodiment of all authority. With power over life and death, it is no wonder that Robin of Loxley's heroic spirit, as a maverick independent, took root in their imagination.

Towards the end of the tenth century, the foundations of local administration were laid across England. Reeves, or bailiffs, were scattered around the kingdom to gather taxes and enforce the king's writs. During Aethelred's reign, the senior one in each shire became known as the Shire Reeve. These were the Sheriffs that the Normans inherited and which over time have reached as far afield as the United States as law enforcers. In fact, the disorder that confronted many sheriffs in America's Wild West was similar to that faced by their Saxon predecessors in bailiwicks more than a millennium before.

Toli was Sheriff of Norfolk when the Normans invaded and for a few years he kept his bailiwick. But by 1076, all shrieval posts had been shared out among the Norman victors of Hastings. Roger Bigod was appointed by William II. Unfortunately, Richard I was not the champion of the masses that fables of Robin Hood make out. He auctioned off sheriffdoms to the highest bidders, to raise money for the crusades, and he gave a clutch to his brother John, which included Nottingham, as a loyalty bribe.

Of the Sheriffs' many responsibilities, the one that interested monarchs most was gathering taxes. As a consequence, Henry I made his new Exchequer Court responsible for supervising the shrievalty of England and it is still on the anniversary of its traditional meetings, the 'morrow of St Michael', that lists are prepared of three new names for each shire's annual appointment. The following March, the Sheriffs Roll is taken to the Queen in Council and she 'Pricks the List', in continuance of the previous Elizabeth's use of a bodkin instead of a pen for this purpose. Many medieval sheriffs avoided arguments with the king over what was due by paying Sheriff-Geld, a set sum. They then had to *ferme* their shires for tax; if they did well there would be a profit. Many families became wealthy on shrieval income and took over more shires. Inevitably, the system was open to abuse.

Magna Carta controlled the sheriffs, because it curbed the king's power under which they operated. The introduction of Justices of the Peace in the fourteenth century reduced them further but the appointment of Lords Lieutenant to carry a military and administrative role, in the sixteenth century, cut their ability to earn money to the bone. During the rest of the century and the one which followed, the workload increased as the income dropped and many did everything to avoid the bodkin's prick. It even became popular for enemies to nominate someone who would be financially ruined by the job.

The Sheriffs Act of 1887 rationalized and defined the duties but it remains a virtually unpaid post that consequently attracts people with resources. Whilst High Sheriffs are now largely symbolic, many aspects of legal power are carried out in their name: for instance, civil writs issued by the courts come to the High Sheriff, whose representatives prepare the warrant with which bailiffs can still arrive at any debtor's door. And, ever since 1254, it is to the High Sheriff that the monarch's writ to hold a General Election in the shire is still sent.

Saxon rulers had Reeves to govern in the shires. From the rural anarchy of post-conquest England to the Wild West of America, **Sheriffs** have held the principal remit of power. Today they act as official returning officers for parliamentary elections, execute High Court writs and greet High Court judges.

Lord Archbishop of Canterbury, Primate of All England and Lord Archbishop of York, Primate of England

Lord Archbishop of Canterbury, in front of St Augustine's throne into which he and most of his predecessors were lifted, including St Thomas Becket, whose desecrated shrine stood where the Primate of All England prays. The grandeur of the principal cathedral in the Anglican Church has witnessed the religious troubles that have been the constant concern of 103 Archbishops of Canterbury.

OVER FIFTEEN HUNDRED YEARS AGO, just as the history of the Anglo Saxon people was starting to take shape, a missionary arrived at Thanet on England's south-eastern shores. He faced a dangerous task in a land where early Christians had often endured torture and death at the hands of rulers who derived their authority from pagan gods and regarded stories of an alternate and jealous God as a threat. The missionary Augustine was seen to have rare gifts as an ambassador for Pope Gregory the Great but he needed all his wit as well as the help of his Frankish interpreters to hold his own at the Court of King Aethelbert of Kent. But there, to an extent, his path had been smoothed by another Christian, Bertha, the king's wife. She, with her chaplain Luidhard, made the monk from Rome welcome at the small church of St Martin on the hill outside the city of Canterbury.

In 597, at the Whitsunday festival to celebrate the inspirational tongues of fire and wind that gave such strength to Christ's disciples, Augustine baptized the king. Many of his people followed him, and were also baptized. In 601 the Pope sent Augustine the Pallium, a simple scarf woven from lambs' wool that symbolized the lamb carried on the shoulders of the shepherd. It was to be the symbol of his authority to act as Metropolitan over all the Christian churches in Britain. At the same time, Augustine set up his cathedra (his episcopal seat) in the new cathedral at Canterbury as the first archbishop.

Augustine was by no means the first Christian missionary to reach the shores, but he was the first to come with the direct authority of the Pope. And the Curia, claiming descent from St Peter, jealously guarded its determination to be the sole arbiter of the true religion. Augustine was therefore the first Roman archbishop, and with his arrival Christianity gained authority. The story of England's Christian tradition had begun. The stage was set for a power struggle between kings and popes, Church and State.

At some stage, each one of over one hundred archbishops has found himself in the eye of such storms.

The archbishop's cathedra, or seat, still sits in the cathedral behind the high altar. Into it each successor to Augustine has supposedly been lifted or dragged. 'Sitting in it for the first time during my enthroning,' explained the 103rd Archbishop, 'my feet left the floor and I felt very small. It reminded me how huge this burden would be.'

When Edgar the Peaceable was crowned in 973, at a time of great unity in the Heptarchy, it was Archbishop Dunstan who wrote and performed the service. His involvement was a master stroke of political positioning. It ensured that kings were seen to take their authority from none but God and that the Archbishop would provide the essential unction that set those kings apart. All subsequent coronations followed this precedent and, after the conquest, Duke William of Normandy legitimized his coronation on Christmas Day 1066 by observing this Saxon rite. However, on this day Archbishop Stigand was in disgrace, and his place was taken by Aldred, Archbishop of York. Tensions grew between the two archbishops over precedence and the right to crown.

One of the most famous incumbents of the see was Thomas Becket. As a clerk in the household of Archbishop Theobald he was groomed for high office. In 1154 he was appointed Chancellor of England to assist the young King Henry II. Immediately they built a strong friendship and Henry benefited from a priest who placed his king's interests above those of the Church. He raised taxes for the king's wars in France and fought for him on the battlefield. He is even said to have unseated a French knight in single combat.

Believing that this single-minded loyalty was his forever, Henry appointed Thomas to the see of Canterbury when it fell vacant in 1162. The bishops were dismayed but held their peace. Henry hoped that in his friend Thomas he had found an ally who would work with him to reduce the Church's power and privileges, but the king was outmanoeuvred. Thomas resigned the Chancellorship and opposed the king's demand to bring the Church courts under secular authority. The king issued the Constitutions of Clarendon, which sought to assert secular law over the clergy, hitherto subject mainly to canon law, and to supervise their relationship with Rome. Thomas fled into exile in France, hoping to gain papal support for his actions and position. In November 1170 Thomas returned to England without any true reconciliation with the king, and a month later four knights, believing they would earn the king's favour, murdered the archbishop in his cathedral as he was on his way to vespers.

The murder sanctified Thomas and all he stood for. It strengthened the Church, and in particular it strengthened Canterbury. Pope Alexander made sure that no opportunity was ever lost for extracting contrition to his own advantage. The king was made to do penance at Becket's tomb, and Canterbury became the principal site of pilgrimage in England.

It was probably never Pope Gregory's intention that Canterbury should always be the senior metropolitan, but that the office should rotate between Canterbury and York. Ever since Thomas of Bayeux was appointed the first Norman archbishop of York in 1070, there was a struggle for supremacy between the two archbishops. York claimed greater age, having had a bishop since the time of the Council of Arles in 314 and, in the curia's eyes, was equal to Canterbury, since Paulinus was sent the pallium in 625. To prevent further discord the archbishops agreed to a compromise by the Accord of Winchester in 1127 whereby the Archbishop of York would be *Angliae primas* (Primate of England) and the archbishop of Canterbury became *totius Angliae primus* (Primate of All England). The Accord has never left Canterbury and it is still in force. York,

however, committed a grave mistake in accepting Henry II's invitation to crown his young son Henry while Becket was in exile. Thomas excommunicated him, which was upheld by Pope Alexander III, who confirmed Canterbury's right to crown English kings.

But the original intentions of St Augustine, that England should be divided with equal precedence between the two archbishops of Canterbury and York, was not altered by this. Each continued to take

Eborius was York's first bishop in 314 and archbishops still sign 'Ebor' after their name. In 627 Paulinus established the Bishopric again after the Dark Ages. In the fourteenth century the **Lord Archbishop**'s official residence was moved to the nearby village, or 'thorpe'.

'Quod Anglicana ecclesia libera sit.'
'That the English Church shall be free.'

MAGNA CARTA, 1215

precedence based upon seniority or length of service in the archiepiscopal rank.

The ascendancy of Canterbury to the position it has held ever since came in the sixteenth century. During this time the powers of the papal legate were exercised through the province of Canterbury, which gave it precedence in the mind of the Vatican. Ironically, following Henry VIII's break with Rome, the new and divided Church that emerged maintained this recently established authority: it was anxious for effective leadership in difficult times. Elizabeth I and her early Stuart successors recognized the usefulness of an episcopacy whose hierarchy they could control, and so Canterbury's supremacy as part of this was confirmed.

Today, membership of the worldwide Anglican communion requires acknowledgement of Canterbury's position as 'first among equals'.

Earl Marshal and Hereditary Marshal of England

The Court of Chivalry in the College of Arms has as its judge England's hereditary **Earl Marshal**. His gold baton with ebony ends copies the one Richard III gave his ancestor. He appoints the Kings of Arms who alone can grant armorial bearings. This court waits to be used: the last case was in 1954.

EACH YEAR THE DUKE OF NORFOLK still takes control of the State Opening of Parliament and he is stood by at a moment's notice to plan State funerals and coronations. The grand ceremonies which express England's life have been the responsibility of the Marshal since the job, which was originally a military appointment, was first granted by William the Conqueror.

Marshal comes from *marescalcus*, a derivation of *marah* (horse) and *calc* (servant). In the ancient courts of Byzantium, the Marshal was responsible for organizing the mounted troops under the Constable's command. Charlemagne's empire of the west adopted many Byzantine practices, which filtered into Europe's evolving structures. As a result, England's first marshal was imported with the Normans in 1066.

In Normandy the Marshal had been hereditary for some time; in 1066 it was held by William the Marshal, whose family married into the Clares, and Gilbert de Clare was England's first recorded Lord Marshal at Stephen's coronation. This hereditary succession in turn ended in five daughters, the eldest of whom, Maude, married Hugh Bigod, Earl of Norfolk. The Mowbrays were presented with the first golden baton, still the Marshal's symbol of office, by Richard II, and they held it until Edward IV's reign, when their male line died out and the title merged with the Crown. Richard III revived it for Sir John Howard, son of Lady Margaret Mowbray, on 28th June 1483, and the Howards have been doing the job, with occasional interruptions, ever since.

Sir John's detractors suggested that his appointment as Earl Marshal and ennoblement to the dukedom of Norfolk implicated him along with Richard III in the murder of the young princes at the Tower of London. However circumstantial it may appear, the evidence is that Howard and King Richard were thick as thieves before their death.

Two years later, the 1st Duke was killed with his king at Bosworth Field, while his son, Thomas, the 2nd Duke, managed one of the sharpest pragmatic moves of side-switching ever, becoming a trusted courtier to Henry VII. He satisfied Henry that serving two masters showed treason to neither because, 'He was my crowned king, and if the parliamentary authority set the crown upon a stock, I will fight for that stock.' And with similar diplomacy, the Howard family set forth through the vicissitudes of England's history: and, despite civil war, religious upheaval and autocratic kings, they maintained position, rank and the Roman Catholic faith.

The Norfolks steered a path of survival through the philosophical peccadilloes of succeeding sovereigns, suffering several attainders and some beheadings. After the Restoration of Charles II and in the ceremonial splendour which surrounded it, the king revived the dukedom of Norfolk and the post of Earl Marshal, which he made hereditary. Unfortunately, the newly honoured duke was described as 'unapproachable…an incurable maniac'. The family asked Parliament to summon the duke from Italy for examination. But, fearing the dangers of an incompetent running its ceremonies, this request was denied.

Among the Marshal's duties is that of judge in the Court of Chivalry. Set up by Edward III, its jurisdiction over chivalric matters pertaining to rank, heraldry and conduct remains extant, but the only hearing in the last few centuries was in 1954. The court's chamber actually exists in the College of Arms, another branch of the Earl Marshal's bailiwick. Here the Officers of Arms, appointed by the Sovereign on his recommendation, conduct heraldic business and support him with the evolution of national ceremonial to meet changing needs: they have the expertise to provide an understanding for the provenance and meaning behind all rituals which the State observes to express itself. With baton in hand, hereditary Earl Marshals conduct Sovereigns to their parliaments, their crowns and their graves.

President of Tynwald and the Lord Bishop of Sodor and Man

THE WORLD'S OLDEST PARLIAMENT in continuous use is on the Isle of Man's Tynwald hill, close to the north-west coast of England. Set on a high plateau, the mound is made up of four large ascending steps over what was probably a Bronze Age burial site. But, since the late 970s when Godred I was king, it has been a place of assembly where law is made and justice given out, while providing a forum for the Manx people to have their say. Tynwald is a derivation from the Norse, meaning parliament field, and its design is similar to a typical *thing-völlr*, or law-hill. The site has been a place of worship for millennia and Celtic chiefs were probably inaugurated here according to the rite of tanistry, whereby power passed into a new chief when he stood over the burial site of former rulers. The idea of power passing from the earth was common, being used by Henry III, who designed the coronation setting in Westminster Abbey beside the elevated burial site of St Edward the Confessor.

Every 5 July, Tynwald still assembles on the ancient hill by St John's church. This gathering brings the Manx community together. The year's legislation is read out by the Deemsters (judges of ancient origin), and if any Act is not read out it lapses immediately. Freemen look on while Coroners, Parish Captains, Members of the House of Keys and the Legislative Council gather to hear the promulgation. There are three seats on the top level of Tynwald. The first is sat on by the Lieutenant Governor, who represents the Lord of Man (who, since 1765, has been the Sovereign); the second is the Lord Bishop's; and the third was added in 1990 for the President of Tynwald. This new appointment, which is elected, was created in response to the constitutional need both for a democratic representative of the people of Man and to separate the executive from the Sovereign's representative. Before the Crown bought the island, and became Lord of Man, the Lordship was given in tenure. In

token of their fealty the Lords of Man presented a cast (pair) of falcons at every monarch's coronation.

The Lord Bishop of Sodor and Man, who tends to the souls of this windswept tax haven, still holds the last remaining Viking barony. Quite when the first bishop established his cathedra on the island is not known. Legend suggests that St Patrick and some of his fellow Celtic saints made visits in the fifth century: pioneering an episcopal church, it is possible they established a bishopric on Man. However, little evidence of Celtic life survived the pagan Viking raids.

Viking raids caused havoc along the Scottish coast, as the Norsemen established a territorial hold over Orkney and Shetland, which they called the Nordreys, and in the Hebrides, known as the Sudreys, or southern islands. Early in the ninth century these longboats beached on the shores of Man, to plunder and then to settle. They established jurisdictions that evolved into eight feudal baronies, and the Barony of Jurby is still held by the Lord Bishop. This may be the oldest ex-officio barony in the British Isles. It is the original source of his continuing right to membership of Tynwald's court.

Such power gave one medieval bishop authority to test the guilt of witches. He tied them to the keel of a boat and rowed them from Peel to St Patrick's Isle, where the remains of St Germain's Cathedral still stand. In this arbitrary ecclesiastical discipline, death proved innocence while survival meant guilt, punishable by death.

The bishops on Man were subject to the archbishops of Trondheim, who originally created

In the Legislative Council Chamber, where part of the Isle of Man's ancient parliament meets in Douglas, sits the **President of Tynwald**. He designed his own robes, which echo those worn historically in England's parliament, both by the Lord High Chancellor and the Speaker. Around his neck hangs his badge as a Captain of the Parish.

St Patrick's Isle with its ruins of St Germain's Cathedral by Peel was the seat of religious power in the Isle of Man. Viking links with Norway survived for nearly one thousand years, which is reflected in the **Bishop of Sodor**'s title and in the Viking barony he still holds.

the diocese of Sodorensis and Mona: the first part of this title refers to diocesan responsibility for the old Norse kingdom of the Sudreys. Even after the island was handed to Scotland in 1266, the ecclesiastical link with Norway was maintained: although Norway's authority has lapsed relations are still friendly.

The Manx respond to criticism of Tynwald with the evidence of stability it has given, proved by names of its members. Over the centuries these surnames are little changed.

'I stole away to St John's, for to see one last time the ancient ceremonies of Tynwald Hill, and secretly to take from its lowest round, one little handful of that earth which has seen, maybe, and heard more history than any other spot on the island.'

THOMAS KELLY, 1827, BEFORE ECONOMIC DISTRESS
DROVE HIM FROM THE ISLE OF MAN

Master and Brethren of the Hospital of St Cross and the Almshouse of Noble Poverty

O N THE OUTSKIRTS OF WINCHESTER is a thriving twelfth-century welfare organization, perhaps Britain's first sheltered housing, certainly England's oldest almshouse.

The colossal Norman tower of the hospital rises above the lazy river Itchen. When Henry de Blois walked this riverbank in *c*.1133, he was not only Bishop of Winchester and Papal Legate, his half-brother was king and he was one of the country's wealthiest men. But England was enduring 'the Anarchy', and food was scarce. The legend goes that a milkmaid carrying a small child came into view, and, momentarily, he thought that they were a vision of the Madonna and Child. He was therefore attentive when she implored him to help her village. So, in the name of the Holy Cross (Sancta Crux), de Blois established the Hospital of St Cross to provide accommodation for thirteen brethren, a number to match Christ and the twelve disciples. He appointed a Master to administer the endowment and he provided resources to feed up to one hundred poor people each day. The brethren (the Poor in Christ) lived out their days in security, with no further care but preparing their souls.

In the twelfth century St Cross was administered by the Knights Hospitaller, and before every crusade knights would assemble and pray there. Therefore Blois' Brotherhood wear black gowns with silver crosses, from the arms of the Kingdom of Jerusalem, established during the crusades.

In 1445 a second brotherhood (the Brethren of Noble Poverty) began, whose members wear dark red gowns and a silver badge engraved with their founder Cardinal Beaufort's hat. He was another wealthy Bishop of Winchester, closely connected with the Lancastrian Plantagenets, who wanted to provide for impoverished noblemen, particularly those in his own family.

The Master is no longer politically influential, and neither does wealth come with the appointment, but his domestic and pastoral responsibilities are unchanged. He administered payments from across the country, which included dolphins from Lincoln – and when the village of Twyford failed to pay up, the inhabitants were excommunicated. One notable royalist Master was forced to flee after Charles I's execution: his place was given to one of the King's judges, but he was reinstalled after the Restoration.

As a boy, Henry de Blois had entered the Cluniac Order. Cluniac monks believed in supporting travellers. To this day, all visitors to St Cross can ask for the Wayfarers' Dole which he instituted. This consists of beer and bread and is given to anyone who asks for it. Drinking the bitter beer in the medieval quadrangle, while the Brethren go peacefully about their business, there is a sense of welcome and shelter all about. Beyond the walls, the roar of the M3 is audible. It beckons non-residents to move on, just as Jerusalem beckoned the crusaders from this safety 800 years ago.

The **Master**, standing on the left, still distributes alms weekly on Fridays of one pound to the **brethren** of both foundations.

Queen's Champion, Lord of the Manor of Scrivelsby

The gauntlet at Scrivelsby Court was last thrown down in 1821 to challenge George IV's detractors. The **Queen's Champion** no longer rides in armour to coronations in order to keep his land but carries the Union Flag.

THE MANOR OF SCRIVELSBY COURT in Lincolnshire has been neither bought nor sold since it was given by William the Conqueror to his friend Robert Marmion after the Battle of Hastings in 1066. It has been passed through the generations and is still today a serious business enterprise for Marmion's descendants. The house has changed a good deal, although the park still has the feel of a once grand establishment, and this piece of Lincolnshire country bears quiet witness to one of the most romantic family stories in the kingdom.

From here, at most coronations and in answer to the terms of the Conqueror's grant, knights have ridden as royal Champions to Westminster, ready to stand and die for their king. This is because the Manor was granted under Grand Sergeanty, in terms described in the 'Inquisitio post mortem' written in Edward III's reign:

'The manour of Scrivelsby is holden by Grand Sergeanty, to wit, by the service of finding on the day of Coronation, an armed knight who shall prove by his body, if need be, that the King is true and rightful heir to the kingdom.'

Norman justice offered the bizarre appeal process of Trial by Combat, by which people could prove their innocence by taking the chance that they might fell a fully armed knight without appropriate weaponry. The dukes of Normandy made use of specially selected knights to stand in and do combat on their behalf, especially to challenge anyone doubting their right to rule. Robert Marmion had been that knight in Normandy and, in the heady days following the defeat of Harold, the Conqueror offered him Scrivelsby on this condition. It was a challenge and Marmion accepted.

Surprisingly, no descendant of Marmion has ever been called to fight for his master. However, when the challenge was made at the coronation of George III in 1761, the crowd fell silent: rumours abounded that Bonnie Prince Charlie was in London and would do mortal combat with the Champion.

The Marmions grew strong with the benefit of royal patronage and became powerful barons in the land. Earl Philip Marmion was a staunch supporter of Henry III throughout his troubled reign but his demise meant confusion for the inheritance of the Marmions. He produced only daughters, so the inheritance had to be divided, the eldest taking Tamworth as her dowry; while the younger retained the estate of Scrivelsby. She married Sir Thomas de Ludlow, and their grand-daughter's marriage to Sir John Dymoke in 1350 brought the Champion's duties to the Dymoke family, which still holds them today.

In return for putting their lives ceremonially on the line, Champions retain the estate of Scrivelsby and were given generous perquisites. They included a horse, 'the best but one' available from the royal stable; a fine saddle, armour and furniture for the horse; a complete suit of armour for the Champion himself, including a shield and lance; twenty yards of crimson satin and the gold cup and cover with which the Sovereign drank his health. Strictly, these fees were only his if combat ensued but, as no King ever wanted a poorly turned-out Champion, no expense was spared on his knightly panoply or the caparisoning of his horse. The last time a Dymoke performed this duty for a king was in 1821, at the coronation banquet of George IV. The doors of Westminster Hall opened and Dymoke, flanked by Great Officers of State, rode in to throw down his gauntlet. Garter King of Arms read the challenge and this was repeated three times. The armour of Champion and horse worn on this occasion now stands as the principal feature in the restored St George's Hall at Windsor Castle.

Coronation Banquets no longer take place in Westminster Hall, so neither does the Champion's ceremonial entry. Instead, for the last four coronations they have carried the Union Flag or Banner of England.

Chief Butler of England and Grand Carver of England

Chief Butler of England.

Outside the royal manor of
Kenninghall in Norfolk stands a
display of the heraldry of its
historic owners. The arms of
King Edward the Confessor
take precedence, along with
the families of Howard,
Mowbray and Dacre, who
provided the butlers of England.

Grand Carver of England.

Until 1821 Peers wore
Coronation Robes at the
banquet as well as the
ceremony. Three rows of
ermine tails signify that
Denbigh is an earl, as does
the coronet with eight silver
balls and strawberry leaves,
which sits on a Coronation
chair from 1953.

NORMAN KINGS HANDED OUT LAND to nobles with strings attached, each manor held of the king in consideration for certain duties. Mostly these consisted of Knight Service, the promise to provide troops or pay in lieu. Others were given under Sergeanty, which required the regular offering of some specific service. This latter group were divided into two: those who offered service at regular intervals or when asked, which was Petit Sergeanty, and those who did service at the coronation only, called Grand Sergeanty.

The manor of Kenninghall was given as a reward by Henry I to William de Albini, in recognition of the support he gave in the king's battle against his elder brother, Robert Curthose, for the throne. Because it was a royal manor it came under Grand Sergeanty and the service expected was *Pincera Regis*, or King's Chief Butler at the coronation banquet. There were perquisites of 'the best gold cup with a cover, which is on the table, and all the wine under the bar of the [Westminster] Hall'. The Butler could rely on none other than the Lord Mayor and Corporation of the City of London as his assistants.

Manors were not vested in families but were feudal in character; hence they could be inherited, bought or sold like anything else. The dukes of Norfolk inherited Kenninghall and the duties with it but in 1872 they sold it to John Oddin Taylor of Norwich. Recently it changed hands again and was bought by a European, who lives in Sweden. His family came from Aquitaine and served Richard the Lionheart in the crusades, while one member attempted to save the French royal family and faced the guillotine.

The last time a coronation banquet was considered was in 1902 for Edward VII, though his sudden illness put a stop to the plans. At the Court of Claims that preceded the event three people claimed the right to act as Chief Butler: the Duke of Norfolk, Mr Taylor of Kenninghall and a descendant of William de Albini. The court did not consider their cases and so no decision was taken.

Nor did they decide on the Earl of Denbigh and Desmond's claim to act as Grand Carver. His claim was up against Scotland's Hereditary Carver, a post fully recognized today. The last person to perform the task at a coronation was the Earl of Lincoln, by right of his earldom, in 1399, at the coronation of Henry IV; as it happened, it was the king himself. However, the Denbighs maintain their right but it would need the Court of Claims to adjudicate. Other banquet appointments of Grand Sergeanty include the manor of Ashele to act as Naperer, the manor of Addington to serve a Mess of Dillegrout, the manor of Nether Bilsington to present three Maple cups and the manor of Sculton to be Larderer.

Lord of the Manor of Worksop

Worksop Abbey is where the new **Lord of the Manor** was christened, schooled and married. Purchasing this feudal history, he hopes to continue Worksop's unique offering. On bended knee his ancestors have presented a single embroidered glove to the new monarch moments before the symbol of kingly power is invested. This is a copy of the one given in 1953.

Because the Normans claimed the throne of England through a promise by Edward the Confessor, the last Saxon king, their apologists worked hard to venerate him and enhance his credibility after death. So successful were they at gathering, or fabricating, evidence of miracles performed in life and after death, that centuries after burial Edward was translated and sanctified as a saint. One of the legends concerns his dream that, on hearing a commotion, he wandered through his Palace at Westminster and discovered that the noise was coming from the Treasury. He opened the door and came face to face with the Devil dancing on tax chests containing coins gathered under the punitive Danegeld: a very unpopular poll tax levied by the Danes when they ruled in England.

When Edward woke the next morning, he repealed the tax and resolved that, because of the misery it had caused his people, nothing similar should ever be collected again. It is believed that the coronation ceremony was evolved to include a symbolic reminder of this lesson: just before the Archbishop puts the Sceptre of Kingly Power in the king's right hand, a single glove is presented as a reminder that the Sovereign power should be exercised with gentleness in taxation and all matters.

In the time of Edward the Confessor Worksop was held by a Saxon noble named Elsi. After the Domesday (1086) survey in the eleventh century it was yielded to the Norman Roger de Bully in return for the knight's service to the king. The Manor of Worksop was granted in 1542 to Francis Talbot Earl of Shrewsbury in Grand Sergeanty. This obliged the Lord of the Manor of Worksop, in the county of Nottingham, to attend the coronation. He was to step forward just before the sceptre was given to the monarch, to kneel and present 'A Glove for the King's Right Hand' and then to remain available to support the arm if necessary. It has been performed at every coronation since medieval times and always by the Lord of the Manor of Worksop or his nominee. It is a silent but deeply symbolic moment in a ceremony full of significance.

Manorial lordships can pass from one generation to another and therefore appear to be inherited, like other titles. However, they are actually property, and can therefore be bought and sold; this appointment is held by whoever has legal title, and whoever owns the Manor of Worksop is entitled to perform the unique services of Grand Sergeanty. As ownership has changed hands over the years, each lord of the Manor has presented his petition to the Court of Claims to present the special coronation glove. At The Queen's coronation this became more complicated, because the Manor was then owned by a limited company, and allowing a commercial organization to take part in the coronation was deemed unacceptable in 1953. Instead, a compromise was negotiated: the Chancellor of the Duchy of Lancaster presented the glove in proxy.

When feudalism ended little remained but the title 'Lord of the Manor', which is intrinsically valueless unless it retains some rights, such as minerals and markets. Nevertheless there is some pride in ownership of a description of such antiquity associated with real territory, even when all the freehold, leases and copyholds have been taken up by others.

The result for Worksop is that, for the first time in centuries, the Lord of the Manor can say he was born there, educated there, made his living there and now resides there. He is someone who has a genuine love for the place. While much else may evolve in the coronations of British kings, it would be a shame to lose the presence of such a claimant, a Worksop man through and through, ready to play his part in reminding the Sovereign, on behalf of us all, to be gentle in taxation and power.

Hereditary Warden of Savernake Forest

In the beech wood, planted by Capability Brown, the **Warden** blows a replica of the Esturmy Horn, which came over with his forebears and William in 1066. This land has never been sold.

IF THE CONTENTS OF THE Battle Abbey Roll are to be believed, then Richard Estormit, or Esturmy, fought with William the Conqueror at Harold's defeat in 1066. By 1083, the *Exeter Book* shows him living in the area which the Saxons called the wood of Savernoc. The *Domesday Book* describes him three years later as a servant of the king and occupying land which, in 1050, was owned by Aluric, who may have been warden, or guardian, of the forest. Whether the appointment came with Aluric's land or not, from this date onwards, until the family ran out of male heirs in 1427, the Esturmys are described as either Wardens or Chief Foresters of Savernake Forest.

Savernake was subject to Forest Law and therefore exempt from Common Law. Its regular courts, or Eyres, required the attendance of the Warden. Here he would receive, among other rents and fines, his equipage. This equivalent of an outfit allowance consisted of saddle, bridle, sword and horn. The 29th Warden said that, 'Today Richard Estormit's... saddle and bridle are dust: his sword is lost to us, and perhaps rusted away... It is, therefore, of peculiar interest to be able to see and handle the horn – 'their great hunting horn, tipped with silver' – ...which very possibly was Richard's own.' This horn is now no longer in the family's possession but is in the British Museum. No longer will the Wardens be able to fulfil their ancient obligation 'to salute His Majesty with a blast of the Esturmy horn' whenever the Sovereign comes to Savernake. This tradition was derived from the traditional fanfare which began the hunt when the king arrived for a day of sport.

The Esturmys proved determined protectors of their royal masters' interests, particularly with the growing pressure from barons intent on deforestation. In 1225 Henry of Cluny and Thomas of Kennett attempted to take royal land over by Perambulation (walking a boundary to make a claim to land that falls within it). Within two years Geoffrey Esturmy had routed their claim. However, the Forest Eyre of 1330 confirmed perambulations which reduced Savernake to sixteen square miles. The last Esturmy in the line died in 1427, his inheritance and bailiwick passing through his daughter to the St Mawr family, better known as Seymour; a family that saw the demesne contract further in the reigns of Edward IV and Henry VII. However, the family fortunes seemed set for recovery when a daughter of the family, Jane, became the favourite wife of Henry VIII. Her son, Edward VI, became a useful nephew for Edward Seymour, first Duke of Somerset, who appointed himself Lord Protector of the Realm, the apogee of the family's power.

In 1675, the 5th duke died. Knowing that this would make Elizabeth Seymour a wealthy heiress, the twenty-year-old Thomas, Lord Bruce, made marriage with her his target. Surprisingly, this union was happy and, as he moved into Tottenham House, Bruce's first act was to appoint a Seymour relative as Ranger of Savernake. In 1747, after spending time with his uncle at Tottenham, Thomas Brudenell inherited the estate and Wardenship: it was the final genealogical leap and again the link was an Elizabeth, his mother, Elizabeth Bruce.

The greatest achievement of this family inheritance is that it has managed to maintain an hereditary office for nearly a millennium when the Wardenship has always depended not upon physical ownership but upon the goodwill of changing sovereigns, a political path of incredible risk. On the few occasions when individuals have slipped from favour, or possession has been vulnerable through minority, forgiveness or rescue was always forthcoming. In these situations responsibility was generally passed temporarily to the Constable of Marlborough. While today's Warden closes the gates for one day each year, to retain the legal independence of Savernake, for the rest of the year it is open to anyone who wishes to enjoy the ancient groves of the only forest in Britain which is still in private hands.

'When my father blew it for King George VI, he was standing inside the entrance hall at Tottenham House, and it was found afterwards that he had set all the dogs barking in Durley, a good half mile away!'

29TH HEREDITARY WARDEN OF SAVERNAKE FOREST, DESCRIBING THE ESTURMY HORN'S LAST ROYAL SALUTE

Verderers and Agisters of the New Forest

'Am I fascinated? Have I lost my senses? Where am I? Had I not a delightful wood here close to Winchester?' So asked the disoriented William the Conqueror, the keen hunter who had chased the Saxon kingdom into oblivion twenty years before. The words are supposed to have been said when the king discovered what his Bishop of Winchester, Walkelin, had done to the royal hunting forest of Hampage, just to the east of his capital city. Given permission to cut trees for three days to rebuild his cathedral, Walkelin took the king at his word and organized carpenters to fell the entire wood. After such a surprise it is no wonder that one year later, the hunt-loving monarch was dead. The story goes on that, following the Conqueror's wishes, a New Forest was opened up for the pursuit of royal hunting in 1097. Whatever the real reason for its name, the vast acreage still enjoyed as a rural wilderness around Lyndhurst in Hampshire took up two pages in the *Domesday Book*.

Forest Law came with the afforestation of the area. What had been a sparse wasteland on which Saxon monasteries eked out a living was cleared for the wild beasts of hart, hind and hare. Vigorous punishment was meted out to poachers or those stealing timber, an oppression of the hungry that became a source of great tension between the king and his people. To impose these penalties, the New Forest had its Attachment and Swainmote Court, where the Verderers' role was to record details of the offences. Their title derives from the French word *vert* (green), which had since Norman times meant any vegetation to feed or shelter deer.

The first of these appointments to what must be one of the oldest judicial bodies in the country are lost in time. From the beginning of medieval times until the 1700s the Verderers Court exercised the unique edicts of Forest Law upon the commoners of the New Forest. Forest Law finally ended with the Wild Creatures and Forest Laws Act in 1971, with the words, 'The forest law is hereby abrogated.'

Another piece of legislation, the New Forest Act, was used to revise the Verderers Court in 1877. After

The Verderer's Hall in Queen's House, Lyndhurst, is where the **Verderers of the New Forest** hold their Open Courts to which anyone may make Presentments. The Official Verderer, standing, is the Sovereign's representative. A stirrup, reputably once owned by King William Rufus, is kept by the court. If a dog is small enough to pass through the stirrup it is allowed to run wild in the New Forest.

'*A certain territory of woody grounds and fruitful pastures, privileged for wild beasts and fowls of the forest... in the safe protection of the king, for his delight and pleasure... and also replenished with wild beasts of venery and chase, and with great coverts of vert: for the preservation and continuance of which said place... there are particular officers, laws and privileges... proper only to a forest and to no other place.*'

MANWOOD, TREATY ON FOREST LAW, 1717

Henry II ordained that '...four knights be appointed for agisting his woods, and for receiving pannage – a levy made for the privilege of allowing pigs to forage for acorns in the autumn'. **Agisters** still do similar work.

150 years in disuetude, when the area had been exploited for timber by builders of the Royal Navy's wooden ships, Parliament revived the institution to fulfil a very different brief. Deer were nearly exterminated in 1851, which had pronounced effects upon the habitat, but the interests of a large area of common land owned by the Crown needed protection. To do the work, the Official Verderer, appointed by the Crown, was assisted by six Verderers elected by the registered Commoners. Today the court is made up of ten Verderers: the Official Verderer, five elected Verderers and four who represent, respectively, the Forestry Commission, Minister of Agriculture, Countryside Commission and Hampshire County Council. They have a responsibility for the health and welfare of the ponies, cattle, pigs and donkeys which the Commoners have rights to graze across the New Forest. They must also take account of the various needs presented by Commoners of the New Forest and an increasing number of visitors, all of whom may attend any of the ten open meetings of the Court and raise issues if they wish.

Since the twelfth century the Lord Warden of the Forest and the Verderers have been able to call upon the Agisters, who were mounted, to act as their agents in collecting all manner of fees and *pannage* from the Commoners who grazed their pigs on acorns in the autumn. Their chief task today is to tend to the animals legally at pasture. This is particularly important during long months of harsh weather. And it is no longer Norman kings who kill animals in the New Forest but the motorists who drive too fast. The six Agisters who are employed by the Verderers are quickly on the scene tending to the injured animals and informing the owners.

Prelate, Bailiff of Egle, Chancellor and Lord Prior of the Most Venerable Order of the Hospital of Saint John of Jerusalem

IN 1095 AT THE COUNCIL OF CLERMONT Pope Urban II called for the First Crusade, urging the faithful to rescue the Holy Land from the grasp of the infidel Turk.

Knights and their indentured servants were therefore mobilized under the authority of the Church: in return, Urban II offered blanket forgiveness of all their sins, an almost irresistible offer in the guilt-ridden middle ages. The Crusaders had to cross the known world on foot. They had no guarantee of return and little idea of what lay ahead. However, on 15 July 1099, led by Geoffrey de Bouillon, this international army of God-fearing troops retook Jerusalem with bloodstained hands and pious hearts.

In the city they had taken was a hospital run by Blessed Gerard, the Custodian of the Poor in Christ of the Hospital of Saint John, offering help to all the wounded. It had been there for half a century at least, its selfless work supported by Turk and Palestinian alike. Many in the crusading army were inspired to offer themselves to the hospital's work and 'serve Our Lords the Sick'. They formed an order of military monks, called the Knights Hospitaller, and their organization was recognized by the King of Jerusalem in 1104 and by Pope Pascal II in 1113.

The English Hospitallers formed one of the eight Langues, or tongues, of the order and controlled the mounted forces and coast-guard, under a commander entitled Turcopilier.

A domestic headquarters was established near London in the early stages of the twelfth century, just north of the City of London, where between 1130 and 1145 Prior Walter of England built the church of St John, whose crypt has survived.

The Second and Third Crusades saw the Hospitallers in full combat beside their brother orders, the Knights Templar and Knights of the Holy Sepulchre. But the Crusaders lost their hold on Jerusalem, moving first to Acre, then to Rhodes, and finally to Cyprus, in 1291, where began a maritime tradition which made the Knights Hospitaller one of the most powerful naval forces in the Mediterranean.

Prior to the Hospitallers' arrival in Rhodes, the Templar knights were implicated in heresy by Philip IV of France. In 1312 Pope Clement V confirmed this and throughout Europe the Templars were stripped of possessions in favour of the Hospitallers. Among the booty which fell into the hands of the English Hospitallers was the large estate near Lincoln called Egle. It became a bailiwick and its bailiff was one of the Order's principal officers until 1999.

It was Suleiman the Magnificent who finally drove the Hospitallers from Rhodes in 1522. Eight years later an English knight, William Weston, sailed into Grand Harbour in Malta to take possession for St John. However, for the English Langue, the order's growth was halted suddenly by the Reformation when Henry VIII dissolved the order, along with the monasteries. Mary I revived it temporarily but soon it was, after all, consigned to oblivion. The order in Malta lived on until the French Revolution cut off vital resources and Emperor Napoleon subsequently took the island and ousted the incumbents.

Britain's Empire benefited from Napoleon's defeat, and with its growth came the need for medical support in the colonies at a low cost for all races and creeds. What better than to dust down the ancient traditions of St John: first unofficially, and then formally by a Royal Charter from Queen Victoria in 1888. The Most Venerable Order of the Hospital of St John of Jerusalem was established in the Priory remnants at Clerkenwell. With the Sovereign at its head, it has become an international provider of first aid.

The order retains a link with its beginnings. It still runs the St John Ophthalmic Hospital in Jerusalem, which provides valuable help close to the religious strife which is still a feature of the Holy City.

The **Prelate**, **Bailiff of Egle** and **Chancellor** are led by the **Lord Prior** in the crypt of their twelfth-century church at Clerkenwell. They run an army of volunteers who all wear the eight-pointed cross of St John, which signifies the four Christian virtues of prudence, justice, temperance and fortitude and the eight beatitudes which spring from their practice.

Archdruid of Anglesey

WHATEVER THE TRUTH MAY BE about the ancient Druids and the effectiveness of their religious practices on Anglesey before the Roman invasion, the Druidic movement today seeks to revive nothing more than the essence of Celtic Welshness from its legacy. As the Archdruid explains, 'We meet today to further poetry and literature on our island.' The Gorsedd stones that used to be the sacrificial altars of the Druids before Christ have become the keystones of literature.

The eighteenth-century antiquarian Henry Rowlands analysed the evidence of Anglesey's Druids both on the ground and in the surviving texts of Tacitus, Caesar and Strabo. His work did much to fan the flames of reviving interest in Welshness: a fire which ignited once more the Druidic tradition. He deduced that the Druids, as a learned class, had established Anglesey as their religious centre in Britain. The island is known as Môn Mam Cymru, the Mother of Wales. The Druids' choice was based upon the island's self-sufficiency in both agriculture and minerals; the former as a result of its clement weather and fertile location, on the north-western tip of Wales. This independence ensured that the Drew, or Archdruid, could give impartial judgement or direction from his high seat without feeling beholden to others when delivering his wisdom. The Drew was surrounded by his fellow Druids, who ruled spiritually over the people and were at the top of the priestly hierarchy. Two further layers included the Offwyr, or Ovates, and the Beirdd, or Bards. Collectively they ruled over and were protected by the Ordovices, or hammer fighters. And it was these warriors who prevented the Roman conquest of Anglesey until the Roman governor, Suetonius Paulinus, gathered his troops across the Menai Straits in AD 60.

The Gorsedd stones of Parc Caergybi in Anglesey are called the 'altars of literature'. Once these were sacrificial altars used by the ancient Druids. Wearing a crown of laurel leaves, Druidic robe and the blue sash of poetry, the **Archdruid of Anglesey** leads his fellow Bards in celebration of Welsh culture. A green sash represents music.

'Around the enemy were a host of Druids uttering prayers and curses, flinging their arms towards the sky. The Roman troops stopped short in their tracks as if their limbs were paralysed...These people regarded it as right to sprinkle their altars with the blood of prisoners and to consult the wishes of the Gods by examining the entrails of humans.'

TACITUS, ANNALS, XIV, 30

Rowlands embellishes Tacitus and tells us, 'For some days, while the Roman general was fitting out his Armada, and expecting time and season for his swimming cavalry, we can expect in this Isle of Mona, but loud invocations and cursings, and dismal screeching of dying victims, echoing one another from the hollow resounding groves; in every corner, altars smoking with horrid miserable burnings of bodies of men, women and children, of rogues, profligates and captives.' The Romans supposedly cast down the stones and altars and felled the groves which surrounded them. Fortunately for the few Druids who survived, Queen Boudicca rose up with her Iceni in the east, drawing the invaders away for another fight. It was Agricola who finished the job, returning in AD 78.

Christians grew to regard the ancient adherents of Druidism with violent distrust. However, with some irony, Bardic rites were used from the second to the sixth centuries by early Christians, who cohabited comfortably with surviving Druidism. But Anglesey was by then empty and abandoned.

The revival of Druidism in Wales was spurred on by two men in the eighteenth century. Religious intolerance was abating in the Age of Reason, and Evan Evans published a book of ancient Bardic poems in 1764, called *Specimens of the Poetry of the Ancient Welsh Bards*, which caught the attention of Edward Williams. He set about elevating Celtic language, literature and philosophy to be equal with the other great cultures of the world. He took on the pseudonym Iolo Morgannwg, and developed a new Druidism, free from screaming sacrifices, to provide a backdrop of credibility for this revival. Iolo's poetry set a standard which Bards and Druids have followed and emulated since. Regularly, the order of Druids holds Eisteddfods, festivals of ritual, music, singing and the recitation of poetry. As part of the celebration, Bards compete for prizes in verse. Meanwhile, archaeologists struggle to find more information to unlock the secrets of the stones on Mona but, for the moment, it would seem that the Romans exercised an effective policy of ethnic cleansing on the last outpost of resistance to their imperial eagle.

Sergeant at Mace and Hornblower of Ripon

THE BORDERS BETWEEN LEGEND AND FACT become increasingly unclear as the centuries turn back. Saxon history may benefit from the *Chronicles* but little else remains of a period from which few parchments were adequately stored to survive the vicissitudes of fire and flood. In this vacuum, Ripon claims its antiquity from a gift of a Bugle Horn by the infamous king of Wessex, Alfred the Great, in 886. The meaning of bugle has changed over the centuries, but in this instance (and originally) it meant 'wild oxen'. Perhaps this claim has as much foundation in fact as the cakes Alfred is supposed to have burned, although the Horn has survived. Like a witness whose testimony could go either way, it could confirm or further upset Ripon's claim.

As the Horn is now extremely delicate, three others have been added over the years to the Hornblower's collection. They share a punishing schedule, with one being blown each evening at the four corners of the Market Place Obelisk and outside the Mayor's House. This signal commemorates the start of the Watch. The Watch was an important part of the most senior citizen's responsibilities: as Wakeman, he organized patrols to ensure there were no thefts in the night. From 9pm until dawn any burglaries would be compensated from his pocket: an incentive to ensure the night patrols were thorough.

When James I issued a further Charter in 1604, many of these traditions and duties were regularized in words which occasionally make reference to ancient custom. It enshrined the need for a Hornblower and, perhaps foreseeing the potential risks the Wakeman might face, it also gives provision for a Sergeant at Mace and two Stave Bearers to provide close protection.

The Charter specifically instructs the Wakeman, whose appointment evolved into today's Mayor, that he 'shall cause a horn to be blown every night…at nine of the clock at the four corners of the cross…And if it happen any house or houses be broken…and any goods to be taken away…then according to old custom the Wakeman for the time being shall make good.'

When considering the start of the seventeenth century, it is worth remembering that civil obedience in the country at large was maintained by Sheriffs and other men-at-arms available for military duties. This was seldom reliable, but for people living in the lee of Reformation this Charter made Ripon an attractive place. The promise of security at night and the benefit of insurance should the need arise helped the city develop. It was a reputation which helped attract a community and it is a tradition which, despite the arrival of a nationwide police force, Ripon choses to maintain. It may no longer do more than help the city and its police set their clocks, but it still attracts visitors to the city centre, with a wish to feel part of an unbroken tradition.

The original Charter Horn is now a venerated object, its original form almost completely hidden by the protection of silver clasps and velvet, and it hangs from a baldric, or belt, covered in the emblems of earlier mayors. Still it is carried before the Mayor when both are guarded by the Sergeant at Mace. Perhaps Ripon will take advantage of carbon-dating to risk seeing how ancient its horn really is. Few believe that the result would confirm a bison's death in 886. However, if it proved to be from that date, the ninth-century Charter and the legends surrounding one of England's oldest customs and appointments would take on renewed importance. In their wake further legends might take shape – perhaps even that Alfred the Great felled the animal himself. But history is no ally to Ripon here: it would seem that the king was busy fighting elsewhere that year.

The baldric worn by the **Sergeant at Mace** has sixty-one silver shields which carry the names of Ripon's mayors from 1570, and from it hangs the Charter Horn from 886. The mace was made in 1607.

'As often as he goes into public, a crown and sceptre are carried before him. He is the eye, the mouth-piece and the right hand of the Sovereign; and the supreme judge of the whole British empire.'

DESIDERIUS ERASMUS, ON CHANCELLOR WARHAM (SIXTEENTH CENTURY)

Lord High Chancellor of Great Britain, Keeper of the Great Seal, Keeper of the Royal Conscience and Speaker of the House of Lords

BEHIND A TRELLIS IN THE COURTS of Ancient Rome sat the scribe, called the *Cancellarius*. Powerful, reforming but illiterate Norman kings needed secretaries and appointed a *Cancellarius*, or Chancellor, to the job. From these humble beginnings, the appointment has become the highest-ranking secular office in Britain, responsible for issues affecting the Executive, the Legislature and the Judiciary, of which the Lord Chancellor is head. Monarchs have always appointed their Chancellors, though since executive power moved from the Crown to Cabinet government, this choice has been made on the advice of the Prime Minister – who then takes precedence beneath the Lord Chancellor.

The advantage of literacy, a skill largely monopolized in medieval times by the Church, was that, in a world of law driven by documents, reading and writing gave access to power. Saxon royalty legitimized its correspondence by using seals, a practice which William I continued. As these Great Seals were deposited with the Chancellor in his chancery, every important document passed under his gaze. This useful responsibility was formalized in the Keeper of the Great Seal. When a new Chancellor is appointed their powers do not become effective until the Sovereign hands over the Great Seal. It consists of two six-inch silver matrices which impress large waxen images of the monarch at the foot of documents: a cumbersome badge of office.

Few appointments can boast three saints, each called Thomas. However, Henry II appointed his mentor and friend, Thomas Becket, as Chancellor in 1155: the first Englishman to achieve high office under Norman rule. The other two were Thomas de Cantilupe, who served Henry III, and the incomparable Thomas More, who was celebrated for standing up for the rights of the House of Commons to another Chancellor, his predecessor Cardinal Wolsey. More was then Speaker of the Commons and Wolsey burst in 'with all his pomp, with his maces, his pillars, his crosses, his pole-axes, his hat and Great Seal too'. No Chancellor has probably ever wielded as much power as Wolsey did. But power so dependent on the whim of King Henry was not secure, and when Wolsey fell from favour no appointment could save him.

Ironically, justice and its good administration have been the Chancellor's staple diet ever since the king's writs were all issued at his behest. Inevitably, responsibility for the administration of the courts followed, and consequently almost all Chancellors have had a good grounding in law. Most appointments to high rank in the judiciary have been made on the recommendation of the Lord Chancellor and he is responsible, as cabinet member for the judiciary, for introducing legislation concerning judicial reform. However, as it is vital for good government that Parliament and the judiciary remain separate, the role of an appointed and unelected Chancellor, holding executive power as head of the judiciary, is an accidental result of history which is vigilantly scrutinized.

As Keeper of the Royal Conscience, the Chancellor is no father confessor to the monarch's soul but instead takes upon his shoulders the sovereign's responsibilities for those unable to help themselves. Blackstone describes that he was 'visitor, in right of the king, of all hospitals and colleges of the king's foundation, and patron of all the king's livings… the general guardian of all infants, idiots and lunatics, and has the general superintendence of all charitable uses in the kingdom'. These responsibilities have now largely been farmed out to the courts.

It is in Parliament that the Lord Chancellor is seen most at work. Here he is the Speaker of the Lords, but one who has little to do in a House which regulates itself. Every year, reflecting that he was once the eyes and ears of the monarch in Parliament, during the State Opening it is the Chancellor who kneels and presents the Sovereign with her Speech.

It was possible to be **Chancellor** and not a Peer of the Realm because sitting on the Woolsack, which is filled with the commodity that made the country rich in the middle ages, is technically not part of the Lords. Therefore, when Chancellors wish to speak in debate, which, as part of the Government they often do, they move to the left of the Woolsack, to the top of the Earls' bench, to reflect their seniority in the House.

Lord Great Chamberlain

THIS IS THE ONLY GREAT OFFICER OF STATE once legitimately entitled to ask for a Sovereign's underwear, bed, furniture and throne. It is also the oldest hereditary office of its kind to remain with direct descendants of the person to whom it was originally granted. The post was established after the Conquest. When William the Conqueror arrived to claim his crown he brought Robert Malet with him to be Chamberlain from the ducal residence in Normandy. While the Tower of London and other fortifications were built, the new king needed someone to oversee the improvements at Edward the Confessor's palace at Westminster.

The Great Chamberlaincy was made hereditary by Henry I in 1133, when Aubery de Vere was granted the appointment, and the de Veres began a male line which, with interruptions, continued until 1526, when the last male died. Mary and Elizabeth Tudor ruled over their heads in favour of a distant male heir. Again the same problem occured in 1626, when the beneficiary was Lord Willoughby d'Eresby. And yet again this line ended in two females, the Great Chamberlaincy being correctly settled in favour of three families after a House of Lords decision in 1902, for the coronation of Edward VII. They share the privilege, taking it in turns. The Marquesses of Cholmondeley have it for the Queen's reign. The Earls of Ancaster served George VI and Lord Carrington's family sit in waiting. The appointment probably survived because its function was largely ceremonial, titular and without much power.

The Palace of Westminster, which was once entirely the Lord Great Chamberlain's domain, is now his responsibility only as far as ceremonial matters are concerned: he plans the domestic arrangements whenever the Queen visits her Parliament. When the Queen's carriage draws to a halt under Victoria Tower, her Lord Great Chamberlain greets her and leads her in. He carries a white stave, which is a little over six foot long, and

on the back of his uniform he wears the golden key, the emblem of his appointment.

One of the privileges for the Lord Great Chamberlain was the archaic right to bring the monarch their shirt, stockings and drawers on the morning of the coronation and to help them dress. In former times monarchs always stayed the night prior to coronation at Westminster, so this made a little more sense. In return for this service, the monarch paid them some extraordinary fees. The Lord Great Chamberlain is entitled to claim the bed, bedding and nightgown used by the King on the eve of his coronation; also all the furniture, valances and curtains of the 'Royal Chamber', where he lay!

In addition he was entitled to demand the clothes worn by the King at the coronation, which include the underclothes, socks and other personal belongings of the stripped monarch. Quite what was done with these extraordinary acquisitions is left to our imagination. Not every monarch took this particularly well, even though there was little room for negotiation as the terms were framed in law. James I, who had just arrived from chilly Edinburgh to claim his English crown, must have raised his eyebrows at the request and would hear none of it, negotiating a sum of £200 in lieu. Queen Anne was, understandably, even more perplexed by the demand and sent £300 to keep her 'bottom drawer intact'. But things are different now, particularly as monarchs prefer a quiet night at Buckingham Palace before the coronation. Since 1821 the complex processions from the Hall to the Abbey are no longer necessary, which reduces the job requirement still further.

The Palace of Westminster is a royal residence in name only. The Lord Great Chamberlain's remit no longer runs far and his ancient functions are carried out by others, such as the Lord Chamberlain, who is the full-time Managing Director of the Royal Household, and Black Rod, who keeps order in Their Lordships' House and its environs.

By 'antient… just and lawful right' the **Lord Great Chamberlain** keeps the Consort's Throne and the Prince of Wales's Chair in the Stone Hall at Houghton: when needed he takes them to Parliament. The symbolic ceremonial key on his back shows that he once ran the palace's domestic arrangements. The white stave of office is carried throughout the reign and broken at the monarch's graveside. When leading the Sovereign to the Lords the Great Lord Chamberlain walks backwards.

High Almoner

The **High Almoner**, in the sanctuary of his cathedral at St Alban's, wearing the badge round his neck which shows the three-masted ship instituted as the symbol of the Royal Almonry by Cardinal Wolsey in 1512. He is girded with towels in remembrance of the days when monarchs, who were anxious to follow Christ's mandate of humility, washed the feet of the destitute. Bishops have filled this post since 1103.

'Where charity and love are, there is God.'

LATIN LITURGY FOR MAUNDY THURSDAY

FROM THE START, IT WAS INCUMBENT upon all Christian kings to remember Christ's example. Their legitimacy came from the coronation unction they received from God and this set them apart as His vicegerent on earth. Just as monarchs were raised above their people by God, so they owed their people a duty to follow Christ's example of humility, symbolized by His washing of feet at the Last Supper. The Christian calendar of high days illuminated specific events in red, and these 'red letter days' required attendance at mass, possibly a crown-wearing ceremony (coronamenta) and maybe some preparatory fasting. Few pages were more heavily inscribed than Holy Week, with its culmination of Christ's Passion. On the eve of Good Friday was the observance of the Mandatum, or commandment, which was spelled out by Jesus, who said, 'I give you a new commandment: Love one another; as I have loved you, so you are to love one another.' Following the ten commandments given by God, this was the eleventh.

To observe this, kings were expected to follow Christ's example when, the night before his crucifixion, at Passover supper with his disciples, he 'laid aside his garments and took a towel and girded himself. After that he poureth water into a basin, and began to wash the disciples' feet, and to wipe them with the towel wherewith he was girded.' Over the centuries, the combination of both dreadful hygiene and other perceived dangers associated with gathering the destitute meant that by 1730 foot washing ended. However, specially minted silver coins were always part of the monarch's charity, as Maundy Money is today. But the tradition of giving out food and objects from the royal wardrobe was replaced with more money, all of which was frankly popular with paupers, who could do more with a full purse than scented feet. To assist in this religious service and to administer the sovereign's obligation, a Lord High Almoner was appointed, whose status is emphasized by inclusion among the Great Officers of State.

Only recently have monarchs revived an active part in the annual ceremony each Maundy Thursday. For years the Lord High Almoner would distribute purses on the king's behalf to a gathering of however many men and women that year equalled the number in the monarch's age. When attending the Maundy Service, he dons towels made in 1883 which symbolize those worn by Jesus. He is responsible for the Royal Maundy each year, as part of the Royal Almonry, which is administered by the Queen's Privy Purse; however, he was once charged with controlling much more.

The Lord High Almoner was a form of lottery-cum-spin-doctor in the middle ages. When the king passed through towns, he would strew the route with money from his master's treasury in order to attract an enthusiastic crowd. He could give the fish dish from the king's table to 'whatever poor person he pleased'. Also, he received all *deodand*, basically any moving thing that had killed a man, which, by dint of its action, became forfeit to God, in the person of His representative the sovereign. So the Lord High Almoner received the hapless horses, carts and ladders which he distributed to the needy after taking a small cut. The practice was abolished in 1846.

Some almonry duties like tearing up and handing out the blue carpet that lined the coronation route went to the Hereditary Grand Almoner. This appointment was originally vested in the barony of Bedford which, before Richard II, was in the Beauchamp family. However, through a complex inheritance it came to the Cecils, as earls of Exeter, who fulfilled the job from James II's coronation in 1685 until 1821. Though the present Marquess of Exeter is still Hereditary Grand Almoner, he is a purely titular figure.

The first Lord High Almoner appeared in 1103. It has always been an ecclesiastical appointment filled mostly by bishops but sometimes by archbishops. Now the High Almoner concentrates solely on planning the Queen's annual act of humility.

Lady Marcher of Camaes and Mayor of Newport

I N 1087 WILLIAM RUFUS reneged on his father's treaty with Rhys ap Tewdwr, the King of Deheubarth. This agreement had held the English border with Wales in peace because it kept the land-hungry Norman barons in check. But with Rhys dead, this policy was replaced with land grabbing violence. All along the Welsh border, from the County Palatine of Chester down to the River Severn, the Normans advanced with small armies across the Marchiae Walliae, or March of Wales.

They deposed the Welsh rulers by sword or drove them into the hills. Their reward was land over which no English king had ever ruled and so consequently they owed no fealty to the Crown. Instead they held *Jura Regalia*, a sovereign power which was theirs by conquest.

One of the furthermost outposts grabbed in this way was Camaes. It was among the seven cantrefs (or hundreds) of Dyfed. Taking its name from the Welsh *camas*, meaning 'river bend or sea inlet', it included the land around the town of Newport. The people here were well used to war and had endured Norse invasions before Norman ones. Wales itself endured a culture of domestic battles between rival princes. They had also heard tales of William I's recent progress to nearby St David's, at the head of a vast army.

Supposedly, Martin de Tours landed at Fishguard. The natives bombarded his ships with boulders as they lay at anchor, forcing him further east 'where the harbour was on the flat and safe from projectiles from above'. The King's Antiquary was sent to Wales in the 1530s to record the country's history: he wrote, 'one Martin de Turribus, a Norman, won the countrey of Kemmeys in Wales about the tyme of King William Conqueror, and that this Martinus foundid the abbey of S. Dogmael in Kemeis and that he lyith buried in the quier there'.

This was an endless saga for Camaes, caught in the fray between Anglo-Norman and Welsh interests that, with the nationalism of the great Princes of Gwynedd in conflict with Norman and Plantagenet aggrandisement, could never be compatible. Camaes was merged into the County of Pembroke, for a long time the possession of English kings.

It was to Pembroke that Henry Tudor came in 1485 to raise support for his stand against Richard III. But it was not until 1536 that Henry VIII gave equal status to the Welsh under the Act of Union between England and Wales. The Act ended the independence of the Marcher Baronies, bringing them into the shires and creating new shires in the north. Camaes was merged fully into Pembrokeshire, though the barony structure remained to administrate the community, as it did all over England until councils took over.

William Owen, fourteenth Lord Marcher of Camaes, was born in 1469 and lived to be 105. As a young man he did well in his legal training at the Temple and met up with Lord Audley, who made him 'Clerk of the courts of Camaes for the rest of his life'. Audley had recently had the barony returned to him, was not much interested in it and was thus happy to offer it in security against a loan from Owen.

The family still hold the Marcher Barony and with it considerable powers over 22,000 acres spread around Newport, most of which lies between the villages of Brynberian and Crymmch. The Lady Marcher describes it as 'quite hard work in that we hold a Court Leet which meets three times a year in the Llwyngwair Arms pub, where it's met for hundreds of years. It deals with things like boundaries, water, grazing and travellers and I always try to be there. Each member of the Court Leet still swears an oath of allegiance to me and the Queen which dates from about 1400. Every November, I appoint the Mayor of Newport. The appointment is agreed between myself and the Court beforehand. At the Court Leet I place the chain of office round his neck and he gives me a red rose in fealty.'

The river bend and sea inlet which gave Camaes its name is now the site of Newport. From its castle the **Lady Marcher** can keep an eye on the community's affairs and confer the mayoralty on one of three names put forward by its community.

2

ORGANIZING CHAOS

1150–1485

THE FIRST CENTURY OF NORMAN RULE was one of consolidation. After brief respite, they began their subjugation of Wales, launched their gradual influence over the Scots and invaded Ireland in 1169. The *Domesday Book* named more than 13,000 settlements in England. The feudal system was headed by the king and his 300 *Rentiers*, or Tenants-in-Chief, who lived off the revenues of estates in turn tenanted to others. At the bottom of the scale came *Villani* (villeins), with just an allotment to their names, who lived in dwellings grouped together (villages), and *Cottars*, who held small landholdings.

This structure gave rise to ambitions among powerful *Rentiers* and, as the landed power base gained strength, challenges to executive royal authority increased. As a result civil chaos often ensued between the king, his barons and the increasingly influential Church. The titles in this chapter resulted from balancing the demands of these three. While democracy was still centuries away and powerful kings would occasionally regain executive power, the balance of power shifted ideologically from the king during this period. Some titles survive from the embryo parliament that was born and others from the palatine powers granted to significant tenants-in-chief who took on demi-ruler status with their own laws and system of justice.

Overseas expansion became an objective. Edward III claimed the crown of France by inheritance through his mother, and he planned to invade to secure his claim. He could not do so unless he was secure at home. To achieve this security he leant upon the discipline of knighthood, which had been a royal honour vested since Saxon times upon proven warriors and which the Church had utilized as the basis for military organization during the crusades. However, the Crusader knights were disciplined still further by oaths that reflected those taken by members of the monastic orders. The result had been a loyal force that contemplated eternal damnation as the price of disloyalty. Therefore, Edward gathered the most powerful knights to his side and, by reviving the chivalrous legend of King Arthur and the Round Table, he created a quasi-religious order of chivalry made up of people upon whom he could depend.

These questions of war and land generated the medieval sciences of genealogy and heraldry because proof of inheritance, birth and ownership became significant. Vibrant heraldic symbolism was developed to differentiate knights in battle. Arguments over privilege, position and status were entrusted by monarchs to their Great Officers of State – Lord Lyon in Scotland and the Constable and Marshal in England; each was assisted by officers of arms, who held important military and diplomatic responsibilities.

Others who enjoyed the riches of great feudal estates were tasked with further domestic duties. Medieval kings in England and Scotland divided up their shores into admiralties, which placed the security of the coastline itself under supervision. The invasion by Louis of France in 1216 was a reminder of the country's vulnerability, so every cliff, cove and port was supervised. The family charged with securing the Wash still farms the lands that originally came with the job.

As commerce and wealth increased, successful speculators and merchants pressured the king for special privileges. The merchant city of London thrived upon its trade with Europe, and the livery companies developed a unique structure to which monarchs, benefiting from their success, were willing to grant privileges. The City's democracy of wealth developed a court reflecting the Crown's blueprint of officers with its own, similarly charged with security, justice and revenue raising within its ancient Roman boundaries. The wealth that came from Cornwall's tin also commanded special privileges, granted with the caveat that they were controlled by an officer appointed by the monarch. This prevented the development of any separatist tendencies within territory so close to France. To tie Cornwall still closer Edward III granted it to his son as a duchy.

To another son, John of Gaunt, Edward III revived the palatine status of the County of Lancaster as a dukedom. This gave authority for devolved powers that stopped short of independent sovereignty, so the Count Palatine could administer his own laws and judiciary. However, it was not always easy to remove feudal grants from those elevated to such power, and Lancaster later became the base for a challenge to the king's power: Lancastrians happily gave their loyalty to their Count Palatine and helped the red rose of Lancaster to victory in the protracted and bloody Wars of the Roses.

When Henry III decided, rashly, to take on a mass of papal debt and a commitment to invade Sicily he placed a massive burden on the English exchequer. The country rebelled under the leadership of Simon de Montfort, and the king was forced to accept an elected

The **Sword of State** was the King's personal weapon. He fought with it, dubbed with it and had it carried before him as a symbol of his power. This is a copy of the Sword of State made in 1678 for Charles II, and shows symbols of four kingdoms: England's rose, Scotland's thistle, Ireland's harp and France's *fleur de lys*. Also Margaret Beaufort's Portcullis Badge, it is now the symbol of Parliament, where the Sword is still carried before the Queen each year at the State Opening.

aristocratic parliament, which met at Westminster Abbey, rebuilt by Henry as a mausoleum for the lately canonized Edward the Confessor. This made the abbey the focus of national life and gave it a unique status, and so it was granted privileges and powers by the king. Among them was the right to grant sanctuary to fugitives, administered by the High Bailiff and Searcher of the Sanctuary.

After Robert the Bruce's Scottish army won the Wars of Independence against Edward on the field of Bannockburn in 1314, the Treaty of Arbroath was despatched to Rome and the Pope acknowledged Scotland's sovereignty by granting the right of unction to its kings. During the war, Scotland's castles had provided his enemies with useful outposts, so Bruce took them under centralized royal control. Responsibility was dispersed through feudal means to loyal lieutenants and their duties became respectively dressed with titles like Governor, Constable or Keeper. He also appointed as Constable the chief of the Hay family, who held lands and influence on the east coast. The appointment was made hereditary and the monarch's personal safety was one of his responsibilities.

Royal power was directly pruned by Magna Carta (1215), which forced King John to acknowledge certain rights of his subjects. This document has influenced constitutional powers of jurisdiction worldwide. The preservation of this document, and all other legal records, were maintained by the Master of the Rolls, and although his function and position have changed radically the pipe rolls that recorded all judgements remain an archive of law in the kingdom.

The Church's influence grew because educated priests ran the complex apparatus of the State; but this was threatened by the plague, which hit clerics ministering to the sick and dying and led to a shortage of literate people. To check this dearth, and to continue the education of the laity, particularly the poor, two great benefactors established foundations: William of Wykeham founded Winchester College, and a century later Henry VI endowed Eton and King's College Cambridge.

The Wars of the Roses destroyed much of the structure and strength that had been carefully amassed around the Crown, which was disabled by aristocratic factionalism. It was only with the end of this civil war and a fundamental reassessment that a powerful monarch could regain the initiative and recreate a strong kingdom.

Knight Grand Cross of the Most Honourable Order of the Bath

BY COMPARISON WITH OTHER ORDERS of chivalry, the Bath, founded in 1725, is relatively modern. Its connections with the ancient orders by that name are circumstantial and not formal. However, the Bath forms part of the evolution of the most enduring form of honour, knighthood. While many honours are often derided, knighthood manages to maintain a credibility of merit, due in some measure to the culture of achievement which surrounds this history.

When it was established, the new order took its name and many of its symbols from the medieval practice of creating knights. It was deemed necessary for a warrior preparing for the accolade of knighthood to undergo certain rituals that would purify his body and soul so that his commitment could be worthy of God, in whose name the honour was conferred. Central to this process, which became increasingly structured during the fourteenth century's age of Chivalry, was the taking of a bath.

First the candidates fasted, spending time in religious contemplation and confession. This prepared their soul for the obligation. The bath was then prepared for the candidate to immerse his body into, which was an act of cleanliness rarely practised in these times, and its purpose was to ensure that the knight was 'of a pure mind and of honest intentions, willing to conflict with any dangers or difficulties in the cause of virtue; to take care both in his words and actions to follow the maxims of prudence; and religiously to observe the rules of fidelity and honour'. After the washing was done, the dripping candidate was led by his squires to a bed where the covers absorbed the wetness to symbolically draw the remaining impurities from his body.

The word knight evolves from *cnight*, the Saxon for youth or military follower. The first recorded knighthood conferred in England was over a thousand years ago when the future king Athelstan was dubbed by his grandfather, Alfred the Great, in token of which a red robe encrusted with jewels was given. While red robes were not always the colour given for the Bath, when the order was revived mulberry satin was selected, with a rich white taffeta lining: these colours symbolizing the blood of Christ and the Virgin Mary's purity.

Before the Norman invasion, Anglo-Saxon knights visited a cleric in some place of worship to spend a night in contemplation before being dubbed with a special sword by the priest at dawn. The medieval knights of the Bath also took vigil with their shield and sword, the latter being symbolically offered at the altar to be the instrument of God's will and surrendered for a fee. A sword is still used when the honour is conferred.

Another link in the history of knighthood and to the spiritual lives of Norman and Plantagenet kings can be found in the upper floors of the Tower of London's White Tower. Built by William the Conqueror, the Chapel Royal of St John the Evangelist remains a silent witness to many of the many vigils which knights observed. Kings too did vigil here before their coronations and, in 1399, before Henry IV's crowning, 46 knights of the Bath were initiated: as Froissart describes, they 'watched all that night, each of whom had his chamber and his Bath, in which he bathed; and the next day the Duke of Lancaster made them knights at the celebration of mass…and the said knights had on their left shoulder a double cordon of white silk, with tassels hanging down'.

The old order slipped into disuetude under James II but, according to Horace Walpole, was revived in 1725 by Sir Robert Walpole as 'an artful bank of thirty-six Ribbands to supply a fund of favours in lieu of places'. The order burgeoned in classes and membership after the defeat of Napoleon at Waterloo in 1815 and serves to express national gratitude to military and civil servants. While bathing is no longer mandatory, it is hoped that all do.

Medieval **Knights of the Bath** frequently kept their vigil in William the Conqueror's private chapel at the Tower of London. Waiting with his sword for dawn and the accolade, the knight was freshly bathed for purification of body and soul. The 1725 Order of the Bath has no formal links with its predecessor but echoes much of this history, including the double cordon of white silk on the left shoulder.

Knight Companion of the Most Noble Order of the Garter

Founded at the onset of the 100 Years War, the Garter's livery of dark blue mimics the royal colours of the defeated French. This **Knight of the Garter**, robed in mantle, collar, Great George Star and carrying his ostrich-plumed hat, also holds the Garter worn by his ancestor, who was the last man to lead an English army to defeat the French. He stands in the Waterloo Gallery, part of the London house given by a grateful nation to their Iron Duke.

QUITE HOW SUCH A STRANGE ITEM became the symbol of the oldest and most senior order of chivalry remains a mystery but the Garter is now over 650 years old and it crops up everywhere, even on cereal packets and marmalade jars. In fact, wherever the Royal Arms are shown, the Garter's dark blue buckled belt with its golden motto neatly encircles the shield.

The actual date of the order's foundation is unclear, as are the events surrounding the occasion. What we do know is that the order is as fine a memorial to its founder, Edward III, as even that romantic and capable monarch could have wished. He fostered chivalry among his nobles, leading them to great wars and sharing victories with banquets, wine and women. The motivation for the order's creation was political but the inspiration was his hero, the legendary King Arthur, and the Round Table. As early as 1344, Edward told his court that a new Round Table of knights would be mustered for jousting tournaments. There would be two teams of twelve: he would lead one, his son, the Black Prince, the other. The meetings would take place at Windsor, and he used the feudal system to summon a workforce to build halls suitable for the festivities.

No sooner had the building work begun than Edward was off to war, this time pushed by an alliance between Scotland and France to defend his interests against the latter's king. His premise for the fight was to claim the French throne for himself: after all, his mother was the late king's sister.

Edward never forgot how quickly domestic problems could develop if the barons were free to plot. First, he knew that conquests must be delivered. His son achieved success at Crécy in 1346 and, subsequently, Calais fell into Edward's hands. Secondly, he needed to secure this advantage. So, on return to Windsor, he evolved his embryo Round Table into an order of chivalry, specifically one which imposed a grave oath of loyalty upon the membership. Few dared to break such bonds in these superstitious times.

The knights' symbol was then, as it is now, a blue garter marked with the motto in gold, 'Honi soit qui mal y pense.' Blue was the French royal colour and its use was a deliberate slight against the French and underlined England's claim to their throne. The motto's provenance is less easy to define. Possibly the fanciful story of Joane, Countess of Salisbury dancing is true. It is said that her garter came loose and fell to the floor, causing laughter among the courtly onlookers. Edward supposedly picked it up, silencing the court and, tying it round the heroic Black Prince's leg, spoke the motto, which loosely translated is, 'Shame to those who think evil of it.' Other sources say it was Edward's queen who dropped her garter and the motto was how she replied when he said it would one day be a symbol of reverence. However, the most tantalizing theory is more recent and points out that witchcraft was still practised in the fourteenth century and that the garter would have been recognized as a symbol of coven membership. Therefore, Edward saved a potentially hazardous situation by stepping in to save a lady's embarrassment.

The Garter has evolved to suit the needs of successive monarchs. The Tudors, anxious to legitimize their dynasty by currying favour with foreign monarchs, used the Garter as a powerful political tool. Henry VIII's excesses led to the most frequent use of Degradation, a ritual that humiliated the treasonable knight, whose banner, sword and helm were throw from their position above the stall in St George's Chapel, to be kicked by heralds out of the gates and into the ditch. For the doomed miscreant such a slight probably went unnoticed.

Today, the Most Noble Order, which is the oldest and most senior in the world, includes former Prime Ministers, retired generals and admirals, and a number of familiar ducal names. Recently, the statutes were evolved to include ladies.

Lyon King of Arms

The Mercat Cross in Edinburgh close to Scotland's old parliament is where all royal statements were made and was often the scene of dissent. Since the Union of 1707, Lyon, as the Queen's representative, has continued to deliver royal proclamations. The Cross is adorned with the arms of Edinburgh, the Kingdom of Scots and the quartered design of the four kingdoms which the **Lord Lyon** also wears. Scotland's rampant lion takes precedence and is repeated twice.

SCOTLAND'S HERALDRY AND CEREMONIAL is run in a very different way from England, by the Lord Lyon King of Arms. He is a Great Officer of State and a judge, with his own Court of the Lord Lyon. Appointed by the Sovereign, he answers to none other and has a unique control over the granting of armorial bearing of the recognition of clan chiefs. On the Queen's behalf, the Lord Lyon makes Royal Proclamations from the Mercat Cross in Edinburgh and it is in this way that news of Parliament's dissolution in far away Westminster is formally announced to the Scottish people; by tradition, it is done three days after the Prime Minister gets the Queen's approval for a General Election, because that was the time taken by a messenger to gallop 400 miles from London with the news. Emphasizing the significance of his role, Scots Law, which is different in so many ways from that practised in England and Wales, criminalizes as treason an assault on the Lord Lyon when carrying out the monarch's work.

Heraldry is a relatively new concern for the Lord Lyon. His predecessors reach back into the ancient history of Scotland's monarchy when they filled the appointment as *Ard Seanachaidh*, or bard-recorder. It was necessary for a scholar to pronounce the king's genealogy, linking him with heroic ancestors for credibility back to Fergus Mor MacErch, who began the royal line in the fifth century. Therefore, the emergence of heraldry in Europe dropped naturally into his lap. Lyon is said to have played a prominent part at Robert II's coronation and one source states that Robert the Bruce appointed a Lyon four years after Bannockburn, in 1318. With certainty, a Lyon Herald received payment from the Exchequer Roll in 1377; another in 1388 styles him royally, as *Leo Regi Heraldorum*; and Henry Greve held office in 1399 and attended celebrations in London connected with Henry IV's coronation.

The title evolves from the use of an heraldic lion by Scotland's kings on their arms. This may date from William 'the Lion', who reigned from 1165 to 1214 and established links with France, which after the Franco-Scottish Treaty of 1295 formed the Auld Alliance. The lion first appeared on the seal of his son, Alexander II, who is depicted with it on his shield, and it has been used ever since. Lyons in the past even had their own coronation; having the crown, one of the three Honours of Scotland, placed momentarily upon their heads.

Such detail has always been the substance of good heraldry and Lyon sits as a judge to oversee any abuse of heraldic law that is brought to his Court by his Procurator Fiscal. His is the only court of chivalry in regular use and is totally integrated within the national legal system. Recent cases include the display of armorial ensigns by the Porsche motor company; as there was no acknowledged grant for the design in Scotland, Lyon ruled that, whilst it would be churlish to demand that the radiator badges be removed, the company was prevented from displaying its shield on garages or publicity material.

At his sole discretion grants for armorial bearings are made and, if evidence of inheritance can be proved, the original grant may be 'matriculated' or altered for the grantee's descendants. He instructs Lyon Clerk and Keeper of the Records to record these in the Public Register of All Arms and Bearings in Scotland. Proven family lines are likewise entered in the Public Register of all Genealogies and Birthbrieves. Amongst these are the Chiefly lines of the Highland Clans who bear patriarchal/matriarchal responsibility for families spread throughout the world. Lyon must be satisfied before a chief has the right to hold sway.

Scotland's State ceremonies are the Lord Lyon's responsibility and he advises the First Minister where necessary. A new Scottish parliament presents opportunities for the nation to celebrate both its history and new beginnings in fresh rituals which the Lord Lyon has the provenance to guide.

Kings of Arms, Heralds of Arms and Pursuivants of Arms in Ordinary and Extraordinary

'And every man Of hem, as I yow tellen can, Had on him throwen a vesture, Which that men clepe a cote-armure, Embrowded wonderliche riche.'

GEOFFREY CHAUCER, 1383

HERALDRY, WITH ITS STRIDENT COLOURS, romantic beasts and strange language, provides one of the brightest illustrations for European history. Since the middle ages, its semiology has been used to celebrate, identify and associate figures and families from the nation's story with buildings, documents and possessions. By enforcing complex rules, it provides a simple system of devices which convey considerable detail to the trained eye. The distinguishing symbols mirror similar systems adopted by tribes and nations throughout the world, each seeking a means to mark the individual out from his peers. Great importance was associated with the study of heraldic sciences and it was once seen as a prerequisite to advancement, just as maths qualifications are regarded as crucial for most jobs today.

In Europe the rapid development of heraldry brought with it the need for regulation and control: in England this became the responsibility of a College, or body of colleagues, consisting of three ranks: Pursuivants, who were attendants or followers; Heralds, whose name, possibly from Hermes, the Greek messenger of the gods, derives from a root meaning 'controller of an army', and Kings, who held administrative sway over vast areas and were given the right to grant armorial bearings in the monarch's name. Collectively, they are still called the Officers of Arms.

The earliest heralds, referred to in the twelfth century, were little more than criers who announced jousts at tournaments. However, as order came to the chivalric world and knights adopted symbols and observed rituals, the heralds became guardians of the new language. They were literate and academic, which outside the monasteries was rare and, by 1350, they were responsible for arranging royal events, negotiating with foreign rulers and delivering proclamations.

All the officers' appointments have names which reflect either the territorial responsibility they held or some symbol closely associated with the Crown. At their head are the three kings, chief of whom is Garter King of Arms, whose appointment was created three months before the Battle of Agincourt in 1415 by Henry V, and who has added responsibilities for running the Order of the Garter. Oldest among the other two is Norroy, short for north king, which dates from 1276. Since 1943, Ulster has been added to his realm. Until then the division between his English responsibilities was the river Trent: he took the north and Clarenceaux (after the Earl of Clare's lands) took land to the south. At one time each king was crowned and anointed with wine pressed from grapes native to the region concerned.

The Heralds are Chester, Lancaster, Windsor, Richmond, York and Somerset, all founded in the

Tabards, or coats of arms, were worn over armour by kings. Henry V wore his at Agincourt in 1415 and heralds wore the king's coat too, to reflect his status in their work. The Corporation of **Kings**, **Heralds** and **Pursuivants** in Ordinary wear tabards of velvet, satin and damask respectively. The Extraordinaries reflect this, with only the lack of a tiny coronet on their wand marking them as junior to the College's Chapter.

fourteenth and fifteenth centuries. The Pursuivants, founded in the latter, include Bluemantle, named after the Garter's robe, and Rouge Croix, Rouge Dragon and Portcullis, all appointed by the Tudor Henrys. They were named after St George's cross, the Tudor dragon of Wales and the Portcullis of Margaret Beaufort, Henry VII's mother (a badge now used by Parliament) respectively.

From 1530 to 1700 officers of arms made visitations to their provinces and audited the heraldry people used. In addition, they supervised ceremonies, particularly funerals, and, like snobbery police, stopped social climbers from outranking themselves with too much undeserved display. When transgressions were uncovered, each case was heard at the Court of Chivalry, where the Lord High Constable and Earl Marshal were judges. Though it has not sat since 1954, the court is still extant at the College of Arms in London.

Anyone can go to the College to have their genealogy researched, check whether armorial bearings already exist in their families and, if not and

they so wish, petition for a Grant of Arms. The heralds check against documents that date back to the fifteenth century. Few are prevented from adding their names to the armigerous, as those with arms are known, and displaying their bearings on anything from letterheads to pyjama pockets.

There are up to thirteen full-time officers, known as Officers in Ordinary, who are assisted by part-timers when called upon, called Officers Extraordinary. The Extraordinaries are named after the many titles held by the College's supervisor, the Earl Marshal of England. All of these officers help the Earl Marshal in his hereditary responsibility as stage manager of State occasions. Just as they supervised early tournaments, the heralds are now the guardians of the way the State celebrates itself, evolving traditions to reflect changing needs. They are the professors of ceremonial provenance, the guardians of the national armoury and pedigree, and the three kings wait to exercise the Sovereign's authority in granting new arms: just as they have since the middle ages.

Lord High Constable of Scotland and Slains Pursuivant

CONSIDERING THAT THE HAYS OF ERROLL have frequently supported the losing side in royal history, it is remarkable that they have held on to the most powerful hereditary appointment in the land, as Lords High Constable, for so long. But their high principles and independent spirit were wisely directed in support of Robert the Bruce at the Battle of Bannockburn, 1314, where Sir Gilbert de la Haye proved a loyal and effective supporter. The grateful king, who believed only a miracle would win him the battle, made Gilbert the Constable of Scotland and decreed it to be hereditary.

Constables appeared in all the western courts that adopted Byzantine Court administration and customs. It implied military command and, in Scotland, asserted jurisdiction which superseded ordinary courts, over offences committed within a certain distance of the monarch or Parliament. The first mentioned was Edward, who served both Alexander I and David I, during the twelfth century. He was referred to as 'Chief of David's Knights'.

The Lord High Constable commands the Doorward Guard of Partizans, the oldest body guard in Britain, and holds a silver baton as a symbol of his office. The appointment takes precedence above all titles bar the Royal Family's.

The ruins of Slains Castle, on top of Scotland's eastern cliffs, stand close to the original fortress of the powerful **High Constables of Scotland**. **Slains Pursuivant** wears the tabard of his master, showing the three red shields that flew over de la Haye's men at Bannockburn. The Earl of Erroll carries the High Constable's baton.

The Chiefs of the Clan Hay, who became earls in 1452, held court in Slains Castle. They had a large household, founded in the fifteenth century, which included an officer of arms named, not unnaturally, Slains Pursuivant. This entourage reflected the influence they held. When Robert Bruce's male heir had no children and his daughter's son, by Walter the High Steward of Scotland, became king, the Constable became more powerful yet. With the Steward's title now merged into the Crown, more responsibilities were passed to the Constable. Thus, when young Mary Queen of Scots was married to the Dauphin of France, her duties included acting as Lord Lieutenant for most of the country in their absence.

Although the Hays often found themselves on the losing side, these were honourable defeats. Two Constables fell in combat fulfilling their obligations against the English army: first defending Bruce's son, David, at Neville's Cross in 1346; then at Flodden Field in 1513, when most who marched south with the king never returned. Catholic loyalty led them to lose again, twice. First, when supporting a Counter-Reformation plan with Philip of Spain to overthrow Elizabeth I and place a 'converted' James VI on the united throne. It fouled up James's plans so badly that the king felt honour bound to blow up Slains Castle to appease Elizabeth's envoys. And in the 1745 Jacobite Rebellion, Lady Erroll, believing herself to be Constable to Bonnie Prince Charlie, sent her sons to fight for his cause.

When James VI left Holyrood for London, the Constable's role altered. In the absence of the king, responsibility for protecting his person and the Verge of his palace switched to the Council, which was exercising power in his absence. A new job title was consolidated in 1681, with a ratification in favour of John, the 12th earl, referring to a 'great constabulary', or 'high constabulary', and establishing his title as Lord High Constable. These changes reflected the inflation in court titles then current on the continent, particularly at Versailles, where levels of deference were becoming a cloying artform. The English Constable was similarly prefixed for James VII/II's coronation. This title was held hereditarily by the de Bohuns, as earls of Hereford and Essex; it passed to the Staffords and, when Henry VIII attainted Edward Stafford, Duke of Buckingham, it merged with the Crown and is now revived only 'from sunrise to sunset' on the day of a coronation. The Errolls are also Assessors to the Court of the Lord Lyon, along with the Dukes of Hamilton.

Master of the Horse

GETTING ABOUT IS AS IMPORTANT TODAY as it ever has been and power depends significantly on mobility. For these two reasons kings have always been keen to maximize their capacity to get around, and those who failed sometimes lost their thrones. For instance, Harold II needed to get his army from Stamford Bridge to Hastings in a hurry when he heard of the Norman invasion. On the other hand, Duke William concentrated on moving his army and horses effectively across the Channel by ship. The duke succeeded but Harold failed. Had the transportation available to either ruler been different, the Normans might never have conquered England.

Ever since man learnt how to break a horse's will to his own, there have been few more reliable forms of transport. They have carried knights into the thick of battle, conveyed messengers from one court to another and enabled monarchs to cover their territory in haste. The Merovingian and Carolingian courts evolved the equine strategies of Rome, particularly where combat-effectiveness was concerned, and combined it with their teutonic efficiency. To streamline this, rulers in the western empire introduced marshals to their courts who were specifically responsible for the stables. This was true of Normandy and it helped to ensure that Duke William's plan was effective.

The Normans managed to rule England from horseback. This was reflected in the increasing prominence given by kings to their Marshals and Keepers of Stables. During the successful campaigns in Scotland and Wales, Edward I's Keeper supplied his king's insatiable demands for new horses through a network of studs both north and south of the River Trent, the traditional dividing line between the north and the south of England.

Edward III's claim to the French throne was catalyst for a war that lasted one hundred years. John Brocas, a Gascon noble who had survived two royal coups and the murder of Edward II, was sent to Gascony to sort out a local supply of horses fast. By turning procurement into a military operation and making it work with crude efficiency, his work secured victory for English knights at Crécy and later at the siege of Calais. The grateful king knighted Brocas and created him Master of the Horse.

At Agincourt, Henry V placed even greater demands on his Master, John Waterton. There was the long autumnal march through France and the battle at Farfleur, to say nothing of the concurrent need to maintain the garrison's horses on the Scottish border prior to departure, all of which placed heavy administrative burdens on Waterton. He retired soon after the battle. His three successors had all seen action with Henry V at Agincourt, serving among the 'happy few' on St Crispian's Day.

On Bosworth Field, Henry Tudor's standard was carried by William Brandon, who died in the battle. In gratitude, the new king Henry VII appointed William's brother, Thomas, as his first Master of the Horse (Grand Ecuyer). His instructions were to run an efficient, frugal stable but to see that it was capable of meeting the demands of Tudor pageantry. Display of royal splendour was a vital art of statecraft, particularly with the onset of the Renaissance.

Henry VIII's Master at the Field of the Cloth of Gold was Sir Henry Guildford, chosen partly because his horsemanship would not rival the king's. Guildford arrived at the spectacle immediately behind Henry VIII leading the king's second charger, as was the custom. The job well done coincided with a wealthier court and so his office became more powerful and better paid.

The Earl of Essex, one of Elizabeth I's ill-fated and foolish suitors, acted as her Master for fourteen years; he was given many other lucrative appointments besides but he still managed to reorganize the Queen's studs.

Five Masters died on the scaffold; one Master, John Claypole, served Cromwell and one, the 4th

From the **Master**'s right shoulder hang golden ropes, called aiguilettes, with two tiny spikes which symbolize the tethering rope and pegs used to tie the queen's horse. Since Henry VIII's time he has kept close to the monarch when horses are about, which might have included hunting here in Windsor's Great Park.

Duke of Devonshire, was also the Prime Minister. The Master of the Horse was a powerful political appointment and, until 1782, was of Cabinet rank, a Privy Councillor and a Peer. It remained a Government appointment, changing with each ministry until 1924, when it became permanent.

Responsibility for the functions of the Royal Mews, which is now as much a case of servicing Rolls Royces as summoning the vet, is carried out by the crown Equerry, a full time executive. Equally, the horses needed for hunting and racing are specializations long since parcelled out to professionals. The Master is now nothing to do with the acquisition of new horses for the army. In fact the role is purely ceremonial and, on his white charger, the Master of the Horse is always close to the Queen when horses are about.

The office reflects a typical progression over the centuries from vital need, through powerful significance, to peripheral unimportance. For the moment, the titular role is vested in a Peer but soon it may seem more relevant to appoint the Crown Equerry to the rank, thus reuniting a once considerable rank with real responsibility.

Master of the Rolls

FEW PROFESSIONS GENERATE more paperwork than the law. The archive produced by lawyers over more than a thousand years is considerable. Yet it needs to be stored. Its existence is the life blood of England's legal system and someone had to be responsible for its maintenance.

The legal structure imposed on England by the Romans was broadly displaced by the migrant races who filled the power vacuum after the Legions left in the fifth and sixth centuries. However, the judicial ideal brought from Rome survived and was used, to varying degrees, by the seven separate kingdoms, known as the Heptarchy, by which England was ruled for three centuries. When the Saxon kings of Wessex achieved a position of supremacy within that Heptarchy, the vine was planted of what we know today as English Common Law: this is the part of England's law that is not embodied in legislation but which derives from the precedent of common custom and judicial decisions.

This could have been cut down when William the Conqueror defeated Harold II's army at Hastings. However, the Norman Duke chose to make good his conquest by respecting Saxon law and one of his sons made an obligation to adhere to the laws of Edward the Confessor, a bargaining point to win himself election as monarch.

The Conqueror claimed the throne by dint of what he held up to be Edward's legally binding promise. He waited for the Saxon Witenamegot, or high council, to 'elect' him as king: a vote that was unlikely to be lost. And, instead of riding roughshod through his subdued territory, he promised to uphold Saxon laws.

English Common Law, which has spread its influence across the globe, is so named because, after the Conquest, this was the law common to the whole country rather than that which was imposed at local level by barons. Its emphasis on precedent ensures that each judgement, assuming it has not been superseded, can be introduced as valid evidence in a legal argument. Subject to new legislation, ancient judgements have always been unearthed to prove the innocent and punish the guilty. Therefore, each judgement has a considerable value and must be stored from generation to generation. Scribes dutifully recorded each one on parchment and, when completed, each vellum was rolled and stored.

A reference in the history of England's Chancery states that parchment rolls, containing the most important judgements and decisions, were being stored there in 1199. However, the court system producing these records began earlier that century, in Henry II's reign. He was the first king of the Angevin empire and respected the legal customs of his disparate lands. The rolls were perhaps in need of order when John De Kirkby was appointed Custos Rolulorum in 1265. At that time, the task appears to have been a purely administrative one and the many different titles given seem to support this, like Clerk or Curator of the Rolls.

Reflecting the growing importance of this archive, the status of its custodian increased during the early fourteenth century. By the end of Edward I's reign, the title Master of the Rolls was in use and its holder was allocated funds for a household. At this time a Master, or Magister, was both a judge and an administrator; he was the senior judge responsible for running the courts and a group of other judges.

The inflation of status was perhaps inevitable and, in 1377, Edward III granted a splendid residence to the Master, called the House for Converted Jews, just off Chancery Lane.

Perhaps because of the gradual accumulation of vellum rolls, this residence became an office and then an archive. Consequently, its site is now occupied by a vast Victorian building where, until recently, all significant documents of State, apart from Acts of Parliament, were stored along with the ancient rolls. Among them are the Coronation Rolls, the only

Until its transfer to the Public Record Office at Kew, a site known as the Rolls Estate – which lies between London's Chancery and Fetter Lanes – was where government records have generally been stored since the middle ages. Historically the **Master of the Rolls** was not a judge but the keeper of the Parchment Rolls, or 'king's filing clerk' of records of the Sovereign's Chancery.

contracts that sovereigns sign, obliging them to rule according to law, as Henry I promised in 1100. This collection came to be known and administered as the Public Record Office with the Master of the Rolls as its custodian.

In the eighteenth century the Master of the Rolls was second in judicial power only to the Lord High Chancellor. Sometimes the Master sat as Vice Chancellor and, for fifty years in the following century, he had his own Rolls Court. But needs have changed and now the Master presides over the Court of Appeal, dealing with civil rather than criminal matters.

The 1990s have seen another evolution in life for the Master and his rolls. The constant need to calibrate information and store it more effectively meant change for the Public Record Office. Most of the documents were moved to Kew, leaving the Master responsible only for the Chancery Records. The title has survived despite yet another alteration in his responsibilities. This is partly because continuity and precedent form the ethos behind England's system of justice; partly because he still has a latent responsibility for the rolls but mainly because it sounds better than President of the Court of Appeal, which is a more accurate description of his role.

Chancellor of the Duchy of Lancaster

BESIDE THE HIGH ALTAR in Westminster Abbey lies the tomb of Edmund Crouchback, Henry III's younger son. Crouchback was so called because he wore a cross on his back as an act of faith during the crusades. He had much to be grateful for, as the Pope had invested him as king of Sicily when he was only ten years old. This investiture proved to be an expense for Henry that led to further domestic discontent in England, and ultimately to Simon de Montfort leading an uprising called the Barons War. The king defeated the powerful traitor barons in 1265, seizing their estates and, before setting off for the Holy Land with his brother, Edmund was given an area of northern England, including much of Simon's attainted land. Two years later, he became Earl of Lancaster and, in 1284, his mother gave him the Manor of Savoy, named after her uncle Peter of Savoy, on the north bank of the Thames.

Edmund's descendant was an heiress called Blanche, whose father had been Duke of Lancaster with palatinate powers (meaning that he was sovereign over his new lands). She married her distant cousin John of Gaunt, the son of Edward III. Through this marriage, he inherited her considerable possessions. He was subsequently created Duke of Lancaster himself and had the palatinate powers restored. Such status and wealth gave him free rein and in 1363 he appointed a Chancellor to act as judge in the courts, with a Sheriff and Justices to assist. Not everything went John's way. During the Peasants' Revolt of 1381 his palace at Savoy was destroyed and later his son, Henry Bolingbroke, was banished from the kingdom. When John died in 1399, because his son was disgraced, Richard II seized the duchy and its possessions.

That summer, a fisherman recognized the commander of a small flotilla sailing into the Humber, and he ran to the village shouting, 'Our noble lord the Duke of Lancaster is come to claim his inheritance.' So began Henry's quest for Lancaster, which became a first step to the crown itself. Within months both were his and, importantly, he declared that the County Palatine should be held separately from the Crown. In order not to leave the duchy bereft of his leadership, Henry elevated the Chancellor to be a chief administrative officer. This arrangement was confirmed by Edward IV, who enacted that the Duchy would be held 'for ever to us and our heirs, Kings of England, separate from all other royal possessions'.

The duchy was a vital resource to the Lancastrians during the Wars of the Roses, sufficiently so for Henry VI to endow both Eton College and King's College Cambridge. When the white and red roses finally conjoined following both Richard III's defeat at Bosworth and Henry VII's marriage to Elizabeth of York, the new king confirmed the duchy's status, with the support of Parliament, as a possession of England's monarchs but separate from the Crown. This is why the Queen is also Duke of Lancaster and its Chancellor, who was originally responsible for administering the Duchy's land, courts and appointments, became a member of the Cabinet.

Henry VII also built a hospital, or home, for the poor on the ruins of John of Gaunt's palace at Savoy. Little remains but ruins of its chapel, now within the Queen's Free Chapel of the Savoy. Here she is referred to as the Duke of Lancaster.

The Lancaster Inheritance brings with it a considerable income for the Sovereign, which is hers 'in Right of Her Duchy'. The Chancellor chairs the Duchy Council, which advises him on the Duchy's administration, and is responsible solely to the Sovereign for its affairs, though he does answer Parliamentary Questions, in order to keep the business open and above board. Ancient dues, like *Bona Vacantia*, or assets from intestate wills, belong to the duchy and now support the Duchy's historic obligations, with surplus going to the Duchy of Lancaster Benevolent Fund. Net income from

running the properties and investments of the Duchy goes to the Privy Purse to meet the Queen's expenditure and any overall profits are taxed.

Separate from the financial assets which the duchy represents, its County Palatine status remains, adding unique administrative duties which must be carried out. While much of the former was swept away in 1971, the Chancellor is still responsible for supervising various affairs on the Queen's behalf, such as recommending a list of Sheriffs for the new regions which represent the old County Palatine, namely Lancashire, Greater Manchester and Merseyside, which the Duke then pricks with a bodkin.

The Prime Minister now appoints the Chancellor, whose real business is always set by the administrative programme of the elected government. There have been pressures to remove a title which is perceived by some to be arcane but there remains a real role to play in the affairs of the Duchy: besides which, there is a strong Lancastrian spirit which appreciates the history maintained by the Chancellor's presence in the Cabinet.

This chapel, lost amongst London's Savoy area, belongs to the Queen as Duke and Count Palatine of Lancaster. Duchy business is supervised, along with the stream of ministerial Red Boxes, by the **Chancellor** from his seat in the Cabinet. The duchy's banner belonged to Edmund Crouchback and shows England's three golden leopards on a red field, debruised with a blue, three-pointed label, each with three French *fleurs de lys*.

Constable of Hungerford

Outside the John of Gaunt pub in Hungerford, the Constable and office-bearers gather for an annual toast to Edward III's fourth son, the man who took time from one of the more remarkable medieval careers to grant their town some excellent fishing.

John was born in 1340 at Ghent, from where he took his name. Owing to his parents' teenage marriage, he had plenty of siblings, but these children went on to create a catastrophically disfunctional family, whose squabbles wreaked havoc over the following centuries, culminating in the Wars of the Roses. John married three times and gained land from two of his wives. The first, his cousin Blanche, brought as dowry the County Palatine of Lancaster and the second, the crown of Castille, although a lifetime of struggle never gave him possession of this Spanish jewel. His elder brothers were all dead by the time Edward III died but John took his responsibility as Lord High Steward seriously in setting his nephew, Richard II, upon the throne. However, despite a lifetime of loyalty, his high profile landed him in the thick of every intrigue around. Often, he was accused of plotting to usurp Richard, though his avuncular work to secure a treaty with France brought the further reward of the Duchy of Aquitaine from a grateful nephew. By the time of his death, John had amassed a phenomenal birthright for his eldest son, Henry Bolingbroke. This wealth and influence was not only politically sensitive, but it also provided John of Gaunt with the opportunity to provide considerable patronage, not least to the good folk of Hungerford.

The market town is set in the beautiful Kennet valley, between the towns of Marlborough and Newbury, where the river and the Kennet and Avon Canal run today. John of Gaunt's fourteenth-century gift of manorial rights to the citizens over their own town, its river and the common land nearby produced the need for an administrative body: the valuable grazing and trout fishing on the Kennet provided useful revenue. To govern in this revolutionarily democratic manor was the Constable, who acted as Lord of the Manor, chief magistrate and coroner. Election was required from a college made up from those who had held rank as Bailiffs or Portrieve.

To mark their special constitution, festivals and ceremonies developed, some of which are still celebrated now. Principal among them was Hocktide, which celebrated John of Gaunt's gift. It falls a fortnight after Easter and probably takes its name from two German words, *Hoch* and *Zeit*, meaning 'high' and 'period of time'. While making one gift, John gave another, in the form of a horn still carried at some of these festivals today. Written upon it is the inscription: 'John a Gavn did give and grant the riall of Fishing to Hungerford towne from Eldren Stub to Irish Stil ecepting som several mil pound.' And as a postscript, it says that 'Jehosophat Lvcas was Cunstabl'.

The Constable today ensures that Hungerford does not forget its patron and on the Friday after Easter a 'Macaroni Supper' at the John of Gaunt precedes a meeting of Hungerford's Hocktide Court in the town hall. This is a gathering of fifteen elected members of the jury who elect the Water Bailiffs, the Overseers of the Common, the Keepers of the Keys, the Portrieve, the Bailiffs and the Ale Tasters. Before the meeting starts the Constable hands ceremonial poles to the Tuttimen, or Tything men. The strange-sounding derivation comes from the West Country word for a bouquet because the poles are adorned with sweet-smelling spring flowers and an orange.

With this extraordinary accoutrement, the Tutti Men proceed around Hungerford gathering rewards from all the residents for services they have performed over the year, and a kiss from all the women who are rewarded with an orange. Later, after a boozy lunch in the Corn Exchange, oranges

John of Gaunt's memory is toasted by (from left to right) the **Constable**, the Tuttiman/Ale Taster, the Bellman and Assistant Bailiff, the Secretary of Commons Committee, the Blacksmith and the Honorary Fishery Manager outside the John of Gaunt pub, beside the River Kennet. They express gratitude for the rights he gave the Town and Manor of Hungerford and for the liberty of Sanden Fee to fish, shoot, hunt and graze.

and pennies are thrown from the window for the children to scramble for. Quite what John of Gaunt might think were he to see the ceremonies which his gift gave rise to, none can tell. However, to conclude all the Hocktide revelry, a toast is drunk to his immortal memory in a remarkably potent punch brewed to a secret recipe known only to the Constables, past and present.

'John a Gavn did give and grant the
riall of Fishing to Hungerford towne
from Eldren Stub to Irish Stil
exepting som several mil pound'.

INSCRIPTION ON SIDE OF HORN

GIVEN BY JOHN OF GAUNT

Lord Warden of the Stannaries,
Rider and Master Forester of the Forest and Chase of Dartmoor,
Keeper of the Prince's Privy Seal and Vice Chairman of the Prince's Council

CORNWALL'S WEALTH LIES UNDERGROUND. It provided the county with a status sufficient to establish its own coinage, courts and parliament. It even provided sufficient temptation for the Romans to set sail from Gaul and conquer England. And it inspired a spirit of independence which survives today. That wealth consisted of tin.

Of what was once a valuable industry, nothing now remains but *knackt bals*, the Cornish for abandoned mines. When they were worked, wealth poured from the earth providing Cornishmen with a strong negotiating hand: one which brought immunity from taxation, a unique royal status and a special governor.

The Latin word for tin is *stannum*, so the rich tin mining areas of medieval Cornwall were called stannaries. Even in the twelfth century it was a rich business, which netted considerable income for the Crown. Until the sixteenth century most mining was done on the surface, in the rich alluvial deposits that nature had thrown up in abundance along valleys, like Red River near Redruth and the Penetewan Valley near St Austell.

The wealth that the miners produced gave them a long-standing sense of independence in the four stannary districts, which had evolved through the ancient laws and courts that existed before the Conquest. So self-confident were they, and so cut off from faraway English kings, that they developed their own coinage.

In 1198, Richard the Lionheart sent William de Wrotham to end this independence. Wrotham was given special powers and the title Lord Warden of the Stannaries. He imposed order and codified the ancient stannary laws in a peculiar jurisdiction for Cornwall. This legitimized the Stannary Parliament, which Lord Wardens had power to convoke. Twenty-four stannators met four times a year in Truro: while the Devonshire stannators subsequently met at

Crockern Tor on Dartmoor. Everything other than issues concerning life, limb and land fell within these parliaments' remit and their decisions were upheld through the Stannary Courts. The Lord Warden, similar to the Lord High Chancellor, presided.

One hundred and forty years after the first Lord Warden established this powerful viceroyalty, Edward III further recognized Cornwall's unique status and wealth by creating a duchy, consisting of much of the county and some other lands, and then conferring it on his seven-year-old son, the Black Prince. This was England's first dukedom: a possession intended to provide the heir with an independent source of revenue which the Lord Warden was directed to run. This situation has not changed, though the duchy's possessions and income have altered out of recognition. On 6 February 1952, in the same moment that his mother became Queen, the three-year-old Prince Charles automatically became Duke of Cornwall and various Lord Wardens have run his affairs since, chairing the Prince's Council and hearing appeals on behalf of the Duke.

Henry III granted the forest of Dartmoor to his younger brother, along with the earldom of Cornwall, and thus, in 1337, it became a part of Edward III's new duchy. Likewise the Lord Warden was charged with responsibility for Dartmoor's extensive forest and chase, famous for its dwarf oaks: in particular he supervised the *Venville* tenure by which people held fishing or grazing rights on the land, in return for the *drift*, which was a sweep of the moor to check cattle numbers and boot trespassers out. It would be a full-time task today.

The Lord Warden's principal duties remained the governance of the independent-minded medieval miners, who endured hideous conditions and great danger. The nation has now grown used to mining hardships, but then it was willing to grant considerable privileges to those selfless gatherers of

The Romans wanted it and for centuries Cornishmen dug for it. Even beneath the Atlantic waves, stanners mined for tin. Its quality was checked by 'coining' under the **Lord Warden**'s auspices. Once virtually an independent governor in the far-flung peninsula, he still ensures that the Duke of Cornwall gets his income. But tin is too expensive to mine in Cornwall now and most mines are flooded.

wealth. They could apply to the Lord Warden for rights to Tin-Bound: staking out territory and working it, in a manner akin to the American gold prospectors. Cornwall provided opportunities for fortunes to be made and this happened while markets were good in tin and copper: not least for the Lord Wardens.

Miners were also excused many feudal obligations to follow the king to fight abroad. However, their skills meant that they might be summoned to burrow beneath the defences of a sieged castle. Whenever stanners were called up, they served only under the Lord Warden's command.

The office attracted some significant holders. Sir Walter Raleigh was appointed Lord Warden by Queen Elizabeth, to administer a duchy with no duke, and Queen Victoria's consort, Prince Albert, was famous for reorganizing the financial mess that the Hanoverians had left. He turned the estate into the efficient model which survives. The Lord Warden now supervises a ducal portfolio which consists of 129,000 acres spread across the south-west and elsewhere, along with residential property in London and other investments. The Stannary Parliament has not sat since the eighteenth century and the *knackt bals* are a reminder that all estates need constant innovative management to keep ahead of economic pressures. However, this title keeps the memory of Cornwall's medieval, wealth-creating mining alive.

Duke

THE FIRST DUKE IN BRITAIN was the Dux Britanniarum, a Roman commander serving his emperor in the fourth century. *Dux* was a Latin word for leader or general and it was a title first given by Hadrian to commanders of major expeditions or garrisons. The Merovingians used dukes, as civil and military magnates, to administer groups of lesser barons, and the Carolingians continued this. However, the decay of the Frankish monarchy's power in the tenth century gave these dukes an opportunity to both consolidate their independent power and make themselves hereditary: among these was the dukedom of Aquitaine, a valuable asset which came into the English crown with Henry II's marriage to the dukedom's heiress, Eleanor.

Meanwhile, the Teutonic warlords created a post equivalent to the Duke, *Heretogas*, which in modern German is *Herzog*. Their tradition was democratic: the strongest and best warlord became the leader and remained so until he failed to deliver victory. The Saxons who invaded England were led by an *Heretogas*, as were the Scandinavian *Northmannus*, or Normans, who adopted the Frankish title as Dukes of Normandy.

However, the domestic appointment of dukes did not begin until 1337. Edward III made the county of Cornwall into a duchy for his son the Black Prince. And in Scotland too, Robert III gave the duchy of Rothesay to his eldest son sixty-one years later. Non-royals were not given this quasi-princely rank until 1448, when the de la Poles were made Dukes of Suffolk. But the dukes were rather exposed by their elevation to later jealous monarchs, and they fared badly under the Tudors, being wiped out completely when Elizabeth I attainted the Duke of Norfolk. But Charles II spread his patronage widely after the Restoration, to reward the nobility he depended upon. It also provided an excellent way of keeping his mistresses in bed: of the fourteen illegitimate children he fathered, six were made dukes.

As the curtain descends on a legislative role for the hereditary peerage, there are twenty-four dukedoms in existence. Among them, two are Irish creations and six are Scots. Few now bother to attend the House of Lords and some believe their rights have lasted too long already. Instead, their work is devoted to maintaining what remains of the great or small estates which sycophancy, whiggery, coal, sheep, canals, illegitimate royal birth or feudal power granted to their ancestors.

Leaning on the ramparts of Alnwick Castle, this Duke is at the heart of a vast agricultural landholding, which started as an administrative feudal responsibility. It was given by William the Conqueror soon after the conquest to his friend, 'William with the Whiskers' from the village of Perci. Thus, the Percy family took a hold in the north which they have kept for generations.

Demonstrating the power of property in Britain's pre-industrial land-based economy, Alnwick Castle proves that while blood may be thicker than water, land is thicker than blood. The Duke of Northumberland today has barely any link whatever with his hirsute Percy 'ancestor'. His forebears were Smithsons, who changed their name to Percy, and the Dukedom says less about the family which fought ferocious battles around these walls and more about the 1st Duke's ambition. But the title grew into itself and now it has a status which successive incumbents fuelled by their effort: today it enjoys a brand of twentieth-century respect which borders on fealty.

Two dukedoms echo directly the original Latin meaning of military commander and were given with the support of a grateful public. The first was Marlborough, who gained his title and Blenheim Palace during the War of Spanish Succession; his descendant Sir Winston Churchill was offered the dukedom of London but turned it down. The second was Wellington, known as the Iron Duke, who destroyed Napoleon's dream at Waterloo in 1815.

Under feudal law, land gave Tenants-in-Chief of the Crown the right to sit in Parliament. The Conqueror granted the dangerous border lands around Northumberland to his friend 'William with the Whiskers' from Perci, who represented this landed interest in court. Percys have continued ever since: sitting as Dukes of Northumberland from 1766 and living behind the ancient ramparts of Alnwick Castle. **Dukes** wear four bars of gold and ermine on the 'temporal' side of their parliamentary robe.

Lord of the Manor of Alcester, with his Court Leet and Court Baron,
including Steward, Chaplain, High Bailiff, Low Bailiff, Constable, Marshall to the Court, Town
Crier and Beadle, Ale Tasters, Bread Weighers, Fish and Flesh Tasters, Affearors, Surveyor of the
Highways, Brook Looker, Hayward and Searcher and Sealer of Leather

ALCESTER HAS MAINTAINED its ancient Court Leet for more than seven centuries, an enduring example of the feudal system by which England was regulated. This gathering no longer performs the functions that once kept them busy in administration throughout the year. Their former duties have now been taken on by local government and related agencies. However, the regular gatherings in Alcester's Town Hall, itself dating from the 1600s, give a good insight into life before councils. They also provide a good example of how the great estates were run in England, from the arrival of feudalism until quite recently. The officers created at a local level echoed the great officers of State in function: it was merely the scale of their operations that was more limited.

The manorial system reached its prime in the thirteenth century, at about the time records in Alcester began, with records of High and Low Bailiffs from 1299. The first was called Roger the Bailiff.

At the centre of this simple feudal system of interdependence would have been a manor house and church with the homes of other inhabitants clustered around. The Lord of the Manor divided out the ground to his tenants, either for rent or in return for military service. Each field was divided into manageable strips, a pole or yard in width (yardland), which extended to contain an acre of land. In that way the Lord, himself the proprietor of land given by the Crown in return for certain duties, was able to meet his obligations upwards while granting a livelihood to those below.

In addition to freemen, the manor would have its share of natives, villeins, bondmen and holders of *virgates*. This social structure implied a complex balance of mutual responsibility, according to wealth and position. In simple terms everyone owed deference and service up the ladder, ultimately to the king, who owed his deference only to God. Meanwhile, the benevolence of security and justice would trickle back down the same ladder. When this operated in balance the feudal system worked remarkably well. Unfortunately, greed, self-interest and other human failings frequently damaged it.

The Steward was responsible for both accounts and the courts, and represented the Lord of the Manor. The Bailiff collected the rents and services, as many still do for the Councils which took over from the manors. The Constable, an appointment which came from the Byzantine Counts of the Stable, was responsible for keeping order. Otherwise, the appointments varied among manors according to what was grown and sold there. Bread, meat, fish, ale and leather obviously formed the ancient economy of Alcester. Today each office holder carries a symbol of their office which is linked to their titles.

The Court Leet now raises money through events which is then distributed to local causes: a benevolent evolution for what once regulated all things.

At the heart of the ancient Manor of Alcester the **Court Leet** and **Court Baron** gather around the seated **Lord of the Manor**. Each carries or wears his symbol of office, and their appointments appear in order from left to right on page 220.

Hereditary Lord High Admiral of the Wash

ON THE WASH'S EASTERN SHORE is the parish church of St Mary the Virgin at Old Hunstanton. Beside it, the village pond is frozen over and there is no relief whatever from the cold when the heavy church door closes the visitor into its voluminous interior. Idle gas heaters and rattling window panes struggle unsuccessfully to keep the icy wind at bay.

Wandering round the aisles, the evidence is clear that this is the pantheon of one family. It was built by them, nurtured by them and their mortal remains have been laid to rest here for nearly 800 years. Beside the altar, under worn carvings of heraldic achievements, lies Henry le Strange dated 1485; in the North Aisle an altar tomb, covered with an intricate brass, celebrates the life of Roger le Strange. Plaques everywhere refer to others in the line, including Henry L'Estrange Styleman le Strange, who restored this freezing building (or desecrated it, depending on your view of Victoriana). What these memorials do not record is that the le Stranges came to England long before any surviving memorial can attest: they came to this corner of Norfolk and they governed the coast as Lord High Admirals.

Roland le Strange supposedly left Brittany during the first decade of the twelfth century. The attraction for many who crossed the Channel at this time was adventure. Duke William of Normandy's son, Henry, had grasped the throne. Seeking riches and land, many knights came to assist in Henry's coup, anticipating the rewards which success might bring. Henry had two elder brothers. The eldest, Robert Curthose, was made Duke of Normandy on the Conqueror's death, while England's Crown was given to the next, William Rufus. However, the latter was killed in a hunting accident in the New Forest. Perhaps not surprisingly, Henry was present at the death of his unfortunate brother and seized the opportunity to take the throne. Robert attempted to claim his birthright but was imprisoned for life.

Many Norman knights founded their fortunes in the largesse which followed: Roland also found himself a wife, the eventual heiress of Hunstanton.

Proving their worth as a knightly family in the campaigns against Wales, John le Strange became Supreme Commander of the Marches in the thirteenth century. And it was at about this time that Plantagenet monarchs reviewed the administration of England's vulnerable coastline, establishing admiralties vested in noble families as part of their feudal obligation. The Welsh wars proved the le Stranges competent and they were given direction over the Wash. Surviving documents confirm little more than the existence of this ancient title but,

Standing on the beach at Old Hunstanton in Norfolk, where the family have lived since the time of the *Domesday Book*, the **Lord High Admiral of the Wash** wears the uniform of an admiral of about 1800. He owns all the land from the high-tide mark to as far as he can throw a spear! This land based admiralty was a feudal responsibility established on the le Strange family in the thirteenth century to supervise the security of the Wash.

typically, these land-based admiralties were responsible for preventing smuggling, administering courts and controlling shipping movements.

None of these responsibilities remain: each has been assumed by other authorities as the centuries passed and monarchs and governments chose to administer things differently. If there ever was grandeur in the hereditary appointment, nothing now remains but the title, which hangs about the le Stranges like an old friend. But the land is still there to be tilled, as it was by the family in the twelfth century.

The Lord High Admiral today is about as gentle, peaceful and unassuming a man as you could meet; nowhere in his bearing can be seen the swaggering bravado of his medieval ancestors. The son of a vicar, it was through his mother that he inherited the Admiralty and, with the hall gone, the Admiral lives nearby in Hunstanton.

Nearby, a lighthouse stands sentinel above the cliff, its famous coloured layers making the rock face appear like the walls of Constantinople. From it can be seen the flat wildness of the Wash, with the plains of Lincolnshire acting like a slipway for the endless westerly winds. The commanding view from this place, over the fishing boats which ply to and fro, is the best evidence for why the admiralty came to the le Stranges of Hunstanton.

Captain of Dunstaffnage, Hereditary Keeper of Dunstaffnage Castle

THE THIRTEENTH-CENTURY FORTRESS at Dunstaffnage rises from a great outcrop of old red conglomerate rock, amid trees on a promontory spurring from the mainland into the Firth of Lorne at the entrance of Loch Etive. This was once a vital strategic defence guarding Scotland's vulnerable Western Approaches. The years have worn down the walls, though good pointing sustains the impregnable appearance of its ruinous structure. But peeking out, looking a little incongruous amid this ancient edifice, protrudes the roof of an ordinary-looking house. And from one of the three chimney pieces streams smoke. This is the Hereditary Captain's residence and has been, in various different forms, since his direct ancestor was appointed to the task in 1490.

Before Ewen MacDougall, the Lord of Lorne, built this castle around 1250 to keep the Norse raiders at bay, legend has it that a series of strongholds stood on this promontory. A local myth suggests that one existed here, built by the mythical King Ewin, before Julius Caesar arrived in Britain. It has long been said that the Stone of Destiny, used at the coronation of Scotland's monarchs and removed for that reason by Edward I to Westminster, originally rested here, until Kenneth mac Alpin, the king whose marriage to a Pictish princess united Scotland, moved it to Scone. When the Queen was recently advised to return it to Scotland there was speculation it might return to Dunstaffnage.

Such was the strategic and historical significance of Dunstaffnage, and the Lordship of Lorne it governed, that when its incumbent MacDougall foolishly resisted Robert the Bruce in 1309, the king attacked and took possession. This was not typical. He usually razed the castles he took, to avoid replays. But in this case he garrisoned it and in 1322 gave Arthur Campbell the custody of the place as Keeper. One hundred and fifty years later, the Campbell Earl of Argyll, now a massively powerful magnate controlling the west coast and its approaches,

decided that he could no longer adequately oversee Dunstaffnage himself. He gave the responsibility to his uncle in a sort of sub-lease, making him Captain.

This was no free gift. While it brought a reasonable acreage and income, it also included clear responsibilities. A charter signed by the 9th Earl to his kinsman, the 10th Captain, in 1667 outlines them: 'holding our said Castell of Dunstaffnies and ever keeping and holding therein six able and decent men with armour and arms sufficient for warr and keeping of the said Castell'. In addition, the Captain had to provide the Earl with free access and lodging if required, and he also had to pass on certain rental payments. The Captain was given a golden key as symbol of his office and his family endeared themselves to those in the area, who referred to them as the Children of Angus the Dun, which in Gaelic is Clann Aonghais an Duin: a reminder of the provenance for the modern word, Clan.

It was this clan system that was so bitterly divided by the religious politics of Britain after the Glorious Revolution, when James II and VII's throne was declared vacant by Parliament. The clans had to take sides. Some stayed loyal to the Stuarts, while others opted for the newly arrived Hanoverians. In each case there was some self-interest involved. Over some fifty years passions rose and the king found Dunstaffnage to be strategically useful again. The Captain was holding the castle for George I while the Old Pretender planned to land there in 1715. Weather and circumstances saved Dunstaffnage from becoming the focus of the uprising's first assault. Then there was the garrisoning task leading up to the Battle of Culloden in 1746, when every redcoat available was scouring these shores for Bonnie Prince Charlie. However, later that year its dungeon received the bold and romantic Flora Macdonald, who risked so much to row the Prince to Skye.

The Earls were soon Dukes of Argyll; it seemed there would be no limit to the honours and feudal

To keep his livelihood and the ancient responsibilities given to his ancestor, the **Captain of Dunstaffnage** meets his obligation of spending a night locked within the castle's ancient walls. Wrapped in Campbell tartan and fortified from cold and ghostly spirits, with his key resting on the hearth, this descendant of Angus the Dun protects his inheritance. He even spent his honeymoon here.

privileges they would gather at nearby Inveraray. But, to the Captain's surprise, one Duke claimed the Captaincy back. Fortunately for the Children of Angus the Dun, who had made the castle and its surroundings their living, the court decision upheld their claim of heredity in preference to the Keeper Duke. However, the decision underlined the special tasks the Captain must meet to maintain his claim: not least, spending three nights a year in the fortress,

nights that, according to local tales, must be shared with the castle's heavy footed glaistig or ghost. This became a particular burden after the fire of 1810 gutted the family's home.

Perhaps for this reason, the roof of a new house now appears above the fortress's old walls. And from its chimney there occasionally rises a stream of smoke and firelight flickers in the windows late into the night, while storms roll up the Firth of Lorne.

Searcher of the Sanctuary and High Bailiff with the High Steward of Westminster Abbey

WESTMINSTER ABBEY IS ENGLAND'S pantheon. It has been inextricably linked with the country's fortunes since Edward the Confessor founded it in lieu of a pilgrimage to Rome, in the eleventh century. Its monastery was dissolved by Henry VIII and the collegiate body, governed by a Dean and Chapter, was founded by Elizabeth I in 1560. This significance has made it arguably the most prominent ecclesiastical building in the country. And for these reasons it acted like a magnet, attracting the influential and disreputable alike.

To deal with this wide range of people some non-clerical appointments were made by Abbots and Deans. They were mostly laymen who acted for the monastery when it was deemed either politic or too dangerous for the brethren to handle. After the monastery was dissolved the High Bailiff and the Searcher of the Sanctuary (now combined in a single appointment) along with the High Steward were appointed by the Dean to carry out these tasks.

The first of these was a policeman. The Abbey once owned lands which extended to most of what is now administered as the City of Westminster. Once a wilderness, this territory now contains the best part of all Government buildings, Buckingham Palace, Soho and the West End. The Abbey's bailiwick needed to be kept in order, particularly when the royal court attracted development and an increasing population, and so the Bailiff was appointed to take responsibility for discipline over the Abbey's vast estate, excluding only the immediate precincts of the church and the Sanctuary.

For millennia there was a belief that holy places offered spiritual, and physical, refuge in their Sanctuary. The Anglo-Saxon king Aethelbert codified Christian Sanctuary at the start of the seventh century; subsequent Canon Law allowed those accused of violent crime a period of grace within Sanctuary: many churches had a Peace-Stool beside the altar for seekers of Sanctuary. Edward the Confessor granted Westminster the right of Sanctuary; Dean Stanley wrote that 'The precincts of the Abbey were a vast cave of Adullam for all the distressed and discontented in the metropolis, who desired, according to the phrase of the time, to "take Westminster".' Indeed, so bad did the surrounding neighbourhood become that it was known as the 'Devil's Acre'. Among well-known fugitives who took Sanctuary were Elizabeth Woodville, the consort of Edward IV who was escaping Richard III, and Henry VIII's poet John Skelton, who hid there after a caustic verse he wrote in satire of Cardinal Wolsey backfired. Sanctuary included Parliament Square, St Margaret's Churchyard and out to Tothill Street, the river and Horseferry Road. This area was later policed by the Searcher of the Sanctuary who checked that all within the defined area had a legal right to remain.

The High Steward was an appointment for a man of gravitas, one who was, if not a statesman himself, able to negotiate diplomatically on behalf of the Abbey with the State. This role became necessary after the Dissolution and the establishment of the Abbey as a Royal Peculiar. Previously, the Abbot had the right to sit in Parliament, but Deans were not accorded the same power, though they are still entitled to sit on the steps of the Throne. The appointment of Sir William Cecil as the first High Steward by the Dean and Chapter in 1560 was inspired: he went on to be Elizabeth's trusted counsellor, which proved an excellent position to advance the Abbey's interests.

As the City of Westminster grew in importance, the Abbey's ancient influence was eclipsed. However, attempts by the City Council to let the Mayor take over the High Steward's role were resisted. The Dean and Chapter said, 'it was of great importance to them that their Lay Arm, so to speak, should not be cut off'. The High Steward is still able to lobby on Westminster's behalf.

The Chapel of St George is at the heart of Westminster Abbey's unique area of sanctuary. The **Searcher of the Sanctuary**, who wears a claret fur-trimmed gown, is also the Abbey's **High Bailiff**. He once policed fugitives hiding amongst the pillars of this influential place, whose affairs were followed up by the **High Steward**, always a respected and influential layman.

Lord Mayor of London, Escheator, Clerk of the Markets and Admiral of the Port of London

UNFORTUNATELY, DICK WHITTINGTON was led by his cat neither to riches nor to the mayoralty of London, but his appearance in pantomimes, with pointy shoes, tights and carrying a hanky-bundle on a stick, resulted from legends of a real life of splendid wealth, all of which he bequeathed to good charitable causes. His enduring, if re-invented, reputation as Lord Mayor put the appointment on the map. In truth, he was no poor boy made good but the third son of a Gloucestershire knight, a mercer by trade and, at a young age, already successful enough to make substantial loans. In 1397 he began his first term as Lord Mayor, a post he filled four times, being mayor of Calais as well. When he died in 1423, having loaned money to three kings (Richard II, Henry IV and Henry V), he left a fortune and neither

King John insisted the **Lord Mayor** present himself for approval. This annual procession gave life to the Lord Mayor's Show and to this gilded coach in 1757. The door panel shows the Genius of the City conferring with Mars, whose spear points to the 1st mayor's name on a scroll held by Truth. Escorted by pikemen in the uniform of 1641, this is the Lord Mayor's most tiring day. He waves from alternate windows to crowds all the way from the Guildhall to the Royal Courts of Justice, returning some hours later to his official residence at the Mansion House.

wife nor child to inherit. All of it went to charity: a new prison at Newgate, almshouses for the Mercer's Company, repairs for St Bartholomew's Hospital and much more.

The City of London has a history of wealth and, from its power to generate money, it has established a tradition of generous giving. Each Lord Mayor, who is elected within the City in a demonstration of defiant independence that stems from its phenomenal financial power, continues to be the figurehead of the related traditions of wealth-generation and charity. To assist with this work, Lord Mayors inherit one of the most splendid titles and a lavish infrastructure to go with it. The Mansion House, almost lost among today's towering banks, insurance companies and brokerage houses, remains a dramatic edifice of wealth, with the Guildhall nearby to provide an arena for display. Following his appointment at a Silent Ceremony, the Lord Mayor has 365 days to live out his office, during which he will have endless dinners, and receive Prime Ministers and Heads of State. In addition, the incumbent engages in a wide range of charitable activities. The purpose of all this is to maintain the profile of the foremost financial centre in the world.

However, for those who are part of the City's rarefied world, these rituals surround a tradition that they thoroughly enjoy, that costs nothing to outsiders (unless they have parked illegally), and that provides a framework for supporting a complex range of schools, hospitals, homes, help groups and other charities. Also it enshrines a real arm of local government.

It continues a tradition which started almost when London began. The City takes its name from two words which describe a pool by a hill and it was this small tidal harbour beside the Tower which attracted the first settlers, which came to be one of England's major trading posts and which ultimately became the centre of an imperial capital city. Twenty-three years after Hastings, the first Mayor, Henry FitzAlwin, is recorded as Chief Magistrate. It was King John who directed that the citizens of London could have the right to choose every year someone, 'faithful, discreet, and fit for the government of the City' to be Mayor, who was then to be presented to him and swear fealty. Largely this has been done since, though the Lord Chancellor steps in for the monarch and sets the year going with bonhomie, cakes and hot spiced wine.

As Escheator for the City (by charter of Edward III) the Mayoralty receives the possessions of all who die without wills or whose estates are seized for treason; he is also Escheator for neighbouring Southwark (by charter of Edward VI).

The markets of the City were its lifeblood, as the financial service markets are today. Once the commodities were sugar, coffee, meat, cloth and other tradeable items from across the globe; inevitably the first citizen presided over them as Clerk of the Markets and, as in many other ports and coastal areas, London needed an admiral to keep its waterways secured, so the Lord Mayor became Admiral of the Port of London.

It is an appointment which garners traditions like a light attracts moths. The Lord Mayor has his own body guard, formed from the Honourable Artillery Company under Henry VIII's charter of 1537. But it was as recently as 1925 that sanction was given for a Company of Pikemen to provide a close escort for the Lord Mayor, and in 1955 the Queen issued a royal warrant to the fully formed Company of Pikemen and Musketeers, a twentieth-century reinvention from the seventeenth century.

As nothing gained is discarded in the City's world, awash with bizarre but meticulously observed rituals, these things have survived and are likely to go on. And with every Silent Ceremony another heir to Dick Whittington takes on this legacy of duties and charitable patronage.

Swordbearer, City Marshal and
Common Cryer and Sergeant-at-Arms of the City of London

THE CITY OF LONDON has always been a law unto itself. Its unique position as the foremost trading area in England generated wealth that provided chestfuls of taxation for royal treasuries up-river at Westminster. The best merchants in the country based their businesses within the protection of the Roman walled city, which was later overlooked by the turrets of William the Conqueror's Tower of London.

Peeking into the markets from these ramparts, medieval monarchs glimpsed the sort of riches they dreamt of; paraded by merchants organized into trading livery companies. Any envy this bred was kept in check by the recognition that England's king needed England's trade for revenue. So the relationship between a king who had power but never enough money and a City whose power only existed because it had money was a tricky one. The City wisely remembered that monarchs were best kept sweet with exotic gifts and revenue when needed: while kings knew that charters granting special powers and privileges were welcome in return. And for a millennium, as London evolved from a market of merchants into one of financial whizz kids, the relationship between the City and Government was maintained through a trade in money for privileges.

Evidence of this can be found in the outward splendour of the Lord Mayor's household. It was felt necessary to display the powers that were granted. What developed around the elective mayoralty was the outward appearance of a wealthy ruling prince: one who was first in the pecking order and who owed fealty only to the monarch. Indeed, he was almost sovereign within this square mile of merchants and even the monarch was expected to ask permission to enter the City bounds.

Dressing this sort of constitutional power into outward appearance is the semiology of authority.

Firstly, the right to have a sword carried before the mayor may seem irrelevant flummery but it was a significant privilege in its time: such privileges were typically given by popes to kings. The honour of carrying it was given to 'A man well bred (one who knows how in all places, in that which unto such service pertains, to support the honour of his lord and of the City)'. This described the City's Lord Mayors' Swordbearers since the fourteenth century: certainly since 1419 when the first mention is made. One of the City's swords was a gift from Elizabeth I to mark her opening of the first Royal Exchange (which the pediment of today's building recalls). When the monarch visits the City formally, it is the Lord Mayor who offers the sword, as a mark of fealty, and then carries it aloft himself. The Swordbearer wears a fur 'Cap of Maintenance', itself a rare privilege which represents royal estate: a symbol which has been worn since the fifteenth century and appears in the City's ancient arms.

Elizabeth I expressed her gratitude to the City in many ways: one was granting powers for a Marshal to keep order within the square mile, thus giving the City further control over its affairs. From horseback he patrolled the City with Marshalmen until the nineteenth-century Police Acts removed the need. He remains responsible for marshalling processions and challenging troops who wish to exercise their right to march through with bayonets fixed and drums beating.

The oldest office is also one most closely connected with the monarch's interest in the safe conduct of the City's affairs. Sergeants-at-Arms were available close to the monarch armed with a club-like weapon for keeping attackers at bay. These guards and their maces have been ceremonialized almost beyond all recognition. In 1338, when the appointment was already well established, it was held by one of the king's Sergeants-at-Arms, implying that

Dwarfed by three engines of finance – the Bank of England, the Stock Exchange and the Royal Exchange, the three ceremonial officers of the Lord Mayor's household help maintain the unique laws and customs that have emerged from a trade-off in money for privileges between the City and the Crown.

Edward III was taking a personal interest in his mayor's safety. By 1419 the City found its own mace bearer and called him the Common Sergeant-at-Arms, which by 1559 was established as Common Cryer and Sergeant-at-Arms.

Changing little with the passage of time, the three ceremonial officers stand strangely in their surroundings. Historical precedent removes any sense of self-consciousness as they perform functions within the bustle of brokers, bankers and traders rushing to and fro with sandwiches or late for meetings. But the Lord Mayor is never late: these three work with the rest of his household making sure all engagements are planned with precision.

Tolly-keepers of Winchester College

THE SHIPS LANDING along the south coast of England in 1348 imported more than cargo; they carried rats that brought bubonic plague which killed off one third of the country's population within a decade, before heading north to slaughter the Scots. Called by contemporaries 'the Great Mortality', it is better known now as the 'Black Death'. Among the worst affected section of society was the clergy, who made the suffering of others their business and caught the incurable contagious disease for their pains.

One young priest who watched this misery was William of Wykeham. He went on to hold some of the most influential and profitable benefices available, including Lord Chancellor and ultimately Bishop of Winchester: the city where he had been educated. With the wealth that accrued, William determined to do two things: first, to found religious houses where chantry prayers could be said for himself and his many patrons and, second, to establish within them colleges for the preparation of priests ready to replace those who fell in the plague.

After the coronation of Richard II, when he was pardoned for previous errors of judgement, William lent money to his new king. The next year, on 1 July, Urban VI's papal bull gave leave for 'a certain college he proposed to establish for seventy poor scholars, clerks, who should live college-wise and study in grammaticals near the city of Winchester'. Thus on 26 March 1388 were laid the first stones of buildings which still form the nucleus of the oldest school in the country, dedicated to 'Seinte Marie of Wynchestre by Wynchestre', now known as Winchester College.

College still exists. It sits at the heart of a large independent school but maintains an aloofness in scholarship, surroundings and language. There are still seventy 'poor and needy' scholars, many of whom are educated on the income derived from wealth bestowed by William. Of these, fourteen boys are in their penultimate year. From among their number it was normal practice for the senior boy in College, the Praefect of Hall, to nominate six as the *Custodes Candelarum*, or Tolly-keepers. This tradition was based upon the ancient utilitarian need for candles to illuminate their study. It ebbed into decline after electricity wired its way into the unique Chambers, where senior and junior boys still study and live together in a mutually supportive society.

However, the Scholars have sufficient ease with the oddity of their lives in a world rife with *notions* (a language based upon evolved tradition) that they willingly revived something which had never been abolished but had merely lain dormant. On the contrary, with great pride in their Roll (the entry of a year's names in the list of admissions, which includes fourteen entered in 1815, known as the Waterloo Roll), the seven Tolly-keepers stepped forward with candles in College Hall, where their predecessors have eaten since the first scholars were admitted to the building in 1394.

The name Tolly-keeper came from the notional word for a candle, which derived from tallow, the mutton fat from which they were made. Under the Senior Tolly-keeper, the seven boys were responsible for keeping the school supplied with Tollies from the Chapel vestry. As the Headmaster explained, 'The Tolly-keepers are best described by what they were not.' They were above juniors but not yet Praefects. College's social structure was laid down in early statute. Boys of all ages lived and studied together as familial units in Chambers, the elder Scholars encouraging and overseeing the younger ones.

William of Wykeham's principal intent, that both Winchester and his theological establishment, New College, Oxford (known collectively as the Winton colleges), would exist for eternity in order to offer up prayers for his soul, was not achieved: centuries of religious turmoil saw to that. However, both foundations survived these vicissitudes as centres of

Before gas and electricity William of Wykeham's College Hall and the 'toyes' in which the seventy scholars studied required plenty of candles.

The Senior **Tolly-keeper**, who carries the snuffer, organized six Tolly-keepers in this logistical enterprise.

learning. Winchester College is now one of the largest and best-known public schools. After the Royal Commission of 1857 the tradition of accepting entry through patronage and nomination was replaced; instead, competitive examination for the whole school was introduced. However, because since 1392 College entrance had always been by competitive 'election' a high standard existed that was mirrored throughout the school, with College always remaining an elite within the elite. However, though many achieve notable careers, few follow William's path to the Church.

Provost, Conduct, Headmaster and Colleger of Eton and the Choristers of King's College, Cambridge

O N 21 MAY EACH YEAR, a group gathers in the oratory of the Tower of London's Wakefield Tower. On this day and reputedly at this place, Henry VI was murdered in 1471. 'Pure displeasure and melancholy' were blamed, but this was disingenous because he died on the very night that Edward IV returned to regain his throne. It was a grim conclusion to Henry's troubled life. As a ruler, he had been naive, burying his head in the sands of pious abstinence and religious observance. Succeeding to the two kingdoms of England and France from his valiant father at the age of nine months, he was almost abandoned by his mother and left in the hands of Richard Earl of Warwick (the Kingmaker), who taught him 'nurture, literature, language and other manner of cunning'. Despite this preparation, his reign is remembered for the loss of two crowns and the foundation of two colleges.

Responding to the success of William of Wykeham's Winton Colleges, Henry was persuaded to exercise his patronage. He used money accrued by his father's confiscation of the alien priories (monastic offshoots of French religious foundations), supplemented with funds from his Lancastrian duchy, and founded a college at Eton in 1440. The next year, he founded another in the hitherto unfashionable university of Cambridge, originally dedicated to St Nicholas but renamed 'Our College Royal of Our Lady and St Nicholas', for a Rector and twelve scholars, reflecting Christ and his disciples. When he laid the foundation stone of King's College on Passion Sunday of 1441, Henry was just nineteen years old.

The first foundation was set in the fields across the Thames below Windsor Castle, where Henry could watch it develop. Called the 'King's College of our Lady of Eton', its religious complement included a Provost, ten Fellows and four Clerks, known as Conducts. They were constituted with six choristers, one schoolmaster, twenty-five poor and indigent scholars and an equivalent number of poor and infirm men; this was a religious house first and a school second. However, after two years, Henry reviewed these arrangements and the number of boys was increased to seventy (the number of Christ's first evangelists), while the bedesmen were reduced to thirteen. The Provost remains a royal appointment today, even if he need not be a clergyman, and the Fellows have evolved from priests to governors, a change formalized in 1870 and including the Provost of King's College Cambridge as an ex-officio Fellow. This confirmed the link which Henry VI established between his two foundations. This link is evident in the visual similarities between the chapels at Eton and Cambridge, where English perpendicular style finds its most glorious expression. It is also shown in their similar heraldic arms. Each shows symbols of the two kingdoms which Henry inherited, but where Eton shows three lilies of the Virgin Mary, granted in 1449, King's College has three white roses, which some say is for St Nicholas.

The Founder's Charter for King's College was illuminated in 1446 with Henry VI at prayer, joined by his combined Lords and Commons. Parliament is thus shown united, which it still was then, in offering praise to God, the Virgin and St Nicholas for the new College. By 1453, its constitutional detail had been established. Much of its form was similar to that of Eton but here there were to be sixteen choristers. As if predicting the magnificent evolution of English sung liturgy, despite the coming Reformation, Henry VI had provided for the existence of boys' voices to help maintain the spirit of worship depicted in that first illustrated manuscript. The number of choristers has never changed. Whilst they are no longer 'poor and needy boys' the doors are open for all to compete by audition. In return for their voices, they receive scholarships and become part of the most famous choir in the world, which has sung praises for five and a half centuries.

These four appointments, gathered in Eton's Lower School, were mentioned in his original Charter. The **Provost**, originally a well-born priest, remains the monarch's appointment and leads the community. The **Conduct** is now the senior cleric. The staple business of this well-known school is represented by the **Headmaster** and **Colleger**.

Henry VI cleared a large area to provide his chapel with this setting on the Backs of the River Cam. As an expression of his pious devotion sixteen **Choristers** were established to sing at its services. They still wear top hats, undergraduate gowns and 'Etons', which consists of 'bum-freezer' jackets and stiff collars, when they go to and from the chapel. The link between King's College and their sister foundation is also evident from their chapels' shared architecture.

'Yet God in his compassion raised up a memorial to this saintly man. For he ordained that two colleges which king Henry founded, here and at Eton, should not fail with the King's fortunes; and to this day they stand so that men shall remember how much this King loved wisdom and learning, and how the fruits of such love long survive the temporal glories of the princes and rulers of this world.'

POLYDOR VERGIL REQUIEM FOR THE FOUNDER,
KING'S COLLEGE CAMBRIDGE

The Chapel at King's was not completed until the middle of the sixteenth century, though the Choristers sang from Foundation. Henry VI's popularity in the country was not sufficient to survive the loss of France or the bickering of nobles that he foolishly favoured. The country fell into the civil wars of the Roses and little building progressed. After holding a chapter of the Order of the Garter at King's on St George's Eve in 1506, Henry VII sent a chest of money, literally, to enable the work to be completed as both a shrine to Henry VI and a celebration of the new Tudor dynasty. But plans for the murdered monarch to be canonized were rejected by Rome; however, his memory was venerated in stone, with chapels at both his colleges and also at Westminster Abbey.

The group that gathers in the Tower of London on the anniversary of his death for the Ceremony of Lilies and Roses are members of both foundations. They lay bunches of the flowers shown on the armorial bearings of their respective colleges.

Master of the Worshipful Company of Skinners and the Master of the Worshipful Company of Merchant Taylors

POPULAR BELIEF HOLDS that the idiom 'All at Sixes and Sevens' comes from the quarrel between two of London's livery companies in the fifteenth century.

The best-dressed merchants in town needed well-cut garments to display their wealth and rank. Among those who supplied these essentials were the medieval tailors and furriers. Although the complexities of Court Dress were yet to establish themselves, successful men wore clothes designed to prove they did not have to get dirty to make a living. Clothing was strictly regulated: not by the social mores of fashion but by clear guidelines of etiquette which were not to be trifled with. Too much fur trimming, some misplaced ornament or the wrong lining could bring about social downfall. Tailoring was therefore a science as well as an art. And the supply of pelts to adorn and line the finest garments was a trade in both warmth and social position.

Ever since Anglo-Saxon times guilds existed in London to do business. When London took over as capital from Winchester, opportunities for the local merchants of this trading port grew. Edward III put the icing on the cake by granting Royal Charters to successful guilds which regulated each one, giving them credibility and in most cases a valuable monopoly. At the same time, these Charters granted position in marketplace precedence. Unfortunately, the Taylors and Skinners (as the furriers were known) were granted theirs in the same year, 1327.

It was essential to be a Freeman in order to do business in the City, so Chartered guilds provided an ideal access point for a fee. This income was self-perpetuating. In time, twelve companies, known now as the Great Companies, controlled the medieval marketplace and from their names it is possible to examine London's economy at this time: among them, apart from Skinners and Taylors, were Drapers, Mercers, Grocers, Fishmongers, Goldsmiths, Haberdashers and Vintners. As this was the age of processions, King John's demand that each new Lord Mayor should present himself at Westminster provided an excuse for jamboree.

It was during the procession of 1483 that trouble flared, although this was not the first time violence had broken out over precedence: in 1226 the Goldsmiths and Taylors had staged a bloody street battle. The combatants in 1483 were the Skinners and Taylors, who ironically should have worked well together. However, to cut costs, each gradually tried to usurp ground from the other's monopoly, a strain further exacerbated by rulings from biased committees of arbitration. Needless to say, these weak judgements aggravated the feud, and to make it more complex, the up-and-coming Taylors' wealth challenged the Skinners' ancient status. So it was no surprise when the 1483 procession to Westminster ended in disaster. The procession moved along the Thames in boats and, as each livery company cast off in order of precedence behind the new mayor, the Skinners and Taylors jostled for sixth position. The scrap turned into a dangerous race: one which led to the collision of oars and vessels, and to bloodshed.

The historian Henry Humperus tells us that the matter was sent for arbitration before the mayor, Robert Billesdon, who decided that for the future the two Guilds should alternately have precedence, and that each year on approaching Westminster, they should lash their two barges together and drink as a toast 'The Merchant Taylors and Skinners; Skinners and Merchant Taylors; root and branch, may they flourish forever.' Billesdon could not make them sixth equal: it would never work. Instead they swapped sixth and seventh place. The wise mayor insisted that they entertain each other to dinner every year, ensuring good relations would flourish.

Few Liverymen now are engaged in the professions anciently operated by their Companies. Instead they are children of former Freemen, new City professionals or others desiring close affinity with the Square Mile's unique constitution. The

The exchange of two gavels, one marked six, the other seven, symbolizes the exchange of precedence between two city livery companies. In this case the **Master of the Worshipful Company of Skinners** must take second place, and the **Master of the Worshipful Company of Merchant Taylors** can take the lead. This solves a crisis between historic rivals competing for tailoring business and supplying fur trim.

Masters of the Skinners and Merchant Taylors are now concerned with running the valuable property portfolios, which burgeon with revenue from banks and brokers, and they supervise distribution of the resources to charitable interests around the country. Each year they process with the new Lord Mayor in his annual show, without tussle, either at sixth or seventh position. This lesson in compromise has always been the core of business life through the ages. Lord Mayor Billesdon in his famous Award did a deal rich in common sense and undeniably long lasting. The two companies and their Masters have been at sixes and sevens for over 500 years.

'This day on the 10th April, 1484, the Master and Wardens of the Misteries of Skinners and Tailors with several worthy men of each Mistery undertook that they would abide by the judgement of Robert Billesdon Mayor and Aldermen of the City of London concerning a matter of dispute between them pending.'

THE BILLESDON AWARD, 1484

3

REFORMATION AND FEAR

1485–1603

Most of the great office holders who served Richard III were either killed or captured on the field of Bosworth. Henry VII had proclaimed himself king the day before the fight, making all the vanquished traitors. With the power of kingship in his hands the first Tudor set about re-establishing unified government and the monarchy, and ending aristocratic factionalism. He used his patronage to grant appointments on merit, not rank. Henry sold some judicial appointments to the highest bidder, such as Master of the Rolls, and even put the Speakership of the Commons up for sale as he worked to fill the depleted treasury.

Pragmatically, he selected a body guard from the most loyal of his soldiers as his first priority. Now the oldest military body in the world, the Yeomen of the Guard still provide close protection to the monarch. Henry needed to ensure his safety because there were still Yorkist claimants about, even though Richard had killed most of them. In the year Henry VIII acceded, he too appointed a body guard, this time from officers of noble blood who took precedence over the Yeomen and were responsible for even closer protection. Both suggest that Tudor policy would make enemies and benefit from the appearance of power.

The Lancastrian Henry married Elizabeth of York to unify his kingdom: by giving their daughter in marriage to James IV of Scotland they hoped to prevent trouble from the north. In turn, the son of Margaret Tudor and her Scottish king was named Prince of Scotland and the Isles, which unified the warring western and northern isles to the crown after centuries of fighting. The Prince of Wales is still Lord of the Isles. The Scottish court was fundamentally similar to England's and stood at the centre of a feudal structure, with its own officers of state. Many of these were phased out after Union but some survived, including the Keeper of the Signet, who was responsible for sealing all the king's business. That post is now merged with Lord Clerk Register, once clerk to the Scottish Parliament.

The court of the Stuarts frequently stayed at Holyrood, the ancient abbey to the east of Edinburgh's fortress, where privileges derived from ecclesiastical law and the baronial powers of its abbots allowed sanctuary to those evading justice. Before formal bail was available, the accused would often seek shelter while they gathered evidence to prove their innocence, and it was into the Bailie of Holyrood's hands that they surrendered themselves.

When Henry VIII defeated and killed his brother-in-law James IV on Flodden Field, his nephew came to the throne, and, after years as the pawn of aristocratic factionalism, James V came into his own with a vengeance. In this respect it is easy to understand the circumstances that led to his encounter with Mr John Howieson in the brig at Cramond, where one of the last feudal gifts began a romantic ritual. However, after two marriages to strengthen the Auld Alliance with France, James's heart was broken by another Scottish defeat. He died leaving an infant daughter in the regency of his wife Mary of Guise, who was to provide the final bastion against Scotland's coming Reformation.

Through the secular and spiritual changes of the English Reformation, Henry VIII gave life to a daring and revolutionary economic realignment of power that changed the nature of his kingdom for ever, setting the foundations for an isolated island within Europe that came to need an Empire for expansion. In taking over the Roman Church's power structure, which had been established through four centuries of monasticism, he filled still further the treasury that his father had worked to rebuild. The countryside is decorated with monastic ruins that once witnessed the moral trials of the Reformation. Their beauty camouflages the stories which made the people of this land contemplate their beliefs, in order to decide upon a faith by which they would live or die. But life was cheap and, fortunately for the superstitiously faithful Tudor Englishman, its loss offered reunification with Christ in heaven. With the dissolution, Henry discovered that many responsibilities once fulfilled by the monasteries lacked patronage, and other patrons had to be found. One such service was that offered by the Carters over Kent Sands on Morecambe Bay.

Perhaps the greatest misunderstanding of this period, a time which gave rise to some of the more extraordinary and portentous appointments in this collection, is that Henry VIII was a protestant: far from it. Indeed, the mere suggestion of such a thought would have added your name to the State Executioner's list in this time of despotic judicial murder. Henry's own book on the sacraments

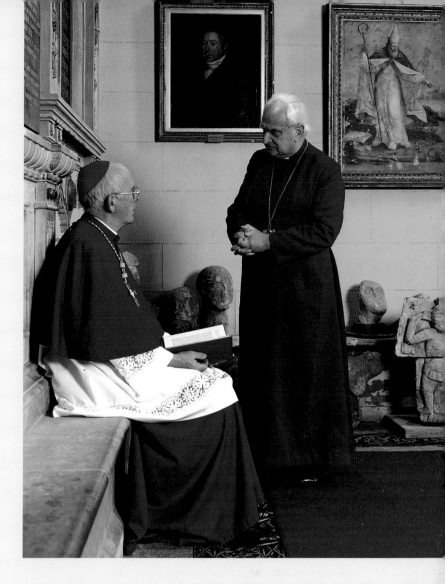

St Patrick established his Bishopric in Ireland at Armagh in 454. His successors, the **Roman Catholic** and **Church of Ireland Archbishops**, who both claim his province in their title, lead communities that have been at odds since the Reformation towards reconciliation. Their Patron Saint's portrait provides an example of unity and purpose on the walls of Armagh's cathedral.

resulted in one of the Sovereign's titles that, in its timing, is perhaps the most ironic: Defender of the Faith. Despite the vicissitudes of this period of religious turmoil and the growing indifference to religious matters since, F·D· (*Fidei Defensor*, Defender of the Faith) is still inscribed about the monarch's head on every coin in Great Britain.

The devotions of monarchs on military missions or progressing their court through the country presented problems. A travelling clergy followed the monarch, with a choir to sing the liturgies. During the Reformation, this courtly group felt the strain of changing doctrine directly, and the pendulum of creed continued to swing violently during the reigns of his three children. The composers too walked the spiritual tightrope carefully, writing music for the children and gentlemen to sing as Anne Boleyn's marriage came, the Act of Supremacy was passed, Mary led the church back to Rome and persecuted the protestants, only for Elizabeth to enshrine protestantism and endure excommunication. The foundations of Edward VI, including St Thomas's Hospital for the sick and Christ's Hospital for educating the poor, were also caught up in this sibling rivalry. But it was particularly difficult for scholars, and the universities, to tread between each creed. In Oxford, the new protestant status quo set by Elizabeth's implacable stand gave one of her supporters, Thomas Bodley, the opportunity to establish a library that houses every book published in England since. England's confidence was greatly boosted by the defeat of Spain's Armada in 1588: the seafaring English were more than a match for the Spaniards, whose ships were dispersed to collide in disarray along the treacherous rocky coastline. England's navy had many advantages, including the navigational aids pioneered by Trinity House that piloted seafarers into and from the Thames.

In order to maintain close links with Parliament, when Henry VIII moved from Westminster he left Black Rod, a functionary from the Order of the Garter, to keep the door as his predecessors had done for the conclave of knights. At the same time Henry made wider use of the Order for political ends, creating knights – who, if they fell from favour, would in turn be 'touched' on the shoulder by the black rod. This doorkeeper's 'tap' heralded 'degradation' from the order, often the first ignominious step on a long road from honour to the scaffold.

The feudal system was increasingly strained in the face of modernization during the Renaissance. The Tudors, recognizing that feudal systems would not efficiently provide the militia they needed, pioneered a new method for summoning men to arms. They appointed lieutenants, who became Lord Lieutenants, in each county to assist the existing sheriffs in both finding and commanding a militia. However, feudalism still had its uses, and in 1565 Elizabeth I granted the island of Sark, in the Channel Island remnants of the duchy of Normandy, as a separate fief that survives with its unique government today.

The Renaissance arrived in England along with the Tudors, who reigned over a period of considerable change. In addition, the Reformation swept from Europe through England, Scotland and into Ireland, where the difficulties were made more complicated by the plantation policies that would further strain relations in the coming centuries and where the missionary inheritance of St Patrick was claimed by both sides. The Dissolution displaced Church wealth and power, though the new Church of England was to be a fervent episcopal successor in the following century, championed by a new royal house. That monarch-in-waiting sat at Holyrood, his protestant education setting the political agenda for an isolationist Britain set on unity and colonization.

Gentleman Usher of the Black Rod, Secretary to the Lord Great Chamberlain and Sergeant-at-Arms of the House of Lords

PAGEANTRY WAS PART OF LIFE for the first twenty-six knights that wore Edward III's Garter in 1348. He constituted an annual assembly for them at Windsor, which coincided with St George's feast day, on 23 April. This required planning and, whenever the Order processed, its stately progress was led by an Usher who carried a black rod. When the knights were safely assembled, the door was closed and their security kept by the same Usher who, with his black rod, became door keeper – *ussarius* being medieval Latin for door keeper.

In this humble manner the well-known 'knocker of doors' steps from the early rituals of the Garter into the history of England. The earliest reference to this door-keeping role comes in 1361: *Letters Patent* state that Walter Whitehorse, who is described as 'usher of the free chapel in Wyndesore Castle' got 12d (pre-decimal pennies) a day for life.

In time, Black Rod moved as part of the court to attend the monarch elsewhere. When a fire in 1512 forced Henry VIII to move from Westminster to York House, his usher was left in the burnt-out remains. He has remained at the palace ever since. Ten years later, Black Rod was directed to have custody over 'all the doors where any councils are held, as well in Our High Court of Parliament, as in other places'.

The role was tricky when the boss was someone like Henry, as Henry Norris found out. He was both Black Rod and Groom of the Stole to Anne Boleyn. In her tragic fall from grace, he was implicated in the web of fanciful accusations that Thomas Cromwell concocted and he was executed after a trial in Westminster Hall. He might have been wise to intrigue less and travel with his monarch more, as Sir William Compton did; he fought with Henry VIII in France and accompanied him to the Field of the Cloth of Gold. But he was still expected to keep up his Garter duties by arresting errant knights with a tap on the shoulder using the Black Rod. If the knight was found guilty a £5 fee would be paid and in Tudor England, an arrest having been made, this reward was virtually guaranteed.

In the celebrations that filled England after the Restoration, Sir Fleetwood Sheppard was handed the Black Rod. He was also steward to Charles II's mistress Nell Gwynn and a *bon viveur* who once invited the membership of the Commons into the king's cellar, to drink a loyal toast. In 1698 Admiral Sir David Mitchell became the first in a lasting run of military appointments. This fulfils the edict of Henry VIII that Black Rod should be a 'Gentleman of Name and Arms'.

As recently as 1971, the role of Sergeant-at-Arms, responsible for discipline in the Lords, was merged with Black Rod's, and he became Secretary to the Lord Great Chamberlain. The latter fits in well with his growing responsibilities as a senior administrator for the Lords. In fact this is an appointment which is growing. The influence Black Rod exercises is greater now perhaps than at any previous time. And each year at Windsor, Black Rod returns to his roots. As an officer of the Order of the Garter he still processes, with Rod in hand, where Walter Whitehorse walked as the first Black Rod.

The public can watch the State Opening of Parliament on television each year when Black Rod walks the length of the Palace of Westminster. He conveys the Sovereign's command for the Commons to leave their chamber and appear at the Bar of the Lords to hear the Queen's Speech. As he approaches the Commons its door is symbolically slammed as a reminder that the Commons guards its independence. It is a rebuff to her messenger that the Queen too can see. However, following a ruling by the Speaker in 1962 the Commons have no power to exclude Black Rod when he knocks three times on the door. So, after the three resounding knocks, the door is opened and Black Rod conveys the Queen's command that 'this honourable House… attend upon Her Majesty immediately in the House of Peers'.

The door of the House of Lords is kept by **Black Rod**, who holds the symbol of his office, while his badge as an officer of the Order of the Garter hangs from the chain around his neck. From the Queen's throne there is a clear view of Black Rod's direct progress towards the Speaker's Chair and the door-slamming incident.

'The king's right hand at the pen, the issuer of the royal
manuscript authority, whether for the ends of state policy,
for transactions of law, or for private purposes.'

HISTORIAN OF THE SOCIETY OF WRITERS TO HM SIGNET, 1890

Lord Clerk Register and Keeper of the Signet

The Signet's matrices are held within an elaborate but utilitarian stamp. It represents the Sovereign's seal, which marks the authority to initiate an action in the Court of Session. Its **Keeper** is a symbolic guardian.

THE OLDEST SURVIVING OFFICER of state in Scotland is the Lord Clerk Register. The Act of Union threw into desuetude many other appointments which no longer carried legislative or executive function now that the sovereign parliament in Westminster had taken over; among these were the Chancellor, Treasurer, Treasurer-depute and Master of Requests. Lord Clerk Register survives as a link with Scotland's independent past. Most of its remaining functions were removed by Act of Parliament in 1879, though as one of the guardian commissioners for keeping Scotland's ancient crown jewels, the Honours Three, it retains a strong symbolic role.

Combined with the title comes the role of Keeper of the Signet; and it is this more junior appointment which tells the story of how the royal writ developed in Scotland. Originally, the king's authority was communicated through the land by warrants, written and read by barely literate people. In order to authenticate these warrants, a system of seals was developed and those matters that related specifically to the monarch, or were private to him, were sealed with the king's own Signet, or finger ring. The oldest impression of the monarch's private Signet survives from 1342, though Laing records one from Robert the Bruce. The volume of paperwork increased, and soon the quantity of medieval documents made it impossible for the king to see every one that needed his Signet. He therefore appointed a secretary to administer it for him. As the burden of work became still greater, the King's Secretary hired clerks to assist in the preparation of writs. These new clerks were first described as Writaries to the Signet; their influence increased as fast as the workload. As the king had not the time to seal everything which needed his Signet, he placed it in the care and protection of his Secretary, who became, officially, the Keeper of the Signet.

In 1532, James V overhauled his legal administration and established the College of Justice. The Writers to the Signet were established as a component part of the new court system, advising applicants for justice on how to proceed. Further legislation that year established regulations by which the growing number of Writers were to be bound. In 1594, Sir Robert Cockburn of Clerkington, who was Lord Secretary to the King and Keeper of the Signet, gave a commission to John Layng to be Deputy Keeper of the Signet, with authority over eighteen Writers, while he retained responsibility for the Signet.

The nature of civil writs in Scotland was such that, to achieve validity in law, they had to be seen by the monarch, and this sight was evidenced by the impression of the Signet on the writ. By the end of James V's reign the volume of legal business needed four Signets. Today there is only one, and all documents involving the Supreme Court must have the Signet's impression. So also must writs summoning subjects to the presence of the Lords of Council and Session, letters of diligence and execution, and letters staying or prohibiting diligence. Each is scrutinized by the Signet Officer to ensure it is 'right and proper' to go before the courts. Then it will 'pass the Signet' and the press is wound down and the seal makes an impression of the Signet.

The ancient appointment of King's Secretary, which had evolved into Lord Secretary, was abolished in 1746, following a shake-up of institutions after the Battle of Culloden, which concluded the Jacobite Rebellion. The office of Keeper of the Signet was not abolished and in 1817 it was given to the Lord Clerk Register. The combined titles have symbolic significance: the first retains ancient links with the original Great Officers of Scotland before Union in 1707 and the second charts the evolution of royal law from Robert the Bruce's signet ring to the hefty impressions which authenticate the business of the Queen's Scottish courts today.

Mr Houison Craufurd who washes the Sovereign's Hands

PERHAPS ONE OF THE MOST morally adroit and reassuring of stories is the one concerning a sixteenth-century king of Scotland, saved from death by an unknowing yeoman farmer who received a dream reward. It was described by Sir Walter Scott in *Tales of a Grandfather* and resulted in a romantic custom which rivals all others throughout Britain for its symbolic simplicity and charm.

Cramond Bridge is now virtually unnoticed by the people who drive on it at speed across the River Cramond between Edinburgh and the Forth Road Bridge. However, it was here in the reign of King James V of Scotland that a farmer threshing his corn heard a noise outside. Investigating, he saw a group of ruffians mugging a well-dressed gentleman on the bridge, probably for his money, but without much care for his life. Fearing that they might murder their victim, whom he didn't recognize, and showing no care for himself, the farmer, John Howieson, ran to the bridge with flail in hand. He could not have known that the unfortunate man was the king in disguise: James V regularly travelled among his people in this way in order to learn what was happening in his kingdom.

After a short struggle, the muggers fled and John invited the injured man back to the cottage and washed his wounds. Later, John accompanied him back towards Edinburgh, in case the muggers struck again. John explained that he was working on the king's farm at Braehead, and the gentleman described himself as the Goodman (or tenant) of Ballengiech, who held a lowly court appointment. The gentleman asked what was the one thing he would most like to own 'and honest John confessed he should think himself the happiest man in Scotland were he but proprietor of the farm on which he wroght as a labourer'. When they parted the gentleman invited John to look over the royal apartments at Holyrood Palace the following Sunday.

John arrived at the gates in his best clothes and asked the guard for the Goodman of Ballengiech. Well briefed, the sentry let him pass and the Goodman stood waiting for his visitor. He was shown all the rooms and his host was 'amused with his wonder and his remarks'. Towards the end, the Goodman asked John if he would like to see the king. The farmer was beside himself with excitement but said he didn't want to cause any trouble. Reassured that it was no bother, John was told that when they came into the royal presence the king would be the only one wearing a hat. They entered the hall together and found it packed with courtiers. John was petrified and searched for his hatted monarch. After looking everywhere, John turned to his escort and said 'It must be either you or me for all but us two are bare headed.'

At this point the cat was out of the bag. 'The king laughed at John's fancy; and that the good yeoman might have occasion for mirth also he made him a present of the farm of Braehead which he had wished so much to possess.' But he gave it on condition that John and his successors should be ready to present a ewer and basin for the monarch to wash his hands, either at Holyrood Palace or when passing by Cramond Bridge.

In 1822 George IV set out on the 'King's Jaunt' to Scotland. It was a significant visit, the first since the 1745 rebellion when much of Scotland's culture had been outlawed. For the first time in nearly a hundred years the king gave permission for bagpipes to be played and, to prove that tartan was also once again a legitimate outfit, George smothered himself in the stuff, even managing to wear his kilt the wrong way round. The preparations for what was deemed at the time a gesture of significant symbolism for Scotland were helped along by Walter Scott. His romantic attitude to history was allowed free rein, and in popular and poetic terms he described the rediscovery of the Honours Three (the country's crown, sceptre and sword), which were found

The ewer, basin and salver, with its fresh linen, have been used to wash royal hands by the **Houison Craufurd** family since George IV claimed his feudal due. This bridge across the River Cramond may have been where their ancestor saved a king from murder by rushing to his rescue from a nearby barn.

wrapped in sheets in a chest behind the panelling of Edinburgh Castle's throne room. This was the first chapter in the romantic reinvention of Scotland that continues to this day.

To give the monarchy relevance as a Scottish institution again, the hitherto 'absentee' Hanoverians (remembered best for the merciless 'Butcher' duke of Cumberland) were surrounded with more Scottishness than you could find at a Burns Supper. The Howiesons were swept up in it all too and were summoned to perform the service on George IV that

his conveniently Stuart ancestor had instigated. There was no mistaking which one was the king this time. William Howieson Crawford presented his ewer and basin and George IV broke the habit of a lifetime and washed his hands.

Whenever called to perform the service, three members of the family [now called Houison Craufurd] come from Craufurland Castle with the silver made for George IV. The senior one holds the basin, while the other two pour the water and offer a linen towel.

Hereditary Falconer

The ancestors of the **Hereditary Falconer** hunted across this land in the southern uplands of Scotland with falcons. Lord Borthwick, the 24th peer and current bearer of the title, is holding a female peregrine falcon into the wind. These are the most popular birds of prey that work these hills.

JUST AS JOHN HOWIESON was presented with a gift from James V in gratitude for the service he had provided at a time of great danger, there were many others who received similar tokens from the Royal House of Stuart for services rendered. Among these tokens, the custom of giving a post within the wider royal court provided the recipient with a useful income and valuable access. When power was vested in the king's court, this was the place to be and, no matter what the task, it was useful to have the ear of those who counted. For this reason, the history of western courts is awash with utilitarian roles granted as hereditary offices to deserving nobles; though it is doubtful whether many were actually fulfilled in anything more than a ceremonial way, the actual task being left to paid servants.

Some of these appointments were given in such informal terms that evidence of them has failed to survive the vicissitudes of history, especially when alterations in the status quo affected the family concerned. One such situation faced the Scottish family of Borthwick. They claim to be hereditary Falconers to the Scots monarch; however, there are no extant charters to prove it, although references survive of their special role before the union of the crowns. In 1672, the 9th Lord Borthwick died. No heir could be identified so the title and all honours fell into abeyance. It was not until 1986 that Lord Lyon recognized it again in a junior branch of the family; the revived Borthwick lords are used to long battles to prove their right.

The Borthwicks claim that, in return for services to the Stuart kings, they received the privilege of serving as hereditary royal Falconers. This was a service associated with leisure and therefore of particular esteem and friendship. When James I of Scots was held hostage, Borthwick offered to be held himself instead of his king: a self-imposed sentence that dragged on for three years. When he was finally returned to Scotland the grateful monarch allowed Borthwick to build his own castle in 1430 and gave the family peerage twenty years later. The 3rd Lord Borthwick fought beside James IV at the Battle of Flodden, and lost his life, as did most of the flower of Scotland's warriors.

Falconry was very popular until about the time that Borthwick's title fell into abeyance. During the eighteenth century, interest in it revived but never to the previous levels. This is emphasized by the medieval rules, which strictly applied levels of rank to the birds of prey anyone could own. For an emperor or king, an eagle; for royalty, a jerfalcon; an earl could use a peregrine, yeomen a goshawk and priests a sparrow-hawk. However, the hopeless kestrel was for knaves and servants.

In England, the appointment of Hereditary Master Falconer was given to the 1st Duke of St Albans in the 1680s, the natural son of Charles II by his mistress Nell Gwynn. Along with the appointment, he was given permission to ride in a coach along Rotten Row, the sandy track that runs through Hyde Park. This was otherwise a privilege restricted to the Sovereign. These honours were all vested upon a boy of just fourteen. His descendant was invited to the Queen's coronation in 1953 but said he would arrive, as Hereditary Master Falconer, with a live falcon. He was dissuaded and consequently did not attend.

'O! for a falconer's voice,
To lure this tassel-gentle back again.'

WILLIAM SHAKESPEARE, ROMEO AND JULIET

Lord-Lieutenant and Custos Rotulorum of Gloucestershire

The **Lord-Lieutenant** of Gloucestershire was once the commander of a large militia and wears a general officer's uniform with silver rather than gold braid. The county has never lost its idyllic rural identity with the Forest of Dean and the Cotswolds, where sheep have been raised for centuries.

EVERY COUNTY HAS HAD A LORD-LIEUTENANT since Henry VIII appointed the first in 1557. Originally responsible for maintaining local defence and civil order, they were quite literally the sovereign's lieutenant, which etymologically derives from the Latin, *locum tenens*, meaning one holding a place for another.

There is a buzz in the air. A small crowd has gathered. Many of them have Union flags and the police watch vigilantly while the royal car approaches. Around the main gate are well-dressed people ready to greet their monarch, but in front of them all is the Lord-Lieutenant. This is a scene played out all over the country by Lord-Lieutenants who are the first to welcome the monarch, her family or visiting heads of state into their respective county. Dressed in a quasi-military uniform, complete with top-ranking officer's sword and braid on their cap, they echo the role Henry originally envisaged for them as local militia commanders. Having greeted the royal visitor and, as it were, handed over the county, he follows the visit and is the last to bid farewell. Once again the Lord-Lieutenant is back at the top of the pecking order.

Feudalism did not die during the Renaissance but it radically evolved and, at the start of the sixteenth century, kings could no longer rely on the feudal system to provide knights and fighting men in time of need. Instead, the money that manors paid in lieu of providing service was centralized and used to pay for a system that became the beginnings of a standing army. The new Lord-Lieutenants were then expected to command the county militias, a role which altered as the army changed, although Lord-Lieutenants have retained a special association with the territorial army and took a leading role in the Home Guard, or 'Dad's Army', of the Second World War.

Until recently, most Lord-Lieutenants were local landowners from the county with large houses and grand titles. This suited the benevolent unpaid nature of their work, especially when their military role declined and only their position at the top of the county's social pyramid remained. There are still parts of the country where this style of lieutenancy is greatly valued and works well. Lord-Lieutenants support the broader life of the community within their county by supporting charities, education and other good works. The people whom the Prime Minister today recommends to Buckingham Palace to become Lord-Lieutenants more closely reflect society at the start of the twenty-first century. In addition, as this reign has seen a virtual revolution in the role of women so has the lieutenancy: however, it has been decided to retain the original title established in the sixteenth century as Lord-Lieutenants.

Some Lord-Lieutenants are also appointed to be the Custos Rotulorum, or the most senior civil officer in the county. Translated loosely this means the custodian, or keeper, of records, and historically this position gave the holder power to appoint senior officials. The Custos Rotulorum is now the senior magistrate in the county and presides over the Lord Chancellor's advisory committee for the appointment of lay Justices of the Peace.

Although it is probably older, Gloucestershire first appears in the *Anglo Saxon Chronicle* of 1016. It technically became a county when Henry I granted it to his natural son Robert, as an earldom: earl being the Anglo-Saxon for count, from which county derives. Ever since, Gloucester has retained a royal association and it was here that medieval kings came for one of the three crowning festivals each year. Since the *Domesday Book* was compiled, the shire has altered its boundaries a lot but the Lord Lieutenant and Custos Rotulorum is still the Sovereign's representative over land including the Cotswold hills, the Forest of Dean and the Severn Basin. The lush rural landscape supports fruit farming, dairy and plenty of sheep.

The Queen's Body Guard of the Yeomen of the Guard

GOING TO BED WAS A DANGEROUS BUSINESS for Renaissance monarchs. There were potential assassins everywhere, and to prevent such assaults the Yeomen of the Guard were drafted in to prepare the bedroom at bedtime and then sleep at the door to keep it safe. Among the extant appointments still shared out amongst the men who line the Queen's ceremonial path are two which reflect this responsibility, the Yeoman Bed-goer and Yeoman Bed-hanger. Then there was the risk of poisoning and here too the Yeomen were drafted, to act as tasters. They generally carried dishes to the dining room from the kitchen and, as they set each one down, took a mouthful to prove it was safe. Exon-in-Waiting (so called because he is a regular serviceman 'exempt' from his duties in order to serve in the

> *'A desperate disease requires a dangerous remedy.'*
>
> **GUY FAWKES**, 6 NOVEMBER 1605

body guard) still stands beside the Sovereign's chair at State Banquets, just in case he is called on to taste again.

However, they were formed to meet a more direct risk. After the Battle of Bosworth Field concluded the Wars of the Roses, the grisly civil war that brought Henry Tudor to the throne, the new king felt insecure. He claimed his crown by right of conquest: indeed it was supposedly lifted from a thorn hedge at the battlefield by Rhys ap Thomas and placed upon his head. This was no time to be complacent about his security because the country remained divided into the red rose loyalties of Lancaster, which had won, and the white rose of York, whose adherents looked resentfully at the upstart Welshman awaiting coronation.

To ensure his safety, Henry VII reorganized fifty of his loyal archers into a body guard in time for his crowning, which were called the Yeomen of the Guard of Our Lord the King. It was not since the reign of Richard II that a monarch had felt it necessary to engage 'a furniture of daily soldiers' to be in constant attendance.

The Roman Catholic Robert Catesby attempted to blow up Parliament at the onset of the seventeenth century. Unfortunately for this conspiracy, one of his accomplices warned a friend away from the Palace of Westminster, and this suspicious message was reported. Searches of the cellar, below the place from which the king was to address his new Parliament, uncovered Guy Fawkes amongst some powder kegs. At most State Openings since, the vigilant Yeomen have carried lanterns into the labyrinthine cellars to check their approaching Sovereign's safety.

Serving the king took on a strange twist for the Yeomen of Charles I. The Queen, Henrietta Maria, was both French and Roman Catholic, and her court was filled with foreigners, most of whom shared her faith. This combination was unwelcome in a country still concerned about the Catholic threat, and when Parliament convinced Charles that her court presented a danger to the country, he instructed his Yeomen to throw it out of his palace and out of the country.

After the Restoration, Charles II established a standing army, at the same time putting the Yeomen of the Guard on a proper footing with their own officers. A portion of the Yeomen accompanied Charles II during his years of exile, which is how they have given the Sovereign unbroken service since 1485, making them the oldest military corps in the world. Their numbers after the Restoration were much reduced from the high days of the Henrys. But, in time, this too was abused, with some civilians purchasing positions among the Yeomen, now known as 'The King's Spears', and royal favourites who had no military experience whatever were granted commissions. However, they provided close protection when George II was the last British king to command an army in the field, at Dettingen in 1743.

They are yeomen still; that is, according to out-dated protocols of class, because the servicemen gathered from the Army, the Royal Marines and the Royal Air Force are all warrant officers or non-commissioned officers. Each must be able to brag of an exemplary service record and none stand on parade without a Long Service and Good Conduct Medal: although they will all tell you that this is an award for undetected crime. There are also five commissioned officers, who command the force under the Captain, as he is known, who takes the appointment by dint of being the Government's Deputy Chief Whip in the House of Lords. They turn out for State functions, Investitures and Garden Parties. But one of these duties has a chilling reminder of the terrorist threat which is ever present.

Lanterns are provided by the Parliamentary Works Department so that the **Yeomen of the Guard** can check that terrorists like Guy Fawkes no longer lurk beneath the Lords while the Queen opens Parliament. The colours red, white and blue on hats, garters and shoes were added to this Tudor uniform after the Act of Union in 1707.

Standard Bearer of Her Majesty's Body Guard of the Honourable Corps of Gentlemen-at-Arms

ALMOST AS SOON AS THE THRONE WAS HIS, the young Henry VIII set about spending the riches his cautious father had put by and reviving a romantic but disastrous struggle for the French throne.

One of his earliest edicts was to establish a close body guard. Henry VII had assembled a body of archers but his son wanted fifty men, armed with spears and lances, to be close at hand if trouble should break out; and he wanted them to be from noble families. They were called the Band of Gentlemen Pensioners, a name which might suit the venerable former officers who fill its ranks today but, in 1509, this was a lean fighting machine made up of the best. Then, the word 'pensioner' had nothing to do with stipendary payments to the elderly; it implied that the king paid for their pension, or board and lodging. They were trained and fit for battle, well drilled and disciplined. Their establishment further demonstrated the change from an army dependent upon feudal arrangements, and it was not long before this new Band was pitched into battle.

The cause was revenge: the booty, two towns costly to defend. The Marquess of Dorset had been sent to France in 1512 with an expeditionary force, to join up with the Spaniards and give the French king Louis XII a bloody nose. Unfortunately, Spain double-crossed the English, leaving them stranded while a cosy Franco-Spanish truce was struck. Henry VIII was furious so, the next June, he landed at Calais at the head of an army of 4,000. In this retinue were his worthies, the Band of Gentlemen, under command of their first Captain, the Earl of Essex. The Band numbered 400 mounted men for this invasion. A painting which depicts the Battle of the Spurs that ensued shows a standard, suggesting that a Standard Bearer was appointed in preparation for war: along with two others, the Harbinger, who ensured the Men at Arms were vitalled with lodgings, and the Clerk of the Cheque, who checked that no one was absent and all were paid.

The next trip to France was for diplomatic display and to impress the great Renaissance monarch François I at the Field of the Cloth of Gold in 1520. Apart from the very real task of defending Henry in a situation which could have gone sour, they pitted their strength against their French counterparts, the Noble Guarde du Corps. This ceremonial role endured and, whenever a State Visitor arrives in Britain, the Queen is surrounded by heirs of the original Band of Gentlemen.

The oldest surviving Muster Roll is dated 1526 and shows Edward Billingham as the Standard Bearer. Standards were first seen in Edward III's reign but became popular under the Tudors. They are narrow and taper to a swallow tail to suit the field of battle when carried aloft on horseback. As foot soldiers generally have squared flags, the one carried by the Standard Bearer now is a reminder of when the Band was a mounted corps.

The last time they served as a military body guard was for Charles I during the Civil War, though they were stood by during the Jacobite Rebellion of 1745 and the Chartist Riots of 1848. King Charles confirmed that the Band had, 'the honor to be our nearest guard and to have their daily access into our presence chamber', a privilege still held today. Even now, the Captain is a member of the Government. At the Battle of Edgehill, in 1642, it was Sir Edmund Verney who was killed as Standard Bearer, his place being taken by Captain John Smith: but strangely neither were in the Band of Pensioners.

Charles II restored the Band, which Cromwell had suspended, but only as a ceremonial guard, the military one being fulfilled by the Life Guards. It became a band of retired officers of merit, which William IV renamed the Honourable Corps of Gentlemen-at-Arms. And at all great occasions, it is the Corps which stand closest to the Queen with their Standard Bearer ready to lower the Standard in salute.

The senior **body guard** in England wears the uniform of Dragoon Guard's officers from the 1840s, with epaulettes to protect from sword blows to the shoulder, and swan feather plumes in their helmets. Their axes were introduced in 1526 to provide more efficient protection when fighting on foot. The three golden tassels represent the cloth that was used to soak up blood and were introduced to keep a reliable grip on the handle.

'His Highness hath ordeyned and appointed to have a Retynue
daily of certaine Speres, called Men of Armes, to be chosen of
Gentlemen that be comen and extracte of noble blod.'

ORDINANCE OF HENRY VIII

Children of the Chapels Royal

TWO MONTHS AFTER LEAVING SOUTHAMPTON, in September 1415, and after a long march through the French countryside with Henry V and his army, the Children of the Chapels Royal sang a dawn mass for the king and his knights in the corn fields beside Agincourt. The Chapels Royal was always a travelling church, consisting of priests who administered to the monarch's spiritual needs, supported by Gentlemen and Children who sang the services.

On that morning, they acknowleged the feast day of St Crispin and Crispinian in their verses – hours before the date became enshrined by battle in England's history. Shakespeare, in *Henry V*, fills the character, Gower, with umbrage after a French raid on the luggage train behind the lines: 'Tis certain there's not a boy left alive; and the cowardly rascals that ran from the battle ha' done this slaughter.' No record survives to describe which Children went with the Chapels Royal in 1415 or how they fared. But that they went and that Shakespeare described the presence of children gives an insight into the manner of fifteenth-century warfare. Kings took much else besides soldiers on their campaigns.

There was a considerable burden upon monarchs to maintain their devotions. Ever since St Augustine converted Aethelbert of Kent, this obligation conflicted with the need for travel. Inevitably royal caravans included priests, and the paraphernalia increased as the ritual developed. Also, the political imperative for travel increased. To keep hold of the monarchy, the early kings had to make progresses and they took priests on the journeys with them.

Edward I made reference to choirboys in his Chapel Royal in 1303, as did both his successors. It is clear from these early references that monarchs took it upon themselves to educate the boys who had given their voices to help with royal worship, arranging for places at Oxford and Cambridge. To attract the best voices, pressure, or 'impressment',

was brought to bear on cathedrals or nobles who had fine singers in their charge. Gradually, the Chapel Royal gained a complement of about half a dozen Children. They were cared for and supervised by a Master of the Children and, if necessary, he prepared them for and conducted them on the monarch's expeditions. The last major journey was to France in 1520 to support Henry VIII's display at the Field of the Cloth of Gold, when ten boys were rationed for 2 pence a day. However, the boys also travelled to Charles I's coronation in Scotland.

Religious strife hit the Chapel Royal as hard as anywhere in the country's religious community. It is best seen from the dexterity of a former chorister of St Paul's, who was appointed to the Chapel Royal in 1569 and stayed until death in 1623. A Roman Catholic by inclination, William Byrd composed music that satisfied Elizabeth I and her Stuart successors, leaving behind a large repertoire of anthems still in constant use.

At high religious festivals, these compositions are often sung under Holbein's painted ceiling in the Chapel Royal at St James's Palace. It was here that the Gentlemen and Children made their choral headquarters after Queen Anne's coronation, in 1702. While they have moved occasionally since, it remains their home, though education had been provided at different places. Since 1923, the Children have attended the City of London School as the Queen's Scholars, on scholarships funded by the monarch, in return for attendance at ceremonies when the Queen still travels the country, such as the annual observance of Royal Maundy during Holy Week, or at the Remembrance Service at nearby Whitehall.

The Chapel Royal has attracted some excellent composers. These include George Frideric Handel, who found the increasingly German court of the Hanoverian kings welcoming. He was in his post as a composer in time to prepare music for George II's

The **Children**, wearing State Coats, as prescribed in Charles II's warrant of 1661, gather in the aisle of the Chapel Royal in St James's Palace, under Holbein's ceiling. With their large packing cases they must be ready to travel with the Sovereign whenever they are needed. Their predecessors even followed Henry V's retinue to the fields of Agincourt.

coronation in 1727, including his famous setting of the scripture explaining how Zadok and Nathan anointed King Solomon.

The Children have seldom missed the chance to make mischief, especially when given licence by James I to act like policemen. He ruled in 1622 that 'No man whatsoever presume to wayte upon us to the Chappell in bootes and spurs' and the Children were encouraged to fine offenders Spur Money. This is now ritualized into the Epiphany Service when the Queen, following the example of the Three Wise Men, makes gifts of gold, frankincense and myrrh to Christ. One of the Gentlemen Ushers who does this wears spurs. A chorister demands the fine but has to recite the gamut, or scale, before the money is handed over. The 1st Duke of Wellington got away without paying on this technicality but none do today.

Queen's Guide Over Kent Sands

THE TIDAL RACE across the vast open sands of Morecambe Bay, on the north-west coast of England, can outrun a galloping horse. As the sea reclaims its territory every twelve hours, waves of chilly water finger their way round the ever-shifting sandbanks. From the shore, they appear to be both flat and inviting, but the landscape they form is one of the most undulating and treacherous. Ever since the forces of nature moulded the Lancastrian coastline, these sands have been lifted and thrown about by each tide. Few people can identify the safe banks from those which will drown a person in quicksand. And many of those bravely walking across have been ambushed by the sea's return.

But good fortune shines on a few and, supposedly, the Roman governor Agricola successfully crossed Morecambe Bay with an army, when heading north through Lancashire, and Robert the Bruce may well have crossed in the other direction when leading his marauding invasion south. The latter had been attracted by the wealth of Furness Abbey, which King Stephen founded in 1127, eight years before taking the throne.

This Abbey of Savignian Benedictines, dedicated to St Mary, took responsibility for the safety of the sands which separated their promontory at Furness from the Lancastrian mainland. The Bay may have been a convenient barrier from the intervention of other powers but it was an obstacle to communication, which many took the risk to cross, cutting their journey by a considerable distance through the sand and over the river Kent, which drained much of the Lake District. If all was well, the sand was firm and the river fordable; but a petition to the king from the Abbot, in 1326, proves that this was often not the case: he asked for a coroner to investigate great loss of life on the sands.

It is not known when the first guide was appointed to show travellers across both bays, that of Cartmell in the west and Kent Sands in the east. But the first record is of Edmonstone in 1501. He was given a ten-acre tenement at Cartmell and was described as the Carter upon Kent Sands. His successor, William Gate, was paid by the Prior of the foundation at Cartmell, which was a satellite of Furness Abbey. This bill was later picked up by the Priory of Conished. However, the future looked bleak when the Abbot of Furness was charged with treason for involvement in the Pilgrimage of Grace in 1536, an uprising in the north responding to Henry VIII's doctrinal changes. The Dissolution followed almost at once, and the vast abbey, the largest Cistercian one in the country, was surrendered with all its wealth, land and satellite priories on 7 April 1537. In 1540 the entire estates of the Abbey were transferred to the Duchy of Lancaster. Along with the Abbey's wealth, the Duchy also took on many of its obligations, including payment for the Guide at Guide's Farm.

One year after the Abbey was surrendered, Richard Carter was given the job, probably taking his family name from the appointment: he drove a cart across the sands. And the Carters held sway, provisionally at ten marks per annum, until 1865. It was a dynasty which helped establish the now-famous horse competition across the sands, known as the Warton Sands Race.

But they also lived with the tragedies of Morecambe Bay, including the death of one Guide, William Carter, in 1672. His son wrote a plea to the Duchy of Lancaster asking for a pay rise. It gives an insight into the Guide's life. He described the expense of maintaining two horses and reminded them that his father had lost his life saving two people from drowning. He explained the hardships of exposure to the winds and driving rain, while constantly seeking fresh fording places over the moving river. This, along with the fear of fog and mist which disorientated him, earned him a sympathetic ear and a few pounds were added to his pay packet.

'Brobs' of laurel, taken from the bushes which surround Guide's Farm, are placed to mark a safe route over the constantly moving sands of Morecambe Bay. Using their eyes, their feet and a stick, **Guides** have been assisting travellers to cross Kent Sands for at least five centuries.

Every day on the sands is different; sometimes the shape of the land itself changes, as the river and sea wash away areas before throwing up new banks. The Guide still lives on Cartmell, in Guide's Farm, where his predecessors have waited for centuries to provide an escort. The house is surrounded by laurel, both to protect it from the bitter winds and to provide brobs, which are the markers for safe routes across the Bay. The Guide takes an armful of laurel and, using his stick to test the sand, he finds a safe path. Every now and then he pushes a brob into the sand, where it will stay as the tide covers it many times.

After five centuries, today's Guide is just a telephone call away from helping travellers across the Bay or taking large parties for a day on the sands. He teaches them how to identify the different types of sand, including caff, slape, slutch and quicksand, which constantly change. Of the latter he says, 'There is a saying by all fisherman including myself which is, 'It'll mire a cat,' meaning that even a nimble cat would go down in such an area.'

The appointment is now funded by the Queen, as a service to the public from her Duchy of Lancaster. But people still ignore the dangers and set off alone, ignoring the brobs. Kent Sands remains as dangerous as ever it was.

Abbot of St Benet-at-Holme

IN SUMMER, THE NORFOLK BROADS become a teeming mass of sailing boats and pleasure craft. The demand for access to this once remote area might seem to endanger the very beauty and solitude that everyone seeks. But away from these crowds, the open and flat countryside is punctuated by characters from the congregation of East Anglian churches, their splendour celebrating faith in God and the wealth of their benefactors. Occasionally, the horizon is lifted by the outstretched vanes of a windmill.

At one point, the waterway curls round the ruins of one of these windmills standing on what was once an island. Surrounding it are the remains of a crumbling grey stone wall. A noble gothic archway provides access to the dilapidated building and adds to its strange appearance. Its incarnation as a windmill was only its most recent one. Transformation to such a utilitarian role was perhaps an act of appalling vandalism. It was certainly brave, considering that it contravened an Act of Parliament. This deserted windmill marks the site of the only monastery that Henry VIII left untouched: indeed he enhanced the influence of its Abbot by enshrining his office in legislation.

During a relatively brief period, all the monasteries and abbeys of the country were taken over by the Crown. The Dissolution resulted in the dismantling of a monastic tradition that had already lasted for about seven centuries, a tradition whose loss resulted in the dereliction and destruction of some of the most magnificent buildings in the kingdom. With them went great traditions of learning and devotion, but it was this wealth, influence and power that Henry coveted and that monasticism had flaunted unwisely.

When the representative of Henry VIII's Vicar General arrived at this gate, the countryside was already filled with dispossessed monks and deposed Abbots, while burning abbeys illuminated the skyline. Abbot Rugge of St Benet's, awaiting the fateful knock, had no resource but prayer to protect his small community. The Reformation in Europe, together with the consequences of Henry's decision to wed Anne Boleyn, fundamentally disrupted society and severed England's links with Rome. There was nothing an abbot could do to resist the demands of a king. Reluctantly, he ordered the door to be opened.

Fortunately for Abbot Rugge, the Vicar General had recently been a guest of the Bishop of Norwich and had seen a life of considerable opulence. In comparison, by either bad management or good fortune, the Abbey of St Benet turned out to be worth virtually nothing. These Benedictines were living in poverty and their pious example of religious life gave Thomas Cromwell an idea.

Instead of dissolving St Benet's, Cromwell persuaded the king to depose the Bishop of Norwich. Taking the wealth of Norwich into the royal coffers, Abbot Rugge suddenly found himself enthroned in the vacated bishop's cathedral. St Benet's was the only abbey that Henry VIII did not dissolve and, by an extraordinary Act of Parliament in 1536, it was protected in perpetuity. This Act, which enshrines one of the most startling conflicts of policy during the Dissolution, went on to stipulate that the Abbot should maintain a Prior and twelve monks 'for all time'.

Unfortunately, this turned out to be just a handful of years. Bishop Abbot Rugge failed in his obligations to his former abbey and gradually its buildings decayed and neighbouring farmers removed its stones. By the mid-nineteenth century all that remained was the ancient gatehouse, which was chosen for a new mill, its agricultural spire camouflaging the old monastery.

The See of Norwich was filled by successive incumbents who, over the years, dropped their unique title of Abbot; the Bishops of Norwich who sat in parliament saw no advantage in continuing to

Ruins only remain of the once mighty abbey church in which was buried the hero of Agincourt, Sir John Fastolff, Governor of the Bastille, Seneschal, Lieutenant and Regent of Normandy. Carrying satchel and crozier, the **Abbot of St Benet's** walks towards the great West Gate's remains, behind which a dilapidated windmill now stands. The abbey was built on an islet – or holme – where Suneman the Hermit founded a small chapel in the ninth century.

use their monastic title, and so it fell into disuse. However, this century has seen a change. Anomalies of history are now enjoyed, and this has provided a will to revive these old quirks and, since Henry VIII's Act is still extant, why not?

The letter of Henry VIII's Act has once again been put into effect: a vicar from a local parish now acts as Prior of St Benet-at-Holme and he has twelve lay monks to assist him in his work. Since 1939 Bishops of Norwich have proudly assumed the title Abbot of St Benet's again. Each August Bank Holiday for the last sixty years, boats have brought a flood of pilgrims to join the Abbot for an open air service. Thus, a unique title, granted by the king responsible for destroying so much, has kept St Benet's alive and, after a long abeyance, it has never been healthier than it is now.

'What mean ye by these stones?'

JOSHUA 4:6

Master Treasurer of the Honourable Society of the Inner Temple

IN 1119 A GROUP OF KNIGHTS undertook to protect pilgrims travelling to and from the newly liberated Holy Land. They gathered others into a religious community, calling themselves the Poor Fellow Soldiers of Jesus Christ, and took oaths of chastity, obedience and poverty, while dedicating their swords to the Patriarch of Jerusalem. Twenty years before, the First Crusade had successfully taken the Holy City and established the Kingdom of Jerusalem. Its king, Baldwin II, gave the knights lodgings beside the mosque of al-Aksa, otherwise known as the Temple of Solomon, from which they took their name as the Knighthood of the Temple of Solomon – or, more simply, the Knights Templar. They were one of the three great military orders associated with the Crusades.

'It pierces my heart. If anyone else abandoned the King, do you know what I would do? I would carry him on my shoulders step by step, from island to island, from country to country and I would not fail him, even if it meant begging my bread.'

WILLIAM THE MARSHAL, ON TAKING RESPONSIBILITY FOR THE CHILD HENRY III, IN 1216

Much of the Round Church in London's Temple survived the Blitz, as did the thirteenth-century figures of Knights Templar including William Marshal, the Earl of Pembroke. The **Master Treasurer** leads a legal community that has occupied these premises since the middle ages. With him is the Head Porter of the Inner Temple, who carries a ceremonial staff surmounted by the Inn's device, the winged horse, Pegasus.

Later in the twelfth century the Knights Templar in England moved their base from Holborn towards the river, to an area of London that is consequently now called Temple. Here they constructed the Round Church, based upon the Holy Sepulchre in Jerusalem that contained Christ's miraculously vacated tomb. And, probably in Henry II's presence, it was consecrated by Patriarch Heraclius in 1185. The international influence of the Knights Templar grew dramatically, and with it their wealth and their need of lawyers. By 1312, when the Knights Templar dramatically fell from grace, there were probably already lawyers in the area. They then became tenants of the Knights Hospitaller. But the Hospitallers too came to a sticky end with the Dissolution and, in 1539, the Crown took back the freehold of the Temple. It finally became the lawyers' possession by grant of James I, though the Great Fire destroyed a number of its buildings.

In 1207 the clergy, who had hitherto provided all educated legal practitioners, were prevented from undertaking temporal business by Canon (Church) Law, so laymen were needed to practise law in the secular courts. Magna Carta stipulated that the king's courts must be at Westminster, so a suitable place was needed to house, teach and administer the growing band of lawyers. This was done informally at first, lawyers being a nomadic breed. But the growing need for efficient justice during the age of chivalry demanded a better solution. The answer was Inns of Court: places where lawyers were trained, fed and lodged as reward for their service. Two were established in the Temple, called the Inner and Middle Temples, each one centred on one of the surviving Templar halls. Records show that both associations were operational by 1388.

The Inns of Court are incorporated; they are societies deriving their constitutions from precedent in a manner similar to the Common Law they practise. At the apex of each are the Benchers, who

are the senior members of the society and are sometimes known as the Masters. Each year, they elect one of their number to be Master Treasurer, who acts as chairman of the governing body. Treasurers have held this position since the end of the fifteenth century and have presided over the association's 'parliament' since at least 1505, when the Inns' records began.

Both Temples keep a weather eye on the ancient Round Church and its nave, an extension consecrated in the presence of Henry III in 1240. The whole church sits heart-like at the centre of the two communities and their higgledy-piggledy boundary meandering through the clutter of buildings marking the end of one Master Treasurer's jurisdiction and the start of another's.

The Round Church is a reminder of the Templars' ancient traditions. The bombing of 1941 destroyed much of its fabric, particularly its marble. But perhaps the most tragic of these destructions were the tombs. These somnolent black figures transport the imagination through the centuries to battles around the walls of Jerusalem, Antioch and Acre. They represent knights of the Temple of Solomon and supporters of the order. Among them is William Marshal, the Ist Earl of Pembroke, who began his career supporting Henry II, was then pardoned by his errant son Richard I, was loyal to the Lionheart's ungrateful brother John and finally acted as regent to Henry III: a phenomenal record of chivalry from a man whose surname derives from having shared the title as Marshal of England.

The principal ecclesiastic at the church is called the Master of the Temple; he is appointed under letters patent from the crown, which carry an implicit authority that all lawyers understand. Just as the Knights Templar had no argument when Edward II's sheriffs arrived at the Temple to arrest their master in England, William de la Mare, on 9 January 1308.

Master Treasurer and Master Reader
of the Honourable Society of the Middle Temple

HISTORY DOES NOT CLEARLY RELATE when or precisely why the Middle Temple separated from the Inner Temple. In 1671 the commentator Dugdale wrote that they were originally joined, dividing in order to cater for the increase in the number of law students. However, the *Paston Letters*, dated November 1440, refer to both Temples as separate colleges but within one Inn of Court. When Charles II finally granted the Temple lands to the two societies, the document referred to 'The Inner and the Middle Temple, or New Temple' as 'being two out of those four colleges the most famous of all Europe'.

As with the Inner Temple, the chief executive officer of the Middle Temple is called the Treasurer. It was the training of this Inn that nurtured Sir Thomas More's concise legal mind and over which he presided as Treasurer between 1512 and 1516. At this time, the office was generally filled for long periods, a practice that was changed in 1596, when annual elections among the Masters of the Society chose the *Summus Thesaurarius*, or High Treasurer. Surprisingly, having been elected to the bench, the future Edward VII was elected Treasurer in 1882. In addition to the Treasurer there are two readers, who serve for six months each, known as the Autumn and the Lent Readers.

The Master Reader has always kept a supervisory eye on the teaching of law within the society. When the Inns of Court were formed, monasteries provided the template for education. Medieval monastic scholars wrote or copied manuscripts, which became the source of legal learning. These documents were rare and, in order to share their contents widely, one monk was selected to read them at student gatherings. The Inns of Court followed this practice, appointing Readers to read out the statutes and legal philosophies which, until Caxton's printing presses made the written word more accessible, provided the only reliable means of developing jurisprudence. The

importance of the Reader's role gave him precedence over Benchers in Hall, even though he was often not a Bencher himself.

Students are no longer expected to 'keep term' for two 'Grand Vacations' by attending a certain number of dinners in Hall. In recent times the practise of 'dining' has been reduced to twelve educational occasions or 'qualifying sessions' (which will usually include dinner). The object of dining is to enable students to mix with barristers and Benchers and learn the ethics and ethos of the profession. Thus they benefit from the experience and wisdom latent within the society they have joined. Originally dining would have begun in silence, while texts were read by the Reader. He then directed the mooting of legal points raised by the text for the mutual learning of all. This tradition is maintained, with the Reader giving a talk or reading on an appropriate subject of his choice. Further advocacy training for pupil barristers now includes a ten-day intensive course provided by Judges and members of the Inn. These take place during the first six months of pupillage, and at least nine hours must be completed before the newly called barrister can go into court on his own account.

The building of Middle Temple Hall commenced in 1562, under the auspices of the Treasurer, William Plowden, and after eight years, it was ready for a visit by Elizabeth I. The first performance of *Twelfth Night*, with Shakespeare himself involved, is said to have taken place in the Hall, and the occasion is recorded in the diary of a member of hall who was in the audience. On All Saints and Candlemas it also provided the setting for great celebrations. The Reader would welcome distinguished judges back into the Society and wait upon them at table before the Master of Revels, sometimes known as the Lord of Misrule, took the Reader's place and hosted a 'masque' during which students demonstrated their dancing and singing in a debauched entertainment.

The book of new Barristers at Law sits on the 'Cupboard', which was made from a hatch-cover given by Sir Francis Drake from his ship *The Golden Hind*. The **Master Treasurer**, on the left, waits to congratulate new Barristers, whose names are read out by the **Master Reader**.

This revel was recreated with great success in 1997.

The Hall was also where the Reader instructed from the Cupboard (the table, or board, in Hall where at meal times empty cups were placed). The timber from which the table was made was the gift of Sir Francis Drake. And, as part of the ceremony of Call to the Utter Bar, which gives students the right to practise as barristers after completing twelve months of pupillage, each one is presented to Master Treasurer by the Master Reader who 'calls them to the Bar'. The newly called barrister signs the book, which waits symbolically on the Cupboard. In bygone times students sat before the Reader on rows

of benches. The most accomplished were placed at the outer, or 'Utter', ends. Hence, when students have passed the examinations they are called by the Treasurer to the Degree of the Utter Bar. Whereas in Elizabeth I's time this heralded a further ten years of study, the ritual is now only the first stage before which a barrister is entitled to practise in the courts. The rights of audience are in the process of being extended to all solicitors and to certain other professions under the Access to Justice Bill brought before Parliament in early 1999. The Barristers' monopoly of rights of audience in the higher courts is now effectively at an end.

Senior Grecian of Christ's Hospital

WHEN CHRIST'S HOSPITAL MOVED from the City of London to Surrey in 1902, the 'Grecians Arch' went too, and the architect incorporated it into the new building. Over a thousand scholars and children made the move, including the two sixth form years, whose members have, since the seventeenth century, been called Grecians. One of them is now appointed from among his or her peers as Senior Grecian.

Nicholas Ridley, the Bishop of London, was himself a scholar of great standing. He preached on charity to the young teenage king, Edward VI, known as 'God's Imp'. His influence over the boy was profound, unsurprisingly for a theologian who was set upon using this impressionable monarch to spur forward the Reformation and who had already assisted Cranmer in the preparation of the articles of faith. As a result of the sermon, Edward gathered the bishop and the Lord Mayor and Aldermen of the City of London together and planned a substantial charity to put these admirable notions into effect. He gave an endowment himself, and the monarch still contributes today.

With the funds gathered, three hospitals were established in 1552, each benefiting from the large legacy of vacant monastic buildings that Henry VIII had left behind. They were Bridewell for the 'Idell vagabondes', St Thomas's Hospital for the 'sore and sicke', which still operates on the Thames's south bank, opposite Parliament, and Christ's Hospital, which was established to educate gifted children and originally occupied the buildings from which the Grey Friars had been evicted, on Newgate Street. The financial endowment was considerable but, within a month of Edward presenting the Charter in 1553, the sickly monarch was dead. England immediately became a hotbed of intrigue, as Bishop Ridley pragmatically proclaimed Lady Jane Grey as the dead king's rightful heir. Her reign lasted for only thirteen days, and she was succeeded by Edward VI's Roman Catholic sister Mary, who burned Ridley and Latimer at the stake in 1555.

This religious turmoil made the first years of Christ's Hospital difficult to say the least. Queen Mary wanted to restore the building to the Grey Friars but fat bribes and an impassioned appeal by Friar John on the Hospital's behalf saved the day: he said that 'he had rather be a Scullion in theire kytchin then Stewarde to the Kinge'. Despite the politics, the new school set about providing education for boys and girls with talent but no financial means to pay for good education. The Christ's Hospital Girls' School is now the oldest in the country, admitting its first 'poor young maiden child' in December 1554. Originally most children were presented by beneficent organizations to be taken in and cared for. Today, similar considerations apply for admission: each is tested for academic ability and financial need.

The doors first opened for 400 children, some of whom were still infants. Most children only stayed in education until they were twelve or thirteen years old, when the demands for clerks in the City drew most away to earn money for their pauper families. Those who remained were destined for Oxford and Cambridge. Because of their obligatory proficiency in Latin and Greek, the ancient name of Grecians was adopted. And their society revered them as intellectuals with their heads in the clouds.

The distinctive uniform, worn by all scholars, earned them another name, the 'Blue Coats'. It dates from foundation and was possibly a development from the habit worn by the dispossessed Grey Friars. The unmissable bright yellow socks were a measure to avoid problems from vermin; apparently it is a colour loathed by rats.

The founder, Edward VI, is surrounded by the statues of four 'Old Blues': Coleridge, Lambe, Middleton and Maine in front of Christ's Hospital's new buildings. The **Senior Grecian** sits with her books while the school band, which plays at a parade before lunch, gathers around. All wear a uniform based on that of a Tudor apprentice.

'God in secreate broughte great things to
passe in the advancement of this foundation.'

FIRST CHRONICLER OF CHRIST'S HOSPITAL

Bailie of the Abbey Court of Holyrood
and the Moderator of the High Constables

A BAILIE ADMINISTERED JUSTICE on behalf of a great land owner. A Constable was responsible for seeing that justice was enforced. The medieval Abbey of Holyrood, with the palace built adjacent to it, was a large estate from early times, and although at its head was a churchman, it still needed to be run efficiently. The Bailie and the Constables are the office holders whose positions have survived from at least the sixteenth century, to the present day.

Scotland underwent considerable change in the reign of David I. As Malcolm III's sixth son he had been sent south for education at the English Court, but he succeeded his brother, Alexander I, in 1124, and brought to Scotland many civilizing ideas. By his death David had introduced the philosophy of the Norman Court, imposed a feudal system on the lowlands and established the foundations for efficient justice. He also strengthened the church with the foundation of six new bishoprics, all occupied by Anglo-Norman bishops committed with him to keeping the Scottish church free from Roman intervention.

On 14 September 1128, David was living at Edinburgh Castle and chose to go hunting in the forest, rather than attend Mass on the feast of the Holy Cross. The legend goes that, while following the chase, he became separated from the rest of the hunt and was set upon by a white stag. Thrown from his horse, he wrestled with the beast but, when grabbing at its antlers, found nothing but a wooden cross in his hand. That night, he dreamt of a voice saying, 'Make a house for Canons devoted to the Cross.'

In response, David founded the Augustinian monastery of the Holy Rood, or Holy Cross. Its foundation charter, which dates from around 1130, grants the Abbot the right to hold a court, where guilt could be tested through a trial of ordeal by fire, water, or duel; it also states that no seizure of goods can be made on Abbey lands.

Like all medieval churches, Holyrood provided sanctuary to men escaping pursuit; having petitioned for protection, unless guilty of premeditated crime, fugitives were safe from their pursuers. Sanctuary prevented summary justice and gave an accused man time to prepare a defence. The first recorded fugitive had killed an English knight during England's occupation of Scotland in the fourteenth century. Holyrood's sanctuary, or girth, became well known as a place of safety and records survive with the names of those seeking protection.

In 1342, David II, the son of Robert the Bruce, raised the status of Holyrood to that of a regality. This made the Abbot a powerful magnate, and the legal burden this must have brought suggests that the office of Bailie may date from this time. No evidence exists to support this date of appointment but it is unlikely that the Abbot sat in judgement himself, given the mass of other matters to attend to. Probably he followed common practice and appointed a Bailie as a legal administrator to run the court and hand out justice. The appointment definitely existed from 1535, when James V by Act of Parliament directed that all sanctuaries be supervised by Bailies.

Four years before this, Holyrood received its first recorded debtor into sanctuary. As it was also increasingly used as a royal residence where parliaments occasionally sat, the noble and great were juxtaposed with the destitute and dangerous. To control the potential conflict of cultures, a police force was needed within the peculiar jurisdiction of the Abbey. In 1504 comes the first recorded constable, who was also in charge of the Queen's Wardrobe, and in 1709 William Robertson was appointed Constable; he had to keep the peace, arrest criminals and run the prison, which frequently was in his own house. Starting with just one Constable, the number has since fluctuated with needs, and now stands at thirty. In 1821 these

When the roof of Holyrood Abbey was removed during its destruction the ancient appointments associated with its monastic privileges survived. The **Bailie of Holyrood** wears the stag's head symbol which alludes to the mythical fight between David I and a white stag. Also his baton is encircled with ducal symbols relating to his boss, the Duke of Hamilton, who is hereditary Keeper of the Palace of Holyroodhouse. The **Moderator of the High Constables** carries similar symbolism on his uniform.

officials assumed the title High Constables, to differentiate them from police bodies forming in the city. Among their most important duties was maintaining order during the election of the sixteen Scottish peers who served in the Parliament at Westminster.

The Duke of Hamilton became hereditary Keeper of the Palace in 1646, and the Bailie is now appointed by the Duke. The Bailie is formally in command of the High Constables. Since 1812 they have elected a Moderator, or presiding officer.

Imprisonment for debt ended sanctuary in Holyrood in 1880. The High Constables are now a ceremonial body responsible for keeping order in and around the Palace when the monarch is in residence.

Bodley's Librarian

WHATEVER THE REPUTATION ENJOYED by Oxford University today, it has been no stranger to hard financial times. The furrows of cultivated learning that it has ploughed for centuries across the field of international consciousness have managed, despite these vicissitudes, to yield a phenomenal harvest. In an institution devoted to teaching, to learning and to research, the source of power is surely its library, storing the very staple of these activities. However, in the middle of the sixteenth century the University of Oxford had no central library. Its collections, built upon those bequeathed by Thomas Cobham, Bishop of Worcester, in 1327, and originally housed in a room over the old convocation house in St Mary's Church, had been dispersed, the final blow coming from the Protestant reformers who in 1550 were said to have given them away or sold them 'to Mechanicks for servile uses'.

Ever since the twelfth Egyptian dynasty assembled the great hieroglyphic archives at Knossos, libraries have been the symbols of civilization. The Medians had theirs at Ecbatana and the Persians at Susa. Religious temples have been reliquaries to the learned texts of their teachers since the beginning of time. And in 1850, while excavating at Nineveh, explorers discovered the carefully arranged and catalogued library of Assurbanipal, the great patron of Assyrian literature.

The first hints of organized learning at Oxford were the theological lectures given by Robert Pullen in 1133, though it is possible that Henry I's palace at Beaumont may have attracted scholars to Oxford's royal court before. The Bishop of Lincoln appointed a Chancellor there in 1214 and the colleges of Balliol, Merton and University appeared in the last decades of the thirteenth century. Cobham's library was therefore established fairly early in the University's life, though funds nearly fell short at the start. Help came from Henry IV and his son Henry V, and the princes Thomas, John and Humfrey Duke of Gloucester, particularly the latter, who donated a tranche of rare manuscripts, many of which were new to England. The library needed a new building and the Divinity School, completed in 1488, was given an upper storey for this purpose. It was this collection that was dispersed during the religious upheavals of the sixteenth century and which left a 'great empty room' for fifty years where Oxford's growing heart had been.

To this shell in 1598 came the Devonian, Thomas Bodley, on his retirement from the court. He was a scholar of Hebrew who had studied at Magdalen College and lectured in Greek at Merton. And, after a lifetime of service to Elizabeth I, he hoped now to serve his university. Twelve years before he had married a wealthy widow, and he was bent on benevolence: his ambition was to restore and restock the library. After just four years the doors were opened to the scholars. They found shelves filled with the books Bodley had collected from all over Europe. And the first Librarian, Thomas James, was waiting to grant them access; his appointment marking the fulfilment of Bodley's ambition. Although he had achieved this within the last year of Elizabeth's reign, it was her successor, James I, who dubbed him a knight.

'I concluded at the last, to set up my Staffe at the Librarie-dore in Oxon; being throwghly perswaded, that in my solitude and surcease from the Commonwealth affayers, I coulde not busie my selfe to better purpose, then by redusing the place (which then in every part laye ruined and wast) to the publique use of Students.'

SIR THOMAS BODLEY

Sir Thomas went on to enter into an agreement which would set his library apart in the world as the first 'deposit library'. He persuaded the Stationers Company to send a copy of every book it licensed to his library. This privilege was forfeited with the collapse of Star Chamber, Henry VII's civil and criminal court, in the Civil War, and after working only fitfully in the half century after the Restoration it was fully restored by the Copyright Act of 1710. Consequently there has since been an unending demand for space. The Quadrangle built in front of the Divinity School between 1613 and 1619 was equipped by Sir Thomas Bodley with a floor

dedicated to book storage, but this was quickly filled, and it has been the responsibility of each succeeding Librarian to arrange further storage as required.

It would be impossible to judge the positive effect of this collection on the increase of wisdom; however, the Librarians charged by Bodley to administer it have enabled some of the greatest minds in the world to pursue their research. And it is easy to conclude that Sir Thomas Bodley's decision to spend the final years of his life turning the remains of a neglected library into the torch of learning that it is today represents more than a testament to his memory: it is a symbol of England's civilization.

The 22nd **Librarian** sits on Sir Thomas Bodley's Chair in Duke Humfrey's Library; while outside the Tower of the Five Orders of Architecture rises above the main gate to the Library. He is supported by four other 'keepers', including the Keeper of the Western Manuscripts and the Keeper of the Printed Books – a resource that perpetually grows.

Deputy Master and Elder Brethren of the Corporation of Trinity House

WHENEVER A VESSEL CARRYING THE SOVEREIGN navigates in home waters, the Elder Brethren of Trinity House can claim the privilege of escorting and preceding the royal craft. This honour is in the monarch's best interest because the Corporation of Trinity House is responsible for directing and maintaining all lighthouses, lightships, buoys and other sea-marks that illuminate the navigator's route through the coastal regions of England, Wales, and the Channel Islands. Arguably, theirs is an escort which could not be bettered.

In 1514, Henry VIII gave the first Charter which established Trinity House as the Master, Wardens and Assistants of the 'Guild or Fraternity of the most glorious and undividable Trinity and of St Clement in the Parish Church of Deptford Strond'. In order to receive a royal Charter, the organization had probably been in existence for some time already but the fraternity's story begins here. Its Brethren could now legitimately demand fees from the ships that plied the Thames and which needed Trinity House Pilots to guide them safely to and from the sea. Deptford was given greater importance when Henry made it a royal dockyard and put the Guild in charge of its operation. This was a quasi-military role and one which they held for nearly a century.

After a relatively inconsequential start to his career the first Master, Sir Thomas Spert, became Comptroller of the Navy and a joint commander of both the *Henry Grace à Dieu* and the *Mary Rose*, both flagships in the English fleet. On a salary of 18 shillings and 4 pence a month (92p) and with the help of eleven other mariners, he used the Guild's revenue to fund the safety and welfare of mariners. The Guild has always upheld the safety and welfare of mariners using the Thames: on a day-to-day basis this is now done by the Port of London Authority.

The Tudors recognized their island's seafaring potential. Whereas, before, shipping had traded or warred with European neighbours; following

Columbus's discovery that the world was round and full of opportunities, England wanted to lay claim to unknown territories and trade with their wealth. Maritime foundations were developed to support a colonial policy which led to the British Empire.

This was all very well but England's treacherous coastline, renowned for dashing the aspirations of many a seafarer upon its hidden rocks, remained one of the greatest obstacles to this plan. Trinity House gained a reputation for its work in the Thames and its approaches, which soon led to greater responsibility.

The Guild, which Henry VIII chartered to make the Thames safely navigable for a fee, was fortunate to avoid Edward VI's attempt to dissolve it along with all other guilds. By changing its name to the Corporation of Trinity House, this threat was avoided and its fortunes were restored by Elizabeth I, who granted the right to place beacons, marks and signs for the sea along the river; and the Coat of Arms, which is still in use today.

In 1604, the membership was divided into two classes: the Elder Brethren, who after 1609 discharged the operational duties, and the remainder of the membership, who were called Younger Brethren. On the fall of Charles I and until Charles II's charter of 1660 Trinity House was dissolved by Parliament. The Restoration brought an increase in power for Trinity House which was further codified in the charter of James II that Samuel Pepys drafted in 1685. Growing income from shipping enabled Trinity House to establish almshouses at Deptford and move its headquarters first to Water Lane, then to Ratcliff, and finally to Tower Hill.

The door opened still further for Trinity House in 1836 when they received power to buy lighthouses from private individuals and to establish a coordinated nationwide navigational system. This was supported by the Board of Trade, through further legislation, with the right to impose charges on shipping that benefited from these aids.

The ensign is lowered in salute and the **Elder Brethren** cheer from their vessel, *Patricia*, after exercising their privilege to escort the Sovereign when afloat on home waters. *Britannia* carries the Queen from Portsmouth on one of its last journeys – passing close to where the *Mary Rose*, the command of Trinity's first Master, sank.

Today, the Elder Brethren direct the Trinity House Vessel *Patricia,* and other tenders and launches, to ply the coast visiting the Trinity House Lighthouse Service, consisting of 72 light-houses, all of which are now automatic, 13 major floating navigational aids, including lightships and lightfloats, 18 beacons and 427 buoys. They are also responsible for dealing with all dangerous wrecks, except HM ships, and this is all paid for by the General Lighthouse Fund: money raised from ships visiting ports in Britain, which is divided between Trinity House, Scotland's Northern Lighthouse Board and the Commissioners of Irish Lights. Since 1685, the Elder Brethren have acted as nautical assessors in the Admiralty Division

of the courts, where their marine experience is placed at the judge's disposal. Finally, they act as trustees of Trinity House's maritime charities. The Younger Brethren, too, have a naval background, which is either civil or military.

Henry VIII might be surprised that the small Guild he established at Deptford has grown to national status and that its Elder Brethren act as trustees of so many maritime charities. Also, there is now no group of distinguished civil and military mariners better qualified to navigate Henry's royal successors into the Solent, through some of the most erratic sand banks which surround the kingdom and where his *Mary Rose* met her end.

Seigneur de Serk

HAROLD WAS HEIR to Edward the Confessor's Anglo-Saxon kingdom when he found himself the virtual prisoner of Duke William of Normandy, who also laid claim to the English throne. To secure his right, Duke William extracted an oath of fealty from Harold, who was anxious to return home. When Edward died Harold took his throne and the Conqueror felt justified in mounting his invasion of 1066. England was conquered and Harold killed. It marked the arrival of Norman feudalism, which perfected the use of sworn allegiance as a means of securing power and maintaining authority. The feudal oath sworn by Harold was probably similar to that sworn to Elizabeth II by the Seigneur of Sark when he knelt before her in 1978 to do fealty for the last feudal constitution in the world: '*Souveraine dame, je demeure votre homme lige à vous porter foi et hommage contre tous.*' ('Sovereign lady, I remain your liegeman to render you faith and homage above all'.)

Sark belongs to the British Sovereign in right of her Duchy of Normandy. The Channel Islands are all that remain of this once powerful dukedom, most of which was lost by King John 'Lackland' to the French, along with most of his Angevin inheritance. It remains a self-governing Crown protectorate, within the Bailiwick of Guernsey but, as a matter of administrative convenience and pragmatic reality, the Duke asks her Government in Britain to keep an avuncular eye on its business, provide defence, and attend to the diplomatic interests of all her Channel Islands, while recognizing that they are not, nor ever have been, part of the United Kingdom.

In the sixteenth century Sark was deserted: raids from the French coast and a short period of occupation had left it derelict. Helier de Carteret, who already held the premier fief of St Ouen in Jersey, petitioned the Crown for Sark as well. However, the Royal Charter of 1565 granted it to him as a separate fief: the first time that Sark's status had been recognized as such. The Charter also formally defined the way this new Seigneur and his island's government would work.

The Seigneur's family have held this tenure since 1852 when, with the Crown's approbation, they accepted it in part payment for a debt. They can hold it in perpetuity, as long as the *rente* is paid to Her Majesty's Receiver General on Guernsey each Michaelmas. But as this only amounts to 'one twentieth part of a knights fee', or £1.79, it is not onerous. The amount has not altered since it was set, being a fraction of what was once the considerable pay of a knight. The Seigneur must also undertake to provide forty armed men, who will stand and defend the island from attack, a task which he achieves by requiring each tenant to supply him with at least one man armed with a 'musket' when required.

The Seigneur is, in his own words, 'like a managing director or the captain of a ship. There's no one else to look after the community: people come to see me if they have any political or civil problems which they can't solve and I am a representative for Sark in the outside world.' His predecessor and Grandmother proved this, as Dame of Sark, in handling German invaders during the Second World War. By sheer force of personality, she insisted that the occupiers respect her feudal rights and issue no edicts until she had seen them first. This way she helped prevent too many ill-conceived restrictions on rural life. The Seigneur explains that 'She'd kick up hell if the German officers were rude or intimidating and say, "Don't you speak to me like that." Also, because they knew nothing about the islanders' lives, she often managed to ameliorate the invaders' absurd instructions.'

The Seigneur must appoint the Officers of the Island, who include the Prévôt, Greffier and Treasurer. A Seneschal was introduced by Order in Council of 1675 to replace the old judge and jurat system and this too is within his appointment. And, in a manner similar to the Queen in Britain, the

The cliffs that surround the island of Sark have provided its main defence. The **Seigneur** maintains his obligation to hold this outpost for the Duke of Normandy by summoning forty armed men from the tenancies. These muskets only have an agricultural purpose today, but as recently as the Second World War they were part of the island's resistance to Nazi Germany's invasion.

Seigneur, with the Seneschal, summons the parliament, which is called the Court of Chief Pleas. Originally this assembly contained just the forty Tenants settled by the first Seigneur. While this was democratically representative of those who owned the land, today the make up has altered to reflect greater diversity: it now includes twelve Deputies, who are elected by other islanders every three years.

Sark appears off the French coast like a fortress. 500-foot cliffs rise to a plateau of just three miles by one and a half, which is covered by a patchwork of small fields. There are no cars and the rural uniqueness is underpinned by endless anomalies – the detritus of an island's story. The Seigneur is the only person allowed to keep an unspayed bitch. This is to control canine proliferation in an area full of

sheep. He also has *droit de colombier*, making him sole keeper of pigeons, for which there is a small dovecote at his residence, La Seigneurie.

The outside world regards Sark with a mixture of fascination, misunderstanding and reforming zeal. To many, it appears an outdated anachronism bogged down with arcane deference. However, the people of Sark do not appear to be in a great hurry for change: they have their own assembly, a peaceful lifestyle and few restrictions. The Seigneur is conscious of his responsibilities and rejects any thought of deference, which has no place in the island's life. For him there is a parliament to call, appointments to make and a *rente* demand arrives each year before Michaelmas. Not forgetting that there is an ancient French oath to teach his son and heir.

4

UNITING A KINGDOM

1603–1750

AGENEALOGICAL COINCIDENCE began the unification of a kingdom from old enemies. Elizabeth, the Virgin Queen, died in 1603, leaving the throne to her cousin James VI. He was waiting at Holyrood for the news of his accession, and when it came he left for England with indecent haste, scattering knighthoods and summary justice as he travelled. He had written: 'God gives not kings the style of Gods in vain, For on his throne his sceptre do they sway,' hinting at the absolutism that would make the Stuart dynasty one of Britain's most controversial. This unification of crowns was the first step to political unity, joining two countries both for economic advantage and to defend their interests against ideological opponents in Catholic Europe.

For Scotland, an absentee monarchy posed constitutional problems. With its single-chambered parliament the country was arguably easier to govern than its southern neighbour, but the growing power of the Kirk since 1560 proved a formidable opponent, particularly when resisting the king's determination to impose his influence through bishops he could control. To maintain his authority from London, James appointed Commissioners to represent him both at Scotland's Parliament and in the Kirk's General Assembly. Despite this, frequent discord erupted between king and Kirk, especially when Charles II, whom the Scots recognized and crowned immediately after Charles I's execution, reneged on promises proffered to recruit support. The Union in 1707 removed any need for parliamentary Commissioners but the relationship with an increasingly independent Kirk was maintained.

England offered negligible resistance to the new dynasty. James I was staunchly Protestant and sought to centralize power in the monarchy, and in due course Charles I's disinclination to consult his Parliament, together with his wife's Catholicism, led to a fundamental breach between the king and Commons. In 1629 Charles instructed his Speaker to adjourn the House but the members prevented this, holding the Speaker in his chair. In 1642 Charles forced his way into the Chamber, determined to arrest five of its Members; this time the Speaker stood up for the rights of the Commons. However, the king was blind to the reality of the political situation and Civil War and Charles's execution followed. Cromwell revived the title of Lord Protector, stopping short of the Crown.

Scotland disagreed with England's regicide, crowned Charles II at Scone and as a result suffered Cromwellian brutality and unification with England in the Commonwealth. Autonomy returned with Charles's Restoration. He gave General Monck, his kingmaker, a dukedom and the Garter while the army was thanked or forgiven, depending on which side they had fought, with the establishment of the Royal Hospital at Chelsea. It provided shelter for elderly men at arms under the military responsibilities of a Governor.

James II succeeded his brother in 1685, having been, as Duke of York, both High Commissioner in Scotland and Lord High Admiral. As king, James fell quickly from favour, facing a rebellion led by Monmouth, and failing to reassure Parliament that he was not seeking to establish a Catholic despotism in the Age of Reason. James's reign was ended by the Glorious Revolution, when Parliament invited his son-in-law, William of Orange, to take over the throne. In the struggle that followed Ireland offered the strategic advantage for James; had the city of Londonderry fallen into his hands in 1688 he might have kept his kingdom. It did not because of the Apprentice Boys who closed the gates and held out against James's French force until help came. Annually, this event and James's subsequent defeat at the Battle of Boyne are marked by opposing religious groups in Northern Ireland.

Many in Scotland did not share the English wish to replace James II, and the imposition of the new regime was carried out brutally, culminating in the massacre of the Macdonalds at Glencoe. To prevent this happening again, Scotland's Parliament refused to accept future decisions on Anne's successor, which she had to accept as she needed Scottish taxes for Marlborough's army on the continent. At this time the queen granted a charter to the Royal Company of Archers, who in time became the monarch's official body guard in Scotland.

The political and economic tensions between the two kingdoms reached a point that only outright union or separation could follow. In 1707, in a state of muddle and intrigue, the Act of Union came into effect, and with the words, 'It is full time to put an end to it', power passed from Edinburgh to Westminster. Scots Law was retained, under the head of Scotland's legal structure, the Lord President of the Court of Session.

The leather-bound **Red Boxes** are symbols of government, conveying business for ministers of the Crown. George I introduced them in 1714, and all Crown matters pass from office to office in similar secure boxes. The Queen's are plum; the Prince of Wales's green; the Scottish Office use blue and Government Whips have black. All bear the reigning Sovereign's cypher of EIIR.

On Anne's death, while the crown of the United Kingdom of Great Britain was passed to George I – a distant Protestant cousin from Hanover – rebellion brewed in Scotland around the figure of James VIII, the Old Pretender. Many rallied to his cause in 1715, and again in 1745 under the leadership of his son Bonnie Prince Charlie. The Jacobite rising was put down at the last battle on British soil at Culloden, after which the Hanoverians broke the ancient clan system for ever.

The new king spoke few words of English and much of his rule was conducted in his name by Privy Councillors, who formed a Cabinet of ministerial advisers. Meanwhile, the king revelled in his new kingdom's wealth, just as James I had. The kingdoms of Scotland and England had become one, and, in 1800, Ireland would join the fold. Westminster was now the seat of Britain's government and the Thames was the capital's thoroughfare: the Worshipful Company of Watermen and Lightermen saw business boom. But as the century progressed the chill wind of revolution began to blow through Europe and the colonies.

Lord High Commissioner to the General Assembly of the Church of Scotland, Pursebearer and Macebearer

AFTER 1603, WHEN JAMES VI left his court in Edinburgh to take possession of his English kingdom as James I, he made greater use of Lord High Commissioners to represent his sovereign authority in Scotland's parliament. This practice concluded with the Act of Union in 1707 which ended the separate Scottish legislature; however, separate Lord High Commissioners were also appointed to represent the king at the assemblies of Scotland's established church, and these appointments continue today. Since 1690, these viceroys have adopted the quasi-royal pomp and splendour that from James VI's departure from Edinburgh until the Act of Union were accorded only to the original Lord High Commissioners. For the week or so of appointment, they drive in cars without number plates, use the standard of the Scots Sovereign and are referred to as 'Your Grace'. With them, since the first was appointed in the sixteenth century, comes a Pursebearer. His symbolic purse once carried money granted by the king to cover the Commissioner's expenses while in office: today he is the principal administrator of the Commissioner's suite and programme. In 1905 Lord High Commissioners, seldom members of the Royal Family, were granted precedence immediately after the Sovereign while in office. Since 1834, they have taken residence in the Palace of Holyroodhouse.

Before leaving her Accession Council, the Queen was required to sign a document promising to 'preserve the settlement of the true Protestant religion as established by laws made in Scotland'. This formality is an historical reminder of the struggle and broken promises between Stuart kings and the Calvinist Covenanters, who reformed the Scottish Kirk in the sixteenth and seventeenth centuries.

John Calvin developed the ideas of Martin Luther that laid the foundations of Protestantism in the sixteenth century. One of his adherents was the outspoken cleric, the forthright Scot John Knox, who helped introduce reform to Scotland's Roman Catholic Church, historically a maverick institution. Protestantism, with its ethos of non-episcopal self-government, posed a very real political threat to the established Church, which had hitherto recognized royal authority in a more hierarchical fashion. Chief among the royal prerogatives was the power to appoint bishops, which monarchs were unwilling to relinquish.

The Confession of Faith (1560) established the Crown's obligation to protect Scotland's reformed church. It also gave rise to a regular assembly to which, in 1578, James VI appointed two commissioners as observers. However, his unwillingness to lose power over the appointment of bishops, a policy enforced variously by his two successors, led to a running conflict between Crown and the growing presbyterian church structure. Charles I did not allow the Assembly to meet and then provoked protest by forcing the 1637 Service Book on unwilling believers, who united against him in the National Covenant. In a final act of betrayal, Charles II, who had relied upon support from Covenanters to regain his throne, demanded the re-imposition of the episcopacy, anathema to the Scottish reformed church whose interests he was committed to protect.

For the Covenanters, the Glorious Revolution could not have come soon enough. With William III and Mary II on the throne, Presbyterian Church Government was formally established in 1690 and a Commissioner has attended its General Assembly's annual deliberations ever since. Occasional interference continued, when Commissioners dissolved the meetings if things disfavoured the Crown but, in 1703, powers were curbed to operate as they do now. The Moderator, appointed by the General Assembly, dissolves the meeting. In so doing he ends the appointment of the Lord High Commissioner, who returns home without the trappings of royal authority that have been his for the duration.

During the General Assembly the **Lord High Commissioner** lives at the Palace of Holyroodhouse and flies the Standard with Scotland's Lion Rampant. She is joined by **Pursebearer,** who once carried the money in a purse with the Scots monarch's heraldry. The symbol of authority is carried by **Macebearer**. The Mace is known either as the Lord President's Mace or the Old Exchequer Mace.

'Their union would be the best security for the prosperity of both, for the internal tranquillity of the island, for the just balance of power among European states, and for the immunities of all Protestant countries.'

MACAULAY ON SCOTLAND'S UNION WITH ENGLAND

Lord Justice-General of Scotland and Lord President of the Court of Session

From his judicial seat in the First Division Courtroom, the **Lord President of the Court of Session**, wearing his robes as **Lord Justice-General**, is symbolically empowered by the Lord President's mace (see page 132) which stands behind him when he sits in court.

DEBATE DOES NOT SLACKEN on the question of the advantages or otherwise of the Act of Union between Scotland and England. On 25 March 1707 there was an outbreak of mob violence in Edinburgh, as Scotland's ancient Parliament considered voting away its sovereignty. The document containing this decision, which was later delivered to Queen Anne, had to be signed in secret by terrified members of the Scottish Parliament in a nearby cellar by the dim light of a single candle, while the crowd cried for their blood on the streets above. In a stroke, the United Kingdom was formed and an impending calamity between two historically quarrelsome neighbours was avoided. However, Scotland maintained her identity in many ways, the most symbolic of which was the continuance of Scots Law.

The Scots Parliament, which voted for union in 1707 albeit awash with bribes from England's Lord Treasurer, had in 1425 called a commission to review the fourteenth century legal codes, Regiam Majestatem, which were revised to incorporate aspects of the French legal system. This understanding was available to the commission because of Scotland's 'auld alliance' with France. Nearly three centuries of Union have integrated many laws within the United Kingdom but the procedure in Scotland remains very different. Since 1532, the supreme court in civil cases for Scotland has been the Court of Session, which was based upon the model of the Parlement de Paris. It has two parts, the Inner House (a court of appeal which is divided into two divisions), and the Outer House, where cases are originally heard. Three judges sit at any one time in the Inner House, whereas only one sits in hearings of the Outer House. Appeals against judgements of the Outer House are heard by a quorum of judges from the Inner House. The Lord President of the Court is the senior judge in the whole of this system.

When the Lord President is sitting with two of his colleagues from the Inner House, the hearing takes place in the First Division Courtroom. The Lord President is also the Lord Justice-General, and in that title he presides over Scotland's criminal court, the High Court of Justiciary. Its decisions are universal and binding: there is no appeal from here to the House of Lords. All judges of the Court of Session are, by definition, qualified to try criminal cases as Senators of the College of Justice and Lords Commissioners of Justiciary. The High Court of Justiciary was completed in 1835, its Victorian architecture speaking vividly of guilt. From its dock many have descended to await execution, including Dr Pritchard, who was convicted of murdering his wife and mother in 1865. His execution that year was the last public execution in Scotland.

Scotland is divided into six sheriffdoms, with a Sheriff Principal presiding over the administration of justice in each of the various sheriffdoms. The office of sheriff can be traced to the Sheriff Depute, a title which dates from the reign of Alexander I, at the beginning of the twelfth century, when Scotland was divided into twenty-five sheriffdoms. The monarch's principal law officer is the Lord Advocate, who is now a political appointment along with his assistant the Solicitor General. The creation of the Scottish Parliament sees a new office of Advocate-General for Scotland, who will advise the Government of the United Kingdom on matters of Scots Law.

Unfortunately there were many bitter pills for Scotland to swallow in the Treaty of Union. One of them was Article XIX, which guaranteed Scots Law only on the caveat that Scotland's courts were subject to changes, 'for the better administration of justice as shall be made by the parliament of Great Britain'. Soon enough, this guarantee was tested by an appeal to the House of Lords by Reverend Greenshields. He was dissatisfied with a decision of the Court of Session in 1711, and his appeal was heard and upheld by the House of Lords. By this precedent, all decisions of the Court are now subject to appeal in London.

Clan Chief, Cameron of Lochiel, 26th Chief of Clan Cameron, Macdhòmnuill Duibh

To the men and women who have this responsibility, no honours or titles can compete with the privilege of leading a great family. Scotland's history, geography and economy gave life to and sustained a large familial system in the wilderness. These groups struggled amid the often inhospitable glens, mountains and lochs of the Highlands. The stories of these families, or clans, and the hardships, battles and dispossession that they have endured, have survived with whisky and oatcakes to form an attractive and marketable ideal that offers identity and acceptance in a world bereft of much belonging.

The wild landscape is a spectacular backdrop for the legends which time and storytellers have passed on. But the truth that hides behind the idyllic Chief and his clan is not always full of glory, particularly after the '45 when they changed from being leaders of a family to owners of land. This meant that their decisions had to be based more upon economic necessity than on historic clan rights. The Highland Clearances at the turn of the nineteenth century will forever remind succeeding generations of how cruel the decisions that had to be taken could be.

In essence, the clan system worked like this: wherever life was sustainable, a group gathered to husband the land and survive from the food they grew. From their number, one would emerge as leader. All would give him their allegiance and in return they would receive his protection. As the unit grew, increased resources were needed and, if they could not be sourced from within, survival compelled a raiding party to go and find what was required. As neighbours seldom had food to spare, these raids became skirmishes. Many died and, human nature being what it is, this bred revenge. On a grand scale this happened to varying degrees all over the Highlands. The great clans were those who wrested adequate lands and attracted the loyalty of sufficient clansmen to survive the vicissitudes.

Tranquillity, like good weather, seldom dominated here and today each Clan jealously guards its identity, formed by the path each trod through this troubled history.

One of the great families is Clan Cameron. Their beginnings are obscure, probably arriving in Lochaber from the islands after leaving the Lord of the Isles' protection to seek their own fortune. Lochiel, as today's Chief is affectionately known, still supervises the lands his family held in the fourteenth century. 'Cam shron' in Gaelic means 'wry-nose' and was an early chief's name. But the fifteenth-century chief, from whom the line has been a constant genealogical descent, was Donald Duibh, or Donald the dark-haired. All his chiefly successors bear the name MacDhomnuill Duibh, or Son of Donald the Swarthy. The Clan and its chiefs gained a reputation which endures today through their heroic support of the Jacobite cause.

It began with the 1688 revolution: Sir Ewen, the 17th Chief, known as the Great Lochiel, led his men to fight. He had secret meetings with the Royalist prisoners when he was under the tutelage of Argyll, and there grew in him a tremendous admiration for the Great Montrose, who had died in 1650, and a firm resolution to follow his example. At about the age of twenty-five he fought the English, who were establishing a fort in Lochaber, now known as Fort William, and in a fierce encounter had to protect his life by using his teeth to tear out an Englishman's throat. Not surprisingly, Lochiel was said to have a 'look so fierce might fright the boldest foe'. And in the steep pass of Killiecrankie, as the Government's army moved through, Cameron's men fell on it and inflicted a heavy defeat, albeit at great cost to the Clan's numbers. Unfortunately, old age prevented the Great Lochiel from fighting in the 1715 Jacobite rising but he told his son John to take the Clan 'out' anyway, an experience that was not so glorious, as there was little fighting to do and the cause was lost.

The 26th **Chief** looks across lands which surround Loch Arkaig, on which Camerons have lived for centuries. Three eagle feathers mark him out as Chief, as does his shoulder-borne 'plaid' of chiefly tartan and his Crimba, or shepherd's crook. His kilt is in Clan Cameron tartan.

As a result, John was exiled leaving his son, Donald, to take the helm as 19th Chief.

Where grandfather had been known as 'Great', grandson was 'The Gentle Lochiel'. When news of Bonnie Prince Charlie's arrival in Scotland reached Lochiel, he was horrified to hear that the prince had landed with only seven men and no French support. Lochiel tried to dissuade the Young Pretender, but royal enthusiasm prevailed and he was persuaded to return to Achnacarry and call out the Clan. He marched them over the hills to Glenfinnan, where the Stuart standard was raised. This started the Clan's defiance, which ended on remote Drummossie Moor, where the Battle of Culloden was fought in 1746. This was the last battle on British soil and it proved a disaster for Lochiel, who was hit by grapeshot. Of the 800 men he led from Lochaber,

more than 300 were killed. Culloden sounded the death knell for the ancient clan system, though the Camerons performed heroically at its end.

Since then ownership rather than stewardship became key and Chiefs as owners were compelled to apply economic criteria to their land management. A collapse in the rural economy towards the end of the eighteenth century led to the Clearances and many Camerons were forced to migrate from Lochaber to America and elsewhere.

Although the idea of the clans has been reinvented, the essential attractiveness of a family system remains. A Standing Council of Chiefs keeps some perspective on this inheritance. To them, the most important part of belonging to the Clan is the chance to savour that most Scottish of associations, kinship.

Captain General of the Queen's Body Guard for Scotland, Royal Company of Archers and Gold Stick for Scotland

FOR MOST OF THE LATE MIDDLE AGES, archery proved the deciding factor in warfare. With the infamous English bowmen as their traditional enemy, Scottish archers faced a formidable foe. Robert the Bruce knew this when he marshalled his small army at Bannockburn, when he could only field the archers from Ettrick Forest to support his line.

The Battle of Flodden, in 1513, tied the association between Scotland's monarchs and their archers still closer. It is said that James IV, who died along with most of the 'flowers of Scottish Chivalry' on that day, fell among a close escort of French archers and that his body, which was denied burial, was dragged from among the bodies of these brave mercenaries.

His great grandson, James VI, respected the skills of archery so much that he passed an edict banning football in favour of bowmanship: a redirection of enthusiasm difficult to achieve then but which might provide a formidable army today. He found two English Body Guards waiting to protect him among the magnificent English Tudor palaces he inherited. He also discovered the appointment of Gold Stick, a military commander specifically tasked with the king's safety.

Despite the absence of the Stuarts, life after the Commonwealth settled in the north. In 1676, records note that the 'Noble and useful Recreation of Archery being for many years much neglected, several Noblemen and Gentlemen did associate themselves in a Company'. They applied for recognition from the Scottish Privy Council, who not only granted this request but also established a prize: there is an annual shooting match each year, and the winner still receives the Queen's Prize from the monarch herself. Also, they were granted the title The King's Company of Archers, which Queen Anne confirmed with a Royal Charter in 1704: ever since, a roll has been kept signed by all Archers.

George IV's visit to Edinburgh in 1822 provided the Royal Company with a chance to bid for the hitherto vacant position of Scotland's official Body Guard. Walter Scott dressed them with a fanciful imagination and the Duke of Montrose swore them in before the Earl of Elgin marched them to the quay at Leith for the king's arrival. Throughout the visit they escorted him in state and three years later the Duke received the first Gold Stick for Scotland from a grateful monarch.

William IV was so glad to inherit his brother's throne that he busied himself signing documents 'William R', eventually having to ease his painful hand in a bowl of warm water. Among these papers was one granting a new Gold Stick, with a Silver Stick and Ivory ones for the Royal Company's council members; also the first set of Colours. And there were more replacement sticks in 1837, when his eighteen-year-old niece inherited the throne.

Royal visits to Scotland were rare and for this reason Victoria's first state visit went badly. Rehearsals had not been made with the Mews and a change of plan meant that, when the young Queen climbed into her carriage, the Royal Company was still shaking itself into formation. Their escort was left in a cloud of dust as the cavalcade sped off and despite a valiant, if undignified, attempt they failed to catch up. Something which was soon put right by the Queen, who ensured that she was properly escorted to claim the keys of Edinburgh Castle the next day.

Each year the Queen's Body Guard parade in uniforms of Border Green at events during the Queen's stay in her Scottish capital. Most ceremonies take place in Edinburgh, against the craggy cliff feature that provides the city's remarkable skyline, called Arthur's Seat. Its name reputedly evolves from Archer's seat because bowmen were supposed to have rested here after practising in the butts valley beneath. This was long before the Royal Company came into existence. Today, the Royal Company retains a competitive involvement with archery.

The archers whom the **Captain General** commands as Gold Stick for Scotland all carry longbows with a 'graith' of three arrows tucked into their belts. Like Clan Chiefs the Captain General wears three eagle feathers and carries a symbolic gold-topped stick. Archers Hall is where the Royal Company meets and practises the skills of toxopholy before shooting matches where each archer tests the accuracy of his bowmanship on targets called 'clouts'. Every summer, the Royal Company of Archers shoot for the Musselburgh Arrow. Started in 1603, this is the oldest continual sporting event in the world.

Speaker

DRAGGED TO HER SEAT, the Speaker must have something to fear. However, this dragging is now a ritual which recalls centuries of tension between powerful kings and an obstinate Commons. Ever since Simon de Montfort forced the profligate Henry III to submit to a representative assembly in his council which, under Edward III, became the constitution's third arm, the House of Commons has grown in stature and influence. It has gradually wrested power from royal hands and deposited it in the arms of universal suffrage. But this path was not an easy one and, at every step, the grim task of conveying the House's decision to furious, autocratic and tax-hungry kings fell to the Speaker.

In 1376, Speaker Peter de la Mare was sent by the Commons with one such message for the king. Bravely, he marched to Edward III and gave him 'what for' about the gross mismanagement of the war with France. He also demanded an end to heavy taxes and the impeachment of certain ministers. To finish this tirade, he insisted that an audited account of royal expenditure be submitted to the Commons forthwith. Within hours, Speaker Peter was staring at the world through a set of iron bars and a new parliament was summoned to reverse these impertinent demands. But the Commons went on pushing at the gates of power, demanding, with ever increasing frankness, the checks and balances that became enshrined in legislation as safeguards for the future. And by the end of Richard II's reign the Commons was powerful enough to join forces with the Lords and impeach the king.

Few Speakers have held their cool better than William Lenthall, whose test came during the Long Parliament. Charles I appointed him because he believed Lenthall to be malleable, and likely to do his bidding. The king ignored convention and burst into the House of Commons on 4 January 1642. A surprised Lenthall vacated the Speaker's chair at the request of the king, who then took his place in it to survey the benches for the five Members he had come to arrest. Failing to discover them in the chamber, the king's chill blue eyes fell upon his Speaker, and he demanded to know the whereabouts of the people he was seeking. The House held its breath but Lenthall replied, 'I have neither eyes to see nor tongue to speak in this place but as this House is pleased to direct me, whose servant I am here.' It put the monarch in his place and both predicted Charles's fate at the House's hands and ensured that no Sovereign would ever set foot inside the chamber again. After the king's execution in 1649, Parliament was supreme and, although he held no real power, Speaker Lenthall found himself the first man in the State.

The Reform Acts of the nineteenth century changed the subtleties of the constitution, chiefly by broadening the franchise. This widening of the democratic base led to a greater sophistication in political life, and to the beginnings of power being vested in the hands of ordinary voters rather than those with huge tranches of land, or other wealth. The apparatus of the state remains to maintain the very checks and balances that the centuries have struggled to gain. These struggles will go on. But, unlike almost all other medieval appointments, which have diminished in the centuries that have passed since their creation, the Speaker's role has grown in relevance with the power of the democracy of which it is so potent an embodiment. In addition, and as a result of Britain's colonial policy, the office of Speaker has been one of the principal constitutional exports of the Westminster system: there are now Speakers around the world, from the United States to New Zealand, either defending the rights of all representatives to enjoy the privileges of free speech or expressing strong moral indignation where this is denied.

The effectiveness of the office derives from popular respect, which has been enhanced in the

'Think of what our Nation stands for,
Books from Boots and country houses,
Free speech, free passes, class distinction,
Democracy and proper drains.'

SIR JOHN BETJEMAN

The **Speaker**'s chair, in black bean, was a gift from Australia. Since Edward III's reign an unfortunate Member of Parliament has been dragged to this seat, to take responsibility for delivering unpopular decisions to furious kings. Not all returned. But then nor did all the kings.

media age by the examples set by fine statesmen selected by fellow legislators to chair their assemblies. Resting on the tenets of fairness and impartiality, the Speaker, who suppresses her own party bias, is chairman of the Commons: responsible for ensuring orderly debate, protecting the privileges of the House and the interests of minorities. Into her appointment have been merged a range of considerable powers and responsibilities, many of

which she shares with the Lord High Chancellor (*see* p. 42). Under the Parliament Acts, which removed many teeth from the Lords, she can decide which Bills do not go to the Lords for consideration and which, when rejected by their lordships, become law anyway.

The role of Speaker achieves such a position of a-political balance that she enjoys a position elevated from the political mainstream yet very much part of it all.

Governor of the Royal Hospital, Chelsea

On Founder's Day Charles II's Romanesque statue is surrounded by oak branches and all In Pensioners and officers wear sprigs of oak. The **Governor** stands in the centre of Wren's riverside 'barracks' on a grassy parade ground. Uniquely, when the elderly soldiers salute here they do so with the hand furthest away from the saluting officer. This maintains the medieval custom of knights raising their helmet visors for identification with the hand that would not hide their face.

CHARLES II'S FUGITIVE WANDERINGS near the town of Tong in Shropshire in 1651, after the Battle of Worcester, might have ended in death had not the Boscobel Oak provided a safe hiding place from Cromwell's army.

When the monarchy was restored, only nine years later, the king remembered the good fortune provided by this tree and recognized the symbolic opportunities in its story. He also remembered the loyalty of Royalist Cavaliers, who had stayed true to his cause during the Civil War, a conflict that pitched brother against brother and divided the land more than at any other time. Cromwell may have won but the puritanism he forced on England and the suppression he inflicted upon both Scotland and Ireland eroded this support.

In this time of spending, reconciliation and gratitude, Charles II searched for grand gestures. Some say that it was Nell Gwynne, the king's lusty cockney mistress, who gave him the idea to build 'an hospitall for maimed soldiers at Chelsey'. However, the famous Hotel des Invalides in Paris had established a standard which he would have known about and been keen to copy.

The king laid the foundation stone for Sir Christopher Wren's design in 1682. Ten years later it was ready to admit 476 pensioners. The In Pensioners, as they are known (to differentiate them from Out Pensioners which include most retired soldiers), are looked after by five Captains of Invalids, who in turn are responsible to the Governor of the Royal Hospital for their welfare.

The Governor finds no holiday from military responsibilities here. He must ensure that the In Pensioners are looked after according to the highest military traditions and he must keep a gentle discipline. However, because many of them served in battles predating his birth, it must be done with sensitivity, not forgetting the thousands of years service which these soldiers represent. Above all, he must ensure that their life is dignified. They are the descendants of Roundhead and Cavalier veterans, who first occupied Wren's vast wings of billets.

The building is one of the great landmarks in London. It was designed to command an uninterrupted view of the Thames and the boggy ground of Battersea beyond. Unfortunately, this idyll has been forced to adapt over the years. Now the proud railings keep traffic at bay, while trees struggle to blot out the ruin of Battersea's power station. However, Wren's interiors have lost none of their drama. In a dining room hung with regimental colours, lined with paintings and surveyed by a vast allegorical portrait of Charles II, the red-coated veterans take meals, provided by the Royal Hospital. In return for being housed, fed and clothed, Pensioners surrender their army pensions. Across the hall, the Chapel is almost always open, with the Governor's stall beside the door: set at a slight angle so he can survey his congregation.

The open quadrangle is colonnaded and lined with memorials to pensioners and governors. Along its length, benches provide rest for the residents and, as the Hospital is open to the public, passers-by converse with old comrades who sit with their thoughts. In the centre of the grassed square, surveying this Valhalla of the living, stands a statue of Charles II by Grinling Gibbons. Rather oddly, the king is dressed as a conquering Roman Emperor, complete with laurels at his temples: symbolism which celebrated the real feeling of relief at his Restoration and which did something to assuage the guilt.

To commemorate the Founder's birthday, the Chelsea Pensioners parade around the statue. It is called Oak Apple Day and each participant wears a clutch of oak leaves, to recall the lucky escape of 1651. But the Governor ensures that the statue keeps the lion's share for camouflage, thus commemorating annually the royal escape at Boscobel Oak.

Gentiluomo of the Cardinal Archbishop of Westminster

WHEN CARDINAL NEWMAN preached in Oscott's new church, near Birmingham, he was celebrating the restoration two years before of a metropolitan See at Westminster and twelve Roman Catholic bishoprics in Protestant England. He called Pope Pius IX's 'restoration of the hierarchy' the 'Second Spring'. It symbolically ended nearly three centuries of Roman Catholic intolerance in England.

Elizabeth I's accession in 1558 heralded the separation of the English Church from communion with the Roman pontiff, and in 1559 the Act of Supremacy committed all office bearers to acknowledge the monarch as supreme 'as well in spiritual things or causes as temporal'. From then on Roman Catholics were seen as potential rebels, many of whom were condemned to burn at the stake. James I attempted to distinguish heresy from treason, on the basis of those who did or did not recognize the Pope's authority to deny the king's legitimacy.

Succeeding Stuart monarchs provided varying degrees of toleration. But James II's reversal of attitude, which included the Declaration of Indulgence, was enough to convince Parliament that he would soon 'subvert and extirpate the Protestant religion'. After the revolution that replaced him with William III and Mary II, legislation was passed to prevent a Roman Catholic, or any person married to one, from sitting on the throne. Neither were they allowed to hold public office or inherit land. The Jacobite rebellions further undermined their reputation for loyalty, though by 1778 attempts to reintegrate them into public life were made, which resulted in riots north of the border. But first Pitt and then Peel pushed for legislative reconciliation as changing circumstances at home and abroad made religious prejudice seem increasingly unnecessary.

The Catholic Relief Act of 1829 overturned most anti-Catholic legislation. However, Pope Pius IX's 'restoration of the hierarchy' was seen by diehards as 'Papal aggression', and the Ecclesiastical Titles Act was passed to stop the new Roman Catholic bishops from taking territorial designations, although this act was never enforced. The first Archbishop of Westminster was Nicholas Wiseman (1850), and he received his Cardinal's hat later that year. With it came a panoply of splendour that was gradually reintroduced into England and included a sword bearer, perhaps a wise precaution in a country still intrinsically sceptical of Rome.

Cardinals derive their name from *cardo*, a hinge. They are princes of the Church and part of the sacred college, which made them powerful men in the politics of Europe. It was because they could not carry arms themselves that the protection of a sword bearer was needed and each Cardinal had a Gentiluomo, a well-born swordsman who stood close at hand ready to fight. The second close attendant was the Cardinal's Secretary, who was a priest. As the Gentiluomo describes, 'I am supposed to defend him from brigands while the Secretary protects him from the Devil. We are the temporal and spiritual protectors of our master.'

The Cardinal Archbishop of Westminster is the last Roman Catholic metropolitan to retain a Gentiluomo, by special permission of the Vatican, conveyed by telegram in January 1968. Cardinal Heenan had appealed against one of the instructions that sought to reduce Cardinals' retinues, ritual and crimson wardrobes, issued by the Curia. While Cardinal Heenan embraced the need to evolve the Church's symbolism, he did not wish to do so at the expense of turning out a loyal servant whose family had served his predecessors since 1932, especially when such niceties of ceremony were very much the art of England and in no way prevented the faithful from understanding the word of God. The last Gentiluomo says, 'I am a sort of Dodo, I am officially extinct.'

The Cardinal Archbishop of Westminster discusses Church business in the Throne Room of Archbishop's House beside Westminster Cathedral. The **Gentiluomo** keeps watch. He wears Court dress with full lace cuffs and *jabot* tied around his neck. A sort of body guard who can bear arms when his religious master may not.

'Canterbury has gone
its way, and York is gone,
and Durham is gone
and Winchester is gone...
Westminster and
Nottingham, Beverley,
Hexham, Northampton
and Shrewsbury, if the
world lasts, shall be names
as musical to the ear,
as stirring to the heart,
as the glories we have lost.'

CARDINAL NEWMAN
SECOND SPRING SERMON, 1852

Governor of the Apprentice Boys, with the Secretary and a Committee Member of the Browning Parent Club

James II faced hostility in the Protestant parliaments of London and Edinburgh during 1686, so he plotted to turn Ireland into a Roman Catholic state. He armed it to the teeth, ready to provide him and his fellow Catholics with a base from which to re-conquer Britain, should the need arise. This pragmatic plan was carried out by his henchman, Richard Talbot, then James's Lord Deputy Tyrconnel, and in two years the job was done. Just in time, because James had crossed the rubicon and Parliament rebelled, inviting his daughter and nephew to take over a more democratic Crown. Making his tactical, if untidy, withdrawal, James journeyed to Ireland to set his carefully laid plan in motion. He sought to restore his three kingdoms of Scotland, Ireland and England as truly Catholic states, subject to his divine right, and satellite to the pan-European Catholicism of Louis XIV of France. One strategic obstacle stood in his way.

Lord Antrim arrived at the Foyle and began to ferry his troops across the river. He led a Catholic army intent upon taking the walled city of Londonderry. The city was built at the start of the century on an ancient druidic site, using money raised by the guilds of London. James I granted a charter recognizing this connection and giving the city a name which remains contentious. Watching Antrim's river crossing from the walls of the city were thousands of people gathered for safety from the changes wrought by James's plan. The Mayor, who was Catholic, planned to admit the army. Thirteen Apprentice Boys had another idea. On 18 December 1688, led by Henry Campsie, they rushed the guardroom of Ferry Quay Gate, took keys and weapons and closed the gate. It symbolically began a resistance which lasted until Captain Michael Browning came to the rescue, smashing King James's boom across the Foyle, which, although he lost his life, raised the siege on 12 August 1689.

Quite apart from the geo-political effects of their successful resistance to King James's planned counter-attack against the vastly more democratic government of William of Orange, the people of Derry had survived a fearful ordeal. One of the heroic joint Governors, Colonel John Mitchelburne, with Benjamin Darcus, flew the 'Maiden Flag' of crimson from the steeple of St Columb's Cathedral: it was said to be stained by the blood of the fallen. Later, military parades were held to mark the closing of the gates and the beginning of the siege. Finally, in 1714, Darcus formed a club guard to celebrate civil and religious liberty, 'with thanksgiving to almighty God for guidance and deliverance during the memorable events of 1688–9'.

The Apprentice Boys of Derry Club was the first of eight which were brought together in 1861 to form the Associated Clubs of the Apprentice Boys of Derry, under a single Governor. The others celebrate the figures who took a lead in resisting the siege, among them the two governors, Mitchelburne and Walker; the latter was killed soon afterwards at the Battle of the Boyne, which finally defeated James. Baker and Murray Clubs recall the part played by an Englishman and a Scot in the siege; Campsie Club immortalizes the Apprentice who shut the gates; No Surrender Club echoes the cry shouted at James from the battlements and the Browning Club enshrines the memory of Captain Browning, who died breaching the boom on his ship the *Mountjoy*. Each is led by a President, with a Secretary and Committee. The rules state that membership can only be granted within the city walls and it implies intent to attend the annual parades.

These parades have been held for over three centuries as expressions of a community's sense of liberty. However, as a celebration of history, they have become a symbolic focus for disagreement in the wider community and its growing conflict. The issues are as complex as the story of Ireland itself, increasingly muddled since the invading Celts were themselves invaded by Strongbow. The Governor seeks to unite Derry, but unfortunately recent events beat a louder drum of menace.

Three centuries have not erased memories in the Apprentice Boys Memorial Hall, as the faces of past governors offer witness. The banner of the Browning Parent Club, carried by its **Secretary**, commemorates the breaking the boom by Captain Browning which enabled relief to reach Londonderry. Today's **Governor** came from the Browning Parent Club and treads a difficult path in Derry.

Member of the Most Honourable the Privy Council

The National Liberal Club has provided many Prime Ministers and statesmen to advise the Crown. Their contributions have been nurtured within the **Privy Council**. All Cabinet ministers must be Privy Councillors to give their powers legal sanction. Once a select band of the closest and wisest, today it numbers 400. Court dress is seldom worn, though it was once the ceremonial dress of imperial potentates who took status from Privy Council membership in exercising power throughout the world.

WHEN LOOKING FOR THE REAL POWER in Britain, a good place to start is the Privy Council: from it, today's Cabinet takes its legal powers. The Anglo-Saxon's strange-sounding Witenagemot, or Witen, preceded the Norman's *commune concilium* from which institutions the status of today's Privy Council takes its shape. It has held many other names during this evolution, like the *curia regis* or *concilium regis*, but the name Privy Council emerged in the thirteenth century because they met in private.

Out of the influence which these royal councils developed, kings were advised, justice was done, royal will was exercised and the monarch's executive power was often kept in check. Thereby, councils guided the royal prerogative. This relationship between monarch and council changed with each incumbent. Like chess, the council was ready to exert greater influence over a weak king, just as a capable monarch could swing the pendulum in the other direction. Early Norman councils consisted of the Chancellor, Chief Justiciary, Treasurer, Steward, Constable, Marshal, the Archbishops of Canterbury and York, and those the king selected: many of these titles still exist, though most only play their part at the Accession Councils and coronations of new monarchs.

The Plantagenet *curia regis* grew fairly large and often misused its power to draft legislation out of petitions sent by the relatively impotent House of Commons. The Tudors believed a small council was vital to good government and it suited Henry VIII to limit any but the most essential Councillors. The Civil War led to the council's temporary disbandment, and Restoration saw its return; but not immediately. Charles II's experiment with thirty new Privy Councillors was not a success: he felt there were too many to keep business confidential and returned to his small inner clique, which helped set another precedent for what was to come. While the Glorious Revolution saw constitutional supremacy move from the Crown to Parliament, the Privy Council provided a suitable body, with its powers vested in precedent, to continue in helping monarchs exercise their lingering powers and to fulfil residual judicial and other responsibilities.

It was the arrival of George I, who spoke no English, which passed greater executive power to the Privy Council. A gathering similar to Charles II's cabal, known as the Cabinet, incorporated the king's ministers.

Constitutional history charts progress from the Hanoverian Cabinet to the parliamentary executive of today. The emergence of an increasingly representative democracy and the decline of royal influence has seen the Privy Council's importance wane and its membership evolve into one of the many national honours.

An oath of confidentiality is critical to membership and provides a means for cross-party briefing by the executive, outside parliament but within the constitution. For this reason, all senior members of the larger parties in the House of Commons are sworn into the Privy Council, using oaths similar to those imposed by Edward I, 'swearing to give good advice, to protect the king's interests, to do justice honestly, (and) to take no gifts'.

The powers which, through membership of the Privy Council, are now enjoyed by the Cabinet in its exercise of the Crown's executive power are potentially limitless. For this reason, Parliament must provide an effective check at all times.

Once a month, or whenever necessary, the Queen meets in Council. On these occasions four Privy Counsellors from the Government witness the Queen give formal approval to Orders in Council: instruments by which much governance is achieved through Royal Prerogative.

In addition, Privy Councilors are available to provide advice on constitutional matters at any time to the Queen and her Ministers.

Admiralty Judge of the Cinque Ports

O N A CLEAR DAY FRANCE is easily visible from the white cliffs above Dover's busy port. Across the often choppy water, the busiest sea passage in the world, the low outline of the continent spills forward like ripe Brie. It is a sight which treats holidaymakers and titillates duty free raiders as they drive down to join the endless procession of ferries to Calais and beyond. However, as the massive fortress of Dover Castle can testify, this proximity was anything but reassuring to England's security, and even in 1945 the sea defences and a tireless Royal Navy were all that stood between Hitler and the Bank of England. The Normans saw and exploited this vulnerability successfully in 1066. They knew that, granted a fresh northerly wind and an unopposed landing, an invader could soon boast a new throne.

'A people which takes no pride in the noble achievements of remote ancestors will never achieve anything worthy to be remembered with pride by remote descendants.'

LORD MACAULAY

Few of the titles, privileges and powers gathered by the Cinque Ports over the centuries have survived. One that has is the **Admiralty Judge** who still administers residual laws over maritime matters in the busy Channel. Dover was once a fortress against the French: it is now a principal link with the Continent. From its white cliffs the judge has a commanding view and holds the symbolic silver oar, with the Lord Warden's cypher.

Dover's castle sits on an Iron Age fort, it has Roman and Saxon features and boasts Henry II's mighty Keep at its centre: all evidence of the strategic importance of this site and the investment that was made in it over the centuries. But this castle was just one part in an extraordinary amalgam of ports and towns, known as the Cinque Ports, which were so successful at preventing the island's invasion and generating revenue for the national exchequer that they gained their own parliament, a wealth of privileges and the right to carry a canopy over all kings at their coronation.

The Cinque Ports were a creation of military logic. To achieve a strategic all-round defence at Dover, there had to be a coordinated policy under a single command. The five ports stretched from Hastings, through Romney, Hythe and Dover to Sandwich, and are described in an extant Charter of Edward I as existing as a federation in the reign of Edward the Confessor. This document also suggests that William the Conqueror, satisfied with his own invasion, saw the need to prevent others following in his footsteps by buttressing the defences of the region. Overall command to coordinate the federation fell to the Lord Warden of the Cinque Ports.

As ever in these situations, a good bargain was struck between Sovereign and vital subordinates. The Cinque Ports were to provide England's navy, a massive commitment which continued until Henry VII's reign, and they had to maintain the security of the kingdom from sea invasion. In return, a degree of independence and considerable judicial privileges were extended, including exemption from tax and tallage. There was a list of odd-sounding legal powers, like *soc* and *sac*, tol and team, flotsam and jetsam, waives and strays, blodwit and fledwit, infangentheof and outfangentheof. Lastly came the right to hold a portmote, or parliament, to which came representative mayors from the five ports and the two 'ancient towns' of Winchelsea and Rye.

While the Lord Warden was a virtual palatine governor, he was also Admiral of the Ports, which gave him full maritime jurisdiction as well. This once considerable clout is now virtually non-existent but the area over which this maritime viceroyalty held sway was only confirmed in a special parliament held by the seaside in Dover, in the seventeenth century: it extends from Shore Beacon in Essex to Redcliffe in Sussex. Cases are heard in the Cinque Ports' Court of Admiralty, which is extremely ancient and perhaps exceeds in age England's High Court of Admiralty, which takes legitimacy from the office of Lord High Admiral, a more recent appointment. The Court originally sat at Sandwich or in the chapel at Dover Castle, though it now finds space in a modern courtroom. Its Marshal carried a silver oar as symbol, an office which has now merged with the Judge.

Whilst the Cinque Ports are still strategically vital to the island, defence policy has long since ceased to rely upon the navy they funded. With the conclusion of the medieval bargain went exemption from taxation and most of the unique jurisdiction. But the Lord Warden remains, a title given to great figures like the 'Iron' Duke of Wellington, Sir Winston Churchill and recently Queen Elizabeth the Queen Mother. The last Baron of the Cinque Ports, appointed from the mayors and councillors for the 1953 coronation, recently died. He took his place and baronial title at the coronation, along with seventeen other mayors and councillors, according to ancient privilege described at Richard I's crowning and enshrined in Charter by Charles II, though since George IV there has been no need for a canopy.

As each ferry comes and goes from the port which remains England's strategically vulnerable under-belly (more from drugs than invasion), the maritime laws of the ancient Cinque Ports remain to be observed and, on behalf of the Lord Warden, the Admiralty Judge will find time from his other work to hear the case should something go wrong.

Sisters of the Hospital of the Most Holy and Undivided Trinity

THE SEVENTEENTH CENTURY was not a woman's world. The Dissolution may have made Henry VIII a wealthy man but its consequences hit the economy hard. There may have been little sympathy for the dispossessed members of religious orders, but the work of these institutions caring for elderly women was sorely missed. Few charities existed to take their place. The sixteenth century closed on ruins where great abbeys had stood, while the destitute elderly wandered in search of food and shelter. Finally, if Hell on earth had not already been established, harsh reinforcement laws to punish the 'idle' imposed a ten-shilling fine upon anyone who did not apprehend a beggar. Into this welfare vacuum stepped patrons of varying wealth, responding to the moral expectation that successful men should perform their Christian obligations as part of the unwritten social contract.

One such beneficiary was Henry Howard, the Earl of Northampton, whose family had gathered wealth through ownership and development of land in Norfolk, particularly at Kings Lynn where a thriving port then attracted good revenue. He was born when Henry VIII's Vicar General was preparing for the Dissolution, and he lived through the Reformation's worst; his brother Thomas, 4th Duke of Norfolk, lost his head after plotting against Elizabeth I. Like most Howards, he held proudly to the Roman Catholic creed and died in the faith. Along with other charitable benefices at Clun and Greenwich, he founded the Hospital of the Most Holy and Undivided Trinity in 1616. He was Lord Privy Seal for James I, as well as Constable of Dover Castle and Warden of the Cinque Ports.

The earl instructed that there were to be twelve ladies cared for in Castle Rising's new hospital, gathered from the local villages, who had to meet strict criteria for admittance. Howard was determined that his money should support the most reputable of the less fortunate, although ironically, in those difficult times many of the worst-off might resort to all manner of morally questionable practices to survive. But morality has always been England's most complex hang-up and there is nothing of Christ's forgiving embrace of Mary Magdalene in the list of qualifications drawn up by the pious patron. 'They must be of honest life and conversation, religious, grave and discreet, able to read, if such a one be had, a single woman, her place to be void on marriage, to be fifty-six years of age at least, no common beggar, harlot, scold, drunkard, haunter of taverns, inns and alehouses.'

Having satisfied this range of requirements and gained admittance, the Sisters were to pray for the lives and souls of Howard's 'noble' family. There is a similarity here to the practice abolished by the Reformation, whereby wealthy people built chantry chapels and funded priests to say masses eternally for their soul: a sort of spiritual life insurance. In return, the Hospital provided a welcome refuge for those admitted to its secure environment at a time of religious upheaval.

Qualifications for membership and the rules to be observed have changed considerably since the seventeenth century in line with evolving compassion and growing respect; in 1959 the building was completely renovated and reorganized to the Charity Commission's approval.

The high-crowned hats look bizarre until they are compared with portraits contemporary with the Earl's foundation, when they were *de rigueur* and worn over a white coif-like headpiece. Originally the gowns were made from dark blue and brown fustian; so it is not surprising that, in the last century, the ladies petitioned for a make-over in red. Full dress is now worn only for celebrations, such as the swearing in of a new Sister, when the event is supervised by the Warden and a member of the Howard family, because Henry Howard's Hospital remains a family concern.

A new **Sister** takes the oath watched by her sorority in the Hospital's Hall. They all wear conical hats and scarlet capes with the embroidered Northampton family crest; except the Warden, who has a three-tiered cape. The Secretary records the event, which is witnessed by a member of the Howard family, whose ancestor was the benefactor.

'My Uncle… hath erected an Hospitall at Rysinge for the reliefe
of certein poore Women… to be likewise governed by a Woman,
Who in respect of her sexe and condicon ys neither fitt nor able
alone wth owte helpe… to pforme the dueties.'

EARL OF ARUNDEL, 7 JULY 1623

Woodmen of the Ancient Forest of Arden

The longbow's range made it a powerful tactical weapon in the middle ages and good bowmanship was a highly prized skill. Archers were encouraged to practise by law, and churchyards throughout England still nurture yew trees which provided raw material for the weapons. A position overlooking the battlefield added both height and the force of gravity to the longbow's effectiveness. **Woodmen of Arden** maintain the art.

AT THE CENTRE of what was once a wooded wilderness in the Midlands, which encompassed the forests of Sherwood, Hatfield, Cannock Chase, Charnwood and Wye, is the ancient forest of Arden. It was one of the wild areas that provided a buffer between the Saxon settlements that formed the kingdom of Mercia. At its heart is the town of Meriden, where, on 15 November 1785, Heneage Finch, the 4th Earl of Aylesford, and five enthusiastic friends gathered at the Bulls Head. In one of England's most traditional settings, they laid the foundations for the Woodmen of Arden. It would become the country's most exclusive society of toxophilites, one which maintained and celebrated the longbow's story.

From the Saxons to the Tudors, the longbow's military effectiveness earned it a significant place in England's history. It was developed from a cumbersome rough weapon into a mass-produced and inexpensive military attribute. In particular, Edward I recognized the weapon's possibilities and ensured that, by his grandson's reign, the improved properties of tensile strength and performance combined to provide English kings with an armament that was almost to win the crown of France in the Hundred Years War. Among the victories it gave to Edward III, Edward the Black Prince and Henry V were the battlefields of Crécy, Poitiers and Agincourt. The records of the Woodmen

of Arden describe how longbowmen were deployed to strategic effect: 'On word of command they shot rhythmic volleys of arrows into the ranks of their charging opponents, shifting their targets successively until every living one of them was killed, or maimed or routed.' Edward III, like each successive monarch until Edward VI, made practising this military skill mandatory after Sunday mass.

When saltpetre and guns marched the efficiency of war a further macabre step along the path of barbarity, archery became more of a noble pastime than a vital military skill. The Tudors developed the sport, with Henry VIII proving a formidable shot. London became a venue for matches, led by the Society of St George. By the middle of the next century small archery societies proliferated as far as Warwickshire.

The 4th Earl of Aylesford had been loosing off arrows at his Meriden estate for years before founding the Woodmen. Since then, succeeding earls have presided, first by the traditional toxophilite title of Captain of the Grand Target, which was changed in 1786 to Warden of the Forest. And, before the year was out, the prefix 'perpetual' had been added. The Lieutenant of the Grand Target was also renamed by the Woodmen as Senior Verdurer. Membership has always been limited to 80, though in 1835 it was increased by one to include Sir Robert Peel. It is a fairly closed shop, with preference given to applicants related to or descended from former members. Each new member is given a number and must record his cresting, a unique mark, on the shaftment of all of his arrows and on the Aschams, or bow lockers. There is both a Captain and Lieutenant of Numbers, offering achievable status below Aylesford's protected salt. The uniform was established in 1786, with the hat following a hundred years later. Forest ground was bought and, according to the records for 1788, 'after a long interval, a Wardmote was first held by the Woodmen'.

'When the Saxons came first into this realm in King Vortiger's days, when they had been here a while, and at last began to fall out... they troubled and subdued the Britons... with their bow and shaft, which weapon being strange... was wonderful terrible unto them.'

ROGER ASCHAM, TOXOPHILUS, 1544

Queen's Bargemaster, Bargemaster of the Company of Watermen and Lightermen and winners of Doggett's Coat and Badge

THE WATER MUSIC, which was performed on the River Thames at one of the most famous musical events in history, is still one of the best-loved works by George Frideric Handel. It was performed for George I while he entertained his guests, among whom was his mistress, Madame Kilmanseck, whose cuckolded husband was left holding a bill of £150 for the musicians alone. George had been on the throne just three years, spoke very little English, and was frankly not very interested in Britain; but he loved his music and his vivacious if ageing mistress, nicknamed 'Elephant and Castle', loved a party.

George I and his great musical event brought together the threads which connect the Royal Watermen, the Company of Watermen and Lightermen and the winners of the annual Doggett's Coat and Badge race. The Royal Watermen, who are led by the Queen's Bargemaster, attended the king at his concert and provided all monarchs with transport when the river was London's best thoroughfare. With Hampton Court, Greenwich and Westminster spaced along the Thames's winding banks, the royal barges frequently ferried the king, his family and business from one to the other. When John signed Magna Carta in 1215, his barge was on hand at Runnymede, and Edward II was supposedly attacked while navigating the River Fleet; on both occasions watermen must have been on hand. The royal appointments begin in the fourteenth century. They facilitated transport until the middle of the nineteenth century, when roads improved and carriages took over. The Royal Watermen now double up as spare royal coachmen, though they occasionally adorn modern craft when the Queen motors along the river.

The Watermen and Lightermen came together in 1700, shortly before the king's party, and made their barge available for Handel's musicians. Since 1514, the Worshipful Company of Watermen provided a reliable taxi service to the City of London's merchants. They regulated the waterway and the fares that Watermen could charge. From 1555, they also ran apprenticeships for boys seeking the skills needed for river life. The Lightermen, who moved cargo around the ships, shared skills with the Watermen. United they worked the merchants' grand city barges, each of which had a bargemaster.

Until 1760 London Bridge was the only crossing point other than by boats crewed from the Company of Watermen, while Lightermen serviced the cargoes of vessels in the port. New bridges were fought off by these companies to preserve their monopoly, but they lost. Before new bridges were built, Watermen, many wearing their scarlet **Doggett's Coat and Badge** (a silver disc on the arm), waited for hire on the river bank. They wait with the **Bargemaster of the Company of Watermen and Lightermen**.

Kings used barges to travel quickly from Westminster to Hampton Court. Their Bargemasters were recruited from the best Watermen in London. Today there are few journeys by boat but the Crown Jewels that once travelled to Westminster by river arrive in carriages staffed by the **Queen's Bargemaster** and the Royal Watermen.

To celebrate the first anniversary of George I's accession, on 1 August 1715, Thomas Doggett, an Irish actor, Whig and comedian, set a wager: something which was then commonplace among the plentiful Watermen who plied their fares across and along the Thames. He offered a red livery and silver badge each year, to be competed for by six young Watermen. The prize included money and was keenly contested. Having set the wager every year until his death in 1721, he willed funds for it to continue: a responsibility which the Fishmongers' Company have maintained. Every August opens with this unique competition to mark the anniversary of the music-loving Hanoverian's arrival. Most Watermen compete and the liveried coats and badges are prized.

'The King expressed a wish to Baron von Kilmanseck to have a concert on the river… By the side of the Royal Barge was that of the musicians… This concert was composed expressly for the occasion by the composer Handel.'

FOREIGN ENVOY AT COURT OF GEORGE I, 19 JULY 1717

5

GROWING AN EMPIRE

1750–1901

AFTER THE KINGDOMS WERE UNITED there was a gradual rationalization of national offices of state, particularly in Scotland. Those with specific historical provenance survived, especially if they belonged with a single family, or if they embodied moments in history, as did the Royal Banner Bearer of Scotland, whose rights carried the hallmark of the wars of independence. Meanwhile, many English appointments were elevated to encompass the whole of the newly named United Kingdom of Great Britain and Northern Ireland: the Earl Marshal took sole responsibility for state ceremonial that encompassed not only his original jurisdiction but the new kingdoms as well.

Britain had united for mutual advantage: to protect itself more effectively abroad, both politically and from the continuing threat of Roman Catholicism, and also to increase its wealth through trade and colonization. Britain sought to establish favourable trading links with distant corners of the world in an ongoing quest for raw materials and markets. Conflicts of interest in these new places often led to the use of arms, either in defence or aggression, and so markets and plantations usually became colonies. More by accident than design, a colonial structure developed that encircled the globe. It was expensive to maintain these new colonies and, although they offered economic opportunity, they were also resented. The Colonial Reform Movement in the 1830s changed this; people believed that there was a moral imperative to invest in the colonies as well as exploiting them, and colonial service became popular, desirable and a moral duty. Public schools and the universities prepared young administrators to serve abroad.

The British government sent blueprints of administration and governors to lead these colonial structures. Communication between the colonies and Westminster was maintained through the Corps of King's Messengers. Britain established colonial structures first in America, but the people of those colonies decided that they would not accept the burden of taxation without representation, and so in 1776 they declared themselves independent. India had been a trading centre for the East India Company since Tudor times, when Elizabeth I granted it a royal charter. India became the focus of imperial effort, and trading administrators became executive Governors; Clive of India advanced British interests and, after the

Indian Mutiny of 1858, Governor Generals became Viceroys. Disraeli formalized the empire's existence by the Royal Titles Act of 1876, by which Queen Victoria became Empress of India. Orders of chivalry were created: the Order of the Star of India was designed to be the sub-continent's Garter. The empire became the largest that the world has ever seen. The rock of Gibraltar, guarding the mouth of the Mediterranean, was vital throughout the period of imperial growth and contraction.

The defeat of the Jacobites in 1746 secured Hanoverian rule. For the first time the United Kingdom could confidently celebrate itself. As a result, the pageantry today recognized as British heritage was largely invented in the eighteenth century. Parliament, the judiciary, the armed services and other institutions took existing workaday practices and gradually adapted them to embody images of stability and longevity. This new ceremonial echoed historical patterns, revived history and instilled into itself ritual that quickly became tradition. The requirements of a growing Empire, hungry for symbolic expressions of established status, reinforced this trend. But it was not until the aftermath of the disastrous funeral of the Empress herself, at which so much went wrong, that British ceremonial was formalized from celebration to artform. Edward VII's coronation was the first to be perfectly choreographed.

Celtic customs also revived during this period. As the nineteenth century wore on people became increasingly interested in local and indigenous customs. In Wales and Cornwall, the Celtic outposts, druidism was revived, no longer as a cult religion but as a means to celebrate cultural inheritance.

The French Revolution in 1789 changed Europe. Its secular and republican ideology and its territorial ambitions set it against most of the continent and, when Napoleon Bonapart's military successes earned him power, his army and navy challenged Britain. Nelson's victory at Trafalgar earned the Royal Navy unchallenged supremacy and influence, enjoyed by the Lords Commissioners of the Admiralty in Whitehall, while Wellington's victory at Waterloo earned him a reputation to match the Field Marshal's baton that the Prince Regent had recently presented to him.

That prince finally succeeded as George IV in 1820. In the euphoria that still smothered Britain after Napoleon's defeat,

Parliament indulged the profligate king's desire for a splendid coronation: not to please him but to celebrate the nation. This was perhaps the most magnificent coronation ever, entwined with plenty of revived or invented tradition, including the appointment of an old friend as Herbstrewer. Later, to heal wounds from Culloden, he visited Scotland to celebrate its highland revival. Quashed pleasures, such as bagpipes and wearing tartan, were resurrected.

Feudal responsibilities that had lingered as a way of administrating the land died away. Cities mushroomed as industry grew to meet the demands of the burgeoning empire, and with these new urban centres came challenges to law and order. Sir Robert Peel's police force was established from the roots of existing constabularies, such as the force responsible for order among the undergraduates at Oxford. Street-walking police 'constables' today carry the same title that was once among the most senior appointments in the Byzantine court. While urbanization continued apace, the countryside remained unassailable and its rural communities followed stag and foxhounds according to strict sporting rules. The Great Reform Bill in 1832, which enlarged the franchise and altered Parliament's make-up, was a further step towards democracy. The Lords remained as the connection between land and power and this was still very significant.

The existence of the British Empire allowed the Church of England's missionaries access across the world, with parts of New Zealand being specifically colonised by the Church itself. Funding for the splendour of Anglicanism was scrutinized by Parliament but administered by Commissioners, while the tidal wave of Victorian morality carried the bishops and their doctrines to ever greater authority, despite the diminution of ecclesiastical courts like the Arches in Cheapside. Since Wesley's conversion, Methodism had grown to challenge orthodoxy and its adherents reflected the shift towards personal empowerment that reform spelled out.

Victoria's Diamond Jubilee in 1897 was the ceremonial apogee of the western empires. Her carriage stood by the steps of St Paul's surrounded by an establishment preening itself in its splendour. From Great Officers, Indian Princes, Ministers and Governors to flag-waving children, this was confidence. It was vulnerable.

Hereditary Banner Bearer for Scotland and Hereditary Bearer of the National Flag of Scotland

THERE IS A FRIENDLY TENSION between two families in Scotland, the Scrymgeours and the Maitlands, who conflicted with each other during the vicissitudes of history. Both claimed the right to carry the Royal Banner of Scotland, and in each case there was a strong legal argument. Only in the last century was a solution reached: one which provided a role for them both and which brought into Scotland's pageantry the two flags that have represented the nation's identity since before the fourteenth century Wars of Independence.

The Scrymgeours, or skirmishers, gained their name when their forebear, Carron, led the army of the Scotland's kings across the river Spey to victory during the twelfth century. In gratitude the king asked Carron to carry his standard.

Little more evidence survives until William Wallace's Charter of 1298, which confirms that Alexander 'called Skirmischur' carried the Royal Banner. He supported Bruce's bid for the crown in 1306 and paid the price with his life. A further charter after Bannockburn, in 1317, confirmed the privileges on his son, along with the Constabulary of the Castle at Dundee. Having served as Royal Bannermen of Scotland through the thirteenth- and fourteenth-century wars of independence, the family turned out for subsequent battles against the English, including the tragic Battle of Flodden in 1513, when John Scrymgeour fell with banner in hand beside his king. The banner was again aloft for Charles II at the Battle of Worcester in 1650 and, after the Restoration, Scrymgeour received the earldom of Dundee. But this glory was shortlived because, on the Earl's death in 1668, his estate's inheritance was not adequately clear. The all-powerful Duke of Lauderdale, head of the Maitland family and Secretary of State for Scotland, therefore seized the Scrymgeour estates and the story goes that he sent a troop of dragoons to Dudhope Castle in order to carry off all the family's deeds of ownership. With the

written evidence of ownership lost, it was no longer possible for the Scrymgeour claimants to regain their lands. In 1790 the Royal Banner and Saltire were added to the Lauderdale arms, confirming their rightful role as the Royal Bannermen.

However, in 1910 at the Court of Claims the Scrymgeours once again asserted their right to carry the Royal Banner for George V's coronation. After hearing the evidence, the House of Lords strictured the Lauderdales for treachery in 1668 and, while the lands were no longer available for return, the Lauderdale successors were asked to pay all the costs of the hearing. Consequently, in 1911 George V was the first monarch since Charles II to have a Scrymgeour as his Royal Bannerman.

After Elizabeth II's coronation in 1953, the year when the earldom of Dundee was restored to the Scrymgeour family, a meeting was held between the Earls of Dundee and Lauderdale, the heads of the feuding families. It was at their request and in his official role as the Lord Lyon King of Arms that Sir Thomas Innes of Learney officiated. A solution to ancient rivalries was agreed in good grace and was subsequently confirmed by the Queen. The intention of the agreement was to enable both of the country's flags to be included in the State's great ceremonies and to recognize that both families held legitimate long-standing claims of precedent. Thus, from 1954 onwards, the Scrymgeours of Dundee have been Hereditary Banner Bearers for Scotland and carry the Royal Banner, showing the lion rampant within a double treasure (two frames), with *fleur de lys* all in red on gold. Meanwhile the Maitlands of Lauderdale have carried the Saltire as Hereditary Bearers of the National Flag of Scotland; their flag shows the white diagonal cross on blue, which brings its colours into the Union Flag of Great Britain. This act of reconciliation reaffirmed the 1603 ruling that the Royal Banner took precedence over all other flags.

The **Hereditary Bearer of the National Flag of Scotland** is standing on the lower part of Salisbury Crags, close to Arthur's Seat, which dominates Edinburgh's skyline and looks over the royal Palace of Holyroodhouse and the site of Scotland's new Parliament. The Maitlands alone were Banner Bearers in Scotland from the seventeenth to the twentieth century.

The saltire symbolizes Scotland's patron, Saint Andrew, who was crucified spreadeagled for his faith, while the Royal Banner represents the spirit of egalitarianism and independence that drove the Scots who fought alongside Wallace and Bruce.

Banners were also the emblem of Knights Bannerets who had been elevated above ordinary knights. The latter flew Pennons, small flags with two tongues on the end, but, after a knight had demonstrated valour on the battlefield, these were torn off by the king himself, producing a square banner, thus promoting the knight to Knight Banneret.

Two years after Wallace was defeated by Edward I, the 'Hammer of the Scots', at Falkirk in 1298, a chronicler described his English royal banner. It echoes Edward's political agenda for the subjugation of Scotland: however, he did not reckon upon his son's failures nor upon the success of the Scottish army under King Robert. The description goes:

'On his banner were three leopards courant [running], of fine gold set on red; fierce were they, haughty and cruel, to signify that like them the King is dreadful to his enemies. For his bite is slight to none who inflame his anger; and yet, towards such as seek his friendship or submit to his power, his kindness is soon rekindled.'

CHRONICLER OF CAEVERLOCK, 1300

Victory on the field of Bannockburn earned Scotland its independence, and the Standard that Robert the Bruce flew as King of the Scots has been borne by Banner Bearers ever since. This century the right to be **Hereditary Banner Bearer for Scotland** was returned to the family who stood beside the King on 24 June 1314. Nestled in the hills behind this battlefield is Stirling Castle. The lion rampant design can be seen in the caparison covering Bruce's charger.

Cock O' The North and the Duke of Atholl with his Atholl Highlanders

Outside Blair Castle the **Duke of Atholl** inspects a guard of honour provided by his private army, the Atholl Highlanders. They all wear a sprig of juniper in their Glengarry hats, the distinctive Highland sporran and the 'Wildman of Atholl' plaid brooch. The Highlanders are armed with Lee and Enfield 303 rifles.

In the 1530s James V of Scotland needed a French alliance, and so he left his kingdom to seek a wife in France. He left regents to rule, among whom was George Gordon, 4th Earl of Huntly, one of the most successful people of his generation. James, fearing his English cousins, appointed Huntly, who was already Lieutenant General of the North, Warden of the Marches (the borderlands between the kingdoms of England and Scotland).

James's first wife died and by the second, Mary of Guise, he had a daughter, Mary (later Queen of Scots). Soon after, English provocation forced James to war and a miserable defeat followed at Solway Moss in 1552, after which he died, leaving his seven-day-old daughter as queen. Fortunately his widow was made of stern stuff. She filled Scotland with French troops and sent the infant Mary to marry the Dauphin of France. Huntly served as Regent again and spent his time keeping order in both north and south. It was on a visit to Huntly Castle at this time that Mary referred to him as 'Cock of the North'. She also made him Lord Chancellor. Such power earned jealousy and, when his patron died and Mary Queen of Scots returned, despite his attempts to welcome the Catholic Queen, the reformist nobles outmanoeuvred him and made Huntly appear hostile.

In 1562, at the Battle of Corrichie, he was defeated and died on the battlefield, either of apoplexy or strangulation. It was a tragic end to an heroic life, but his achievements live on: as a tribute, his descendants are known as Cocks O' The North.

Among the forces that defeated Huntly at Corrichie was the Earl of Atholl with his Highlanders, a military force that still serves as the only private army in Europe. For Atholl, the battle at Corrichie was a chance to settle old scores in a neighbourly dispute that had rumbled on since Celtic times. After 1745 no military forces other than the Crown's were permitted.

In 1777, a regiment of Atholl Highlanders was raised on the understanding that it would serve with the British army for three years or the duration of war in America. Having fulfilled the service agreed, instead of being disbanded its volunteers were sent to Portsmouth for duties in India. The Athollmen had been double-crossed and mutinied; their special status saved them from punishment, and they were disbanded. Ever since, their role has been private and predominantly ceremonial, a situation legitimized by Queen Victoria, who in 1845 took the unprecedented step of giving Colours (a banner symbolizing regimental spirit) to this maverick force.

The **Cock O' The North**, a titular sobriquet, stands in front of Aboyne Castle. The present estate is just a small part of what was once a million acres of Huntly land. 'The Cock O' The North' is the regimental march of the Gordon Highlanders, who were raised in 1794 and commanded by the Marquis of Huntly.

Dean of the Arches, Official Principal of the Court of Canterbury and Auditor of the Chancery Court of York

THE CHURCH OF ST MARY LE BOW is famous because it was the seat of the Archbishop of Canterbury's court. Consequently, its story is both ecclesiastical and legal.

St Mary's was described originally as Beata Maria de Arcubus, or St Mary of the Arches, because of the design of its crypt, built between 1077 and 1087, though some say it comes 'by reason of the steeple thereof raised at the top with stone pillars in fashion like a bow bent archwise'. It became a 'peculiar', that is, a church subject to unique jurisdiction, in this case the Archbishop of Canterbury's. The Archbishop had thirteen peculiars around London and administered them from St Mary's, the most convenient. Here the Court of Peculiars was established, under the authority of the Dean of the Arches. In 1279, Archbishop Pecham of Canterbury passed to Master Roger de Rothwell the right to exercise full jurisdiction over all things belonging to the deanery of the Blessed Mary of the Arches.

Before the Reformation, Canon Law was administered by the Church with appeals to the curia of Rome. It was independent of secular law, which touched on temporal matters outside the Church's possessions or beyond its spiritual province. The Archbishops of Canterbury and York both had courts, supervised by Official Principals, to hear appeals sent up from the diocesan Consistory courts. St Mary's provided the Archbishop of Canterbury with a suitable location close to the City of London, the king's Courts of Chancery and Government at Westminster. By the late thirteenth century the Court of Arches was established as the senior ecclesiastical court in the Province of Canterbury. Archbishop Stratford, in the next century, ruled that the Official must appoint the Dean of the Arches as his Commissary General when summoned to appeals in Rome. Ultimately the two were merged, with the senior title of Official Principal being subsumed by the junior one, Dean of the Arches.

After severance from Rome, in 1536, the king became 'of the Church of England and also of Ireland, on Earth the Supreme Head'; thereafter, appeals from the Court of Arches went not to Rome but to the Court of Delegates, and, since 1832, to the Judicial Committee of the Privy Council. At this point, according to Garth Moore, 'because the Church of England is established, the Church's courts are courts of the state and the State's courts are courts of the Church'. A gradual shift towards State law and away from Church law still continues; this was particularly manifest when the Church's power over matrimonial matters was passed to the State and when the Toleration Act of 1688 curbed the power of the Church to punish people who did not worship, which had been compulsory until that time.

Since the Public Worship Regulation Act of 1874 one person has been Official Principal of both provincial courts: he no longer needs to be a cleric. Appointment is by both archbishops and has to be approved by the Crown. Today the Arches court is an appellate court, deciding appeals from diocesan chancellors, mainly relating to changes in the structure and ordering of churches and from the decisions of diocesan disciplinary proceedings. The Dean of the Arches and Auditor is also the Master of the Faculty Office, in which capacity he is responsible for the appointment of Notaries in England, Wales and many parts of the Commonwealth. While the Dean can be a clergyman, it is necessary only for him to be a communicant member of the Church of England who has at least ten years' experience as a barrister or has held high judicial office. The case load, whilst fascinating to those with a taste for such things, is quite small, and consequently, the Dean of the Arches is a part-time appointment. Although the boiler has taken some of the ancient space, the Court of Arches at St Mary's has survived the Great Fire of 1666 and the Blitz of 1940 in much the same form as the Norman builders intended.

The powerful court of the Arches, which once wielded considerable power, is now a café in the crypt of St Mary le Bow. Occasionally the catering equipment is cleared to one side and the **Dean of the Arches** resumes his seat of judgement. Many of the architectural features that gave this place its name were destroyed in the Blitz but have since been restored.

'A little out-of-the-way place where they administer what is
called ecclesiastical law, and play all kinds of tricks with
obsolete old monsters of Acts of Parliament.'

CHARLES DICKENS, DAVID COPPERFIELD, ON ST MARY LE BOW

First Church Estates Commissioner

FEW INSTITUTIONS FIND THEMSELVES more challenged by the changing moods of this century than the Established Church of England. Its history is one of logical and inevitable integration, making it now so much a part of the constitution that, while severance remains an option, it does not present an easy path. However, the Church has been acutely aware of its own need to reform, responding to changing circumstances that challenge its principal task, making the ministry of Christ's gospel available in every square mile of England. One evolutionary step came in 1948, when two traditional sources of funding, both vital to underpinning this principle, were united under a board of ninety commissioners,

to be administered by the First, Second and Third Church Estates Commissioners; appointments which were not new, having been created nearly a century before.

Both sources of funding were themselves pragmatic evolutions, established in response to the changing situations and demographics which affected the Church's ministry. The first was Queen Anne's bounty. Established by Royal Charter in 1703, it was set up to relieve the plight of poor clergy. Since Norman times the local priest was given land to farm for income, called his glebe, and he supplemented this with tithes, which were taxed tenths of the parish's income from agriculture or

The Church Commissioners' building is situated between the Christian foundation of Westminster Abbey, where monarchs have been crowned since the Norman Conquest, and the seat of temporal authority, the Houses of Parliament. The view symbolizes the balance between spiritual and material needs that is the **First Church Commissioner**'s responsibility to maintain.

'It's a job of balance: on the one hand there are the needs and requirements of the Church, and on the other the expectations and scrutiny of Parliament. The Commissioners are accountable to both for making these assets work wisely.'

FIRST CHURCH ESTATES COMMISSIONER, 1998

industry. But Rome insisted on receiving the first year's income from each priest and a tenth of what followed, called *Anales et Decimae*, or 'First fruits and tenths', which, after Henry VIII's break with Rome, came to the Crown. Queen Anne's bounty diverted this money back to the Church as a resource from which to pay clergy who ministered in places that had no adequate funding. Because this was the State's money, Parliament still retains a keen interest in its management.

Industrialization at the start of the nineteenth century moved large numbers of people into cities, where the Church's traditional funding was non-existent. The 1832 Reform Act produced a mood for change and the Church responded by redirecting excess diocesan assets to fund both poor benefices and the new urban churches. The Episcopal and cathedral riches were given in trust to a new body, called the Ecclesiastical and Church Estates Commissioners for England, in 1836. Along with several bishops, the commissioners of these historic Church assets included various officers of state and links are still maintained today. In 1850, three joint treasurers were appointed to administer the corporation of the Ecclesiastical Commissioners. They were the First Church Estates Commissioner, appointed by the Crown; the Second, with a seat in Parliament, selected now from the back benches of the governing party in the House of Commons; and the Third, a nomination of the Archbishop of Canterbury.

Because the work of both organizations overlapped, they were united to form the Church Commissioners for England in 1948, with the three administrative commissioners continuing their work. Since then, they have managed the combined assets of Queen Anne's Bounty and the Ecclesiastical Commissioners, in order to support the costs of funding the clergy, chiefly their stipends (pay) and pensions. The Church Commissioner also reviews the Church's pastoral organization, acting as impartial arbiters when there are no objections to local plans to reorganize parishes (and consequently patterns of ministry), and decides the future of redundant churches.

None of this was made any easier by investment errors in the 1980s, which reduced endowment values considerably. Dramatic management changes endeavour to ensure that remaining resources continue to provide approximately one quarter of the Church's annual running costs. In doing so, the First Commissioner must maintain the balance between a financially strapped church and a rightly inquisitive Parliament.

Field Marshal

THE PRINCE REGENT wrote to Wellington: 'You have sent me, among the trophies of your unrivalled fame, the staff of a French Marshal, and I send you in return that of England.' By these words the campaigning general learned of his promotion to the rank of Field Marshal following his victory at Vittoria. It was a flamboyant gesture from the master of flamboyance. However, the communication brought no baton, as is proved by a letter to him written eighteen days later from the Commander-in-Chief's office: '…It does not appear that there ever has been an English Baton; and no better occasion can ever occur of establishing one than the present…and if I am not interfered with from the Fountain of Taste, I trust it will be found an appropriate badge of command… you must have the "baton of England".' A red velvet baton, topped with a golden St George killing the dragon, its length scattered with crowned lions and bearing the recipient's name on the base, has been presented by Sovereigns to all Field Marshals ever since.

It was the result of a natural evolution from the Byzantine beginnings of both the appointment and its symbol. Richard III gave England's Earl Marshal a baton of office in the fifteenth century and, while the link between this great officer of state and the military rank is tenuous, there was an historic link in Europe. Here the *marescalcus campi* carried out certain executive responsibilities on behalf of the Marshal, who was the monarch's military leader immediately beneath the Constable. In England the Marshal, while also technically inferior to the Constable, took command of the king's troops in battle. It therefore runs contrary to logic that it took George II to import the military rank from Germany. He made the 1st Earl of Orkney a Field Marshal on 12 January 1736. Two days later, the honour was extended to the Duke of Argyll, who had defeated the Old Pretender's army at Sheriffmuir in 1715 and had served with

Marlborough; on whom had been bestowed the former honour of Captain-General.

For Wellington, the rank must have come as a surprise. At forty-four, he was much younger than any previous recipient, most of whom had received their rank almost more as a mark of longevity than military prowess. Lord Drogheda was ninety-one when George IV celebrated his coronation by handing out batons and, until the end of the nineteenth century, it was rare to find any Field Marshals younger than seventy. Excluding members of royal families, there has never been a younger appointment than Wellington, though, at fifty-two, Lord Alexander of Tunis came close. Few others went on to command an army in the field after appointment, as Wellington did at Waterloo, though Lords Raglan in the Crimea, Roberts in South Africa, Haig in the First World War and Montgomery with Alexander in the Second World War are the exceptions. Nor has there been another who became Prime Minister as well, though Smuts was Prime Minister of South Africa.

Three Field Marshals became leading enemies of Britain: Kaiser William II of Germany, Emperor Franz Joseph of Austria-Hungary and Emperor Hirohito of Japan. All three were deprived of the rank, while an ally, Tsar Nicholas II of Russia, received his within months of abdication and murder.

The rank is described as 'five star' and is seldom granted by the United States; Eisenhower and Bradley being the last equivalent, as Generals of the Army. In consequence, Britain as a member of NATO became aware of a growing imbalance in the ratio of these ranks to its military power. Before the Cold War ended Britain's forces were numerous. However, political demands for a Peace Dividend reduced the army to such a size that the Bett Report recommended, in February 1996, that further 'five star' appointments should cease. Batons have not been abolished but, short of monarchs, no new appointments are likely unless Britain goes to war.

The baton, designed by the Prince Regent in the nineteenth century, is topped with a golden St George killing his dragon and has the **Field Marshal**'s name inscribed on its base. Crossed batons appear within laurel wreaths on his shoulders and cap badge, and his 'five star' rank is placed for recognition on his vehicle. Though today's batons are ceremonial, they were used by medieval marshals to direct troops in the field – as used here on military training grounds with the Royal Green Jackets near Aldershot.

First Sea Lord and Chief of the Naval Staff

THE QUEEN HAS BEEN LORD HIGH ADMIRAL of the United Kingdom since 1 April 1964. On that day the Board of Admiralty, consisting of Their Lordships the Commissioners, ceased to exist, their duties subsumed into the Joint Chiefs of Staff in the Ministry of Defence, where the three service chiefs are chaired by the Chief of the Defence Staff, the senior serving officer in uniform.

However, the Board Room of the Admiralty remains in use because the business of Admiralty continues. From here the Royal Navy which won supremacy at sea for Great Britain and explored much of the globe was sent forth 'By the Commissioners for Executing the Office of Lord High Admiral of the United Kingdom of Great Britain and Ireland, etc'. Two roles that survived the establishment of the Ministry of Defence were the ringing appointments of First and Second Sea Lord. The First Sea Lord had also become Chief of Naval Staff during the First World War and the Second assumed the responsibilities of the Commander in Chief, Portsmouth (see p. 201).

In medieval times, the English navy was supplied by the Cinque Ports under same feudal system by which the monarch administered the land: the barons of these wealthy Channel ports did service to the king by supplying ships. In Henry III's reign, they were expected to supply fifty-seven fighting vessels with 1,197 men and boys for fifteen days at sea every year, after which the king would pay the expenses. But unfortunately this feudal fleet was prone to engage in piracy and, in 1297, while travelling to Flanders, they attacked and demolished twenty ships from Yarmouth as Edward I looked on in horror.

The first Admiral of all England was William de Leyburn in 1294. In 1360 Sir John Beauchamp combined his military responsibilities with the judicial elements of Admiralty. Forty-six years later John of Gaunt's natural son, John Beaufort, was appointed the first Lord Admiral. He ruled a navy already dependent on men who were forced to sea by impressment under the Laws of Oleron, the 'custom of the sea', and the practice of seizing people from the streets to serve on ships for indefinite periods continued until the conclusion of the Napoleonic wars. Under Edward III the Lord Admiral's duties and jurisdiction were fixed; he selected the ships offered under the feudal system, and chose the officers who would take them to sea. The choice of captains to command in the Royal Navy remains a responsibility of the First Sea Lord.

Henry IV was forced to apply to private enterprise in the fifteenth century to protect his shores. This maverick fleet was commanded by two admirals, Richard Clitherow and Nicholas Blackburn. Henry VIII reorganized his navy completely, placing it upon the foundations from which it still evolves. He built ships with the money he plundered from the monasteries and established the Navy Board on 24 April 1546, chaired by the Lord Admiral and his deputy, the Lieutenant of the Admiralty. It was not until 1623 that the title Lord High Admiral was first granted to the Duke of Buckingham.

When James II was Duke of York and Lord High Admiral, he was served ably by the energetic reformer Samuel Pepys, as Secretary. After 1688 power passed from the Navy Board to the Admiralty Board, created in 1690 by William III, who appointed nine Commissioners to act as if they 'were the Lord High Admiral'. Chief among these was the political post of First Lord of the Admiralty, until 1806 sometimes occupied by senior admirals. From this time on, the senior serving officer on the Board of Admiralty was called First Naval Lord, an appointment which evolved into First Sea Lord. By appointment this person became the senior serving officer in the Royal Navy.

The post of First Sea Lord lives on, not just as a link with the past and tradition but because geography does not change – Britain remains an island and needs a strong navy to protect the nation's interests and further its aspiration.

'He who would be secure on land must be supreme at sea'.

OFFA, EIGHTH-CENTURY KING OF MERCIA

The Admiralty Boardroom is dominated by the weather-vane which still spins with the wind to inform whether it is 'Fair for France', although invasion by sail is no longer a threat. Chunky naval symbolism, carved by Grinling Gibbons, includes ropes and anchors, astrolabes and bearing rings – instruments which Captain James Cook used to fulfil commands drafted here to explore the globe. The **First Sea Lord** directs a vastly different navy today.

Governor and Commander-in-Chief of Gibraltar

The Convent's state dining room awaits the **Governor**'s guests, its walls illuminated with his predecessors back to the Moorish Caliphs of the eighth century. The Port Sergeant hands him the Keys to the Fortress of Gibraltar: the strategic base, which proved so vital in building an empire and in two world wars, is secure for another night.

THE BRITISH EMPIRE was the largest the world has ever seen: it once included much of the United States, Africa, India, Australia, New Zealand and the Carribbean. It was built through trade and then the exploitation of opportunity, mixed with a sense of duty and purpose. Started by accident in the seventeenth century, it was seen as a mixed blessing in the eighteenth, became a valued and popular policy in the nineteenth and finally proved to be politically, financially and militarily untenable in the twentieth. This spread of territories presented a major administrative challenge, and it became necessary to improve communication and strategic support from the mother country.

In 1704, one such opportunity arose during the War of Spanish Succession. English troops, under the command of Prince George of Hesse Darmstadt, attacked the Rock of Gibraltar, as a step in their plan to put Archduke Charles of Austria on the Spanish throne. However, when Admiral Sir George Rooke made good the assault, he took possession in Queen Anne's name rather than Charles's: a pragmatic step ratified by Westminster and then confirmed in the Treaty of Utrecht of 1713, which Spain has never accepted. This did three things: it gave the growing Empire a strategic hold on the Mediterranean's entrance, started a long-running feud with Spain over sovereignty and produced another outpost which had to be governed.

Britain thought it governed colonies well, but it took time to get the attitude and balance right. Mirroring Britain's constitution, representatives of royal authority were needed and were called Governors from the Latin, *gubernare,* to steer, direct or guide a ship. According to the size of the territory they were graded from Lieutenant Governors through Governors up to Governors General. In both Ireland and India they were given added status as Viceroys.

Some early governors were as powerful as medieval monarchs, with all the dangers that absolutism could pose. This occurred because constitutional lessons in Britain's evolution, concerning the growth of individual liberty, were often deliberately overlooked. Executive powers were sometimes subject only to limited domestic checks and a Secretary of State in London, thousands of miles away. Over time, checks and balances were introduced and each colony followed its individual path to democracy and independence, while Governors became constitutionally aloof. But, in the case of the few remaining dependent territories, of which Gibraltar is one, this aloofness retains diplomatic clout.

Gibraltar's strategic importance meant that, until the late 1990s, the Governor was always a senior officer from the armed forces. This continued a line of military governance back to 711, when Al Walid Ibn Abdulmalic was the first moorish Caliph on the rock.

That military significance is now marked on special occasions by a ceremony. Marines who secured the Rock had to defend it from a succession of Franco-Spanish counter attacks, notably during the Great Siege of 1779 to 1783, and when Captain Fisher and seventeen men defended the Round Tower from 500 French grenadiers. In those days, to demonstrate that the Rock was secure, the Port Sergeant delivered the Keys of Gibraltar to the Governor in the Convent, his official residence. The Colony's coat of arms thus consists of a fortress and keys.

The Governorship's diplomatic role has increased to reflect the wider European outlook and to address Spain's continued claim: for the first time a non-military diplomat has filled the post. Gibraltar's House of Assembly, which opted for membership of the European Union, must leave responsibility for external affairs, defence and internal security to the Governor and, thereby, the United Kingdom's Government. Gibraltar may choose to end its governance by Britain at any time, but sovereignty would then revert to Spain. Gibraltarians are unhappy with this 'Catch 22' and beneath this historic gubernatorial dignity the difficult work of colonial governance goes on.

Superintendent of the Corps of Queen's Messengers

WHEN ENGLAND SANK INTO CIVIL WAR, loyalty was rare and prized. It was vital for Charles I to maintain communications with his supporters across the country, as well as over the border in his Scottish kingdom and abroad. From the beginning at Hull, when the gates were slammed in his face, through the battles of Edgehill, Marston Moor and Naseby, the king struggled to maintain his strategic position. He relied on his Corps of Kings Messengers, formed one hundred years before, to fulfil this need in a nation sick with intrigue. The Corps traces its history through entries in the the Royal Household's clothing accounts to 1199: early Messengers were drawn from noblemen or proven and trusted courtiers. They provided a range of services from collecting taxes to escorting felons accused of High Treason.

Each British embassy needs a reliable passage of information with government that is often sensitive in nature. Under the Vienna Convention for Diplomatic Relations, such communication can be carried out without fear of interference and in Britain the Corps of Queen's Messengers still undertakes the task. No longer are they the Gentlemen of the Great Chamber in Ordinary, or Extraordinary, who were formed by Henry VIII into the first Corps in 1547: nor are they still part of the Royal Household. Instead, when monarchs' powers began to decline in favour of the constitutional system and ministers took responsibility for government, the Corps served their political masters. On 6 May 1722, sixteen of them were transferred into the King's Foreign Service Messengers and the Corps followed from the palace to the Foreign Office.

Medieval heralds provided the first royal messengers and conducted basic diplomacy. But the demands of ever greater communication and the need for permanent ambassadors abroad caused change. The first King's Messenger recorded was Robert Asshewell, whose appointment was signed by Henry VI in 1454, and Richard III appointed John Norman in 1485, within months of his fall at the Battle of Bosworth.

The victor, Henry VII, selected the silver greyhound of Richmond as one of the heraldic beasts to support his royal arms and it was embroidered across the chest of Tudor messengers. When Prince Charles was in exile during the Civil War he is supposed to have broken silver greyhounds from his dish and given one to each of his English and Dutch couriers, to enable them to be recognized. Then, it is said, he decreed that greyhounds should be suspended around the neck of his messengers from Garter blue ribbon, though many were stolen and many were lost when falling from horses. Today they are worn only on special occasions.

Flying around the world, it is possible that the two neighbouring seats will be occupied by a taciturn retired officer, keeping his eyes on bags that enjoy their own seat. A diplomatic incident would result if these bags were tampered with.

During both world wars, Kings Messengers worked hard as encoders and decoders. But during the build-up of Hitler's Germany, the passage of secret hand-carried communiques was essential in assisting the government understand what was going on.

Each Messenger covers, on average, more than 250,000 miles a year but the Corps undergoes continuous financial review. Recently the title of Superintendent has been replaced by the less poetic sounding Head of Classified Bag Services. Even though the confidentiality of electronic communication is improving, hand carriers remain the most reliable means for communication. The Queen's Messengers will probably continue to be needed to carry sensitive and often bulky items of Her Britannic Majesty's diplomatic business around the world, safely, politely and discreetly.

'Neither snow, nor rain, nor heat, nor gloom of night shall stay these couriers in the swift completion of their appointed rounds.'

HERODOTUS

The **Superintendent** holds one of six special passports that he needs because visas take two to three weeks to process. The silver greyhound badge around his neck is suspended from an oval containing the Queen's cypher. Most journeys begin from the Grand Staircase of India House that dominates the Foreign Office.

Senior Constable and Constables of Oxford University

CHARLES THE WISE OF FRANCE supposedly established the first police force in the fourteenth century, 'to increase the happiness and security of his people'. Unfortunately, it did quite the opposite by suppressing them with an engine of torture. In England, Edward I passed a statute of 'Watch and Ward' in 1285, which established a formal watch on the streets of London; and it is here that most evolutionary steps towards a national police force have been taken. However, the Constables of Oxford University claim to be the oldest police force in the world, predating Edward's 'Watch and Wards' by seventy years, when Proctors patrolled the city.

Civil order until the nineteenth century was maintained outside London by the lords of each manor and the civil authorities which gradually took their place, with officers and courts through which to keep the peace. Serious offences were referred to higher courts and ultimately to the king's mercy. Within these manor courts the office of Constable was an influential one. It stemmed from the Byzantine structure where emperors had dignitaries to look after their horses, called 'counts of the stable'. These Constables often commanded large and powerful armies for the emperor, and the title is now the first rank held by policemen in Britain.

In the same year that Proctors first patrolled Oxford, the barons forced King John to sign Magna Carta, which curtailed royal power in favour of justice for the individual. Justice can only be exercised when the law is enforced but, despite this, British culture consistently rejected an organized force of law. It was, and still is, often distrusted; a suspicion stemming from the national instinct for freedom. However, the gradual decline of civil order in the nineteenth century, brought about by the industrial revolution's urbanization and a decline in awe for heavenly retribution, led to a public will in favour of law enforcement. In 1829, London's police force was reorganized by the Home Secretary,

Robert Peel. They were known as 'Peelers' or 'Bobbies' after their founder. Opposition was strong, with many rejecting the State's adoption of such power, which became the foundation for a national police force. And it remains part of Britain's social contract, which needs constant scrutiny, to ensure that the power to enforce law is always exercised within the law.

In the same year that Peel's legislation was passed, the Vice Chancellor of Oxford signed the 'Plan for the Establishment of an efficient University Police'. It formalized the duties and powers of the Oxford Constables.

University Constables, and the Proctors before them, were principally responsible for the supervision of scholars. These new powers gave them the ability to be both issuers of avuncular reprimand and also quasi-policemen within the University precincts. Undergraduates throughout history have juxtaposed academic study with mischief and revelry, which was enhanced by the challenge of avoiding a Constable's detection. Up until the end of the Second World War, the university was in *loco parentis*, which gave them a parental power and responsibility over students: this included kicking them out of pubs and getting them to their own bed on time. Misdemeanours were punished by either the college or the university, on evidence presented by the Constables, who are known now as 'Chief Sniffers of University Bulldogs'. A common misdemeanour was failing curfew, or being found with the opposite sex, the latter being treated with varying judgement according to the social mores of the time. However, cheating has always been the worst malevolence and Proctors were originally allowed to send down a student, without referring the matter any further.

The Oxford Constables are now trained by Thames Valley Police Force. The Senior Constable said, 'The last time we were out in any force was last Tuesday; the students occupied one of our buildings.'

The **Senior Constable** is surrounded by the **Constables of Oxford University** between Christopher Wren's Sheldonian Theatre and the Old Library. They have worn bowler hats since 1946, when the top hat and cape were dropped. Behind them stands the Clarendon Building, designed by Nicholas Hawksmoor, and topped with statues of the nine muses. The University Police are now the last private police force in Britain, and carry warrant cards with the power of arrest within Oxford City or on University property.

'That they be also nominated to act as Vice-Chancellor's Men, in
order that they be enabled more readily in this capacity to conduct
irregular Gownsmen to their respective Colleges and Halls,
without taking them into custody in their capacity of Constables.'

ESTABLISHMENT OF POLICE FORCE, 1829

'*About a quarter before nine, while he was describing the change which God works in the heart through faith in Christ, I felt my heart strangely warmed. I felt I did trust in Christ.*'

JOHN WESLEY'S
CONVERSION,
24 MAY 1738

Wesley's pulpit stands at the centre of his church in London's Old Street. Methodist symbolism surrounds the **President**, whose outstretched arm mirrors those of Christ and his disciples. From Alpha α to Omega Ω it was Wesley's determination that the Gospel was for everyone, as his hymns spelled out: 'for all, for all, my saviour died'.

I**T ALL BEGAN WHEN A FIFTEENTH CHILD** was born to the Reverend Samuel Wesley. The infant John was to become an English divine, whose life began with the eighteenth-century advantages of clerical position. When the Rectory was burnt to the ground, the Duke of Buckingham provided money for his Charterhouse education, which led to Oxford. In 1729, aged twenty-six, John was appointed Father of the 'Holy Club': a small society which met to study the Greek Testament every Sunday and which fasted each Wednesday and Friday. They followed a simple 'rule', the Greek word for which is 'Method', which became the foundation of the Methodist Church.

The evangelical pursuit of Jesus Christ amongst the precepts and rituals of the established church has often been a cause for tension within the Anglican communion. This was particularly true when John became an ordained member of England's dominant church. He did not find fault with the thirty-nine articles, which form the foundations of Anglican faith, or with Archbishop Cranmer's *Book of Common Prayer*. However, this was the Age of Reason and his egalitarian belief that the word of God should reach beyond the church door, out into the kingdom's roughest communities, was one which contradicted established practice. He led a revival which 'spread Scriptural holiness over the land'. Methodism was to become another strand of factionalism: one which was identified more by the zeal of its adherents than by the nature of their faith, although their conviction that the Gospel is for all flew in the face of Calvinism.

The doors of Anglican churches were slammed in the face of Wesley and his adherents, who made street corners their pulpits and crossed the oceans to America in search of souls. They found a population hungry for ministry, many of whom had been cast from churches when they could no longer pay the rent demanded for pew space. Travelling preachers visited communities and established Methodist Societies with their own local preachers. Each was dedicated to worship, fellowship, service, prayer, Bible study and responsible giving. Shunned from the stiff comforts of Anglicanism, Wesley had to ordain his own preachers: thus Methodism took its independent root.

All human institutions developed for the worship of God seldom match the demands placed upon them by individual members: this was true of Methodism, which could not contain the aspirations of its fast growing Societies, many of which splintered off into different groupings, among them America's Episcopal Methodists, the Calvinistic Methodists and, later, even the Salvation Army. Wesleyan Methodists maintained their links with John's original vision, but today they take their place as equals within the wider Methodist community.

Wesley understood mavericks, having been one himself. He may have anticipated the natural process of disintegration that followed his stipulation in 1784 that a 'Yearly conference of People called Methodists' should meet. And whilst this was initially the institution against which many rebelled, it subsequently provided a means for uniting them all.

John died leaving no nomination for his Church's leadership and so, in default, responsibility fell to the Methodist Conference. During the period of disunity, the appointment of President was held by Wesleyan Methodists, often for long periods. However, by the time all Methodists were reunited into the Connexional structure that is Methodism today, this system had been changed. Each year, a new President is selected from the wide membership, who inherits many things. Among them is the tradition of pulpit evangelism that continues at Wesley's Chapel which he built in the City of London. Every President may reflect that, during the first sermon there on All Saints' Day in 1778, John launched a tirade against the sea of expensive hats that filled the building. To him, they symbolized wealth and privilege — at odds with Gospel simplicity.

Herb Strewer

The **Herb Strewer** sits at the West Door of Westminster Abbey, the coronation church of England's monarchs since Christmas Day 1066, when William the Conqueror celebrated his coronation. The Herb Strewer led the procession of the most flamboyant coronation Britain has ever seen when George IV was crowned in 1821.

'My elder sister... had the nomination of the six ladies who were to strew flowers...A more interesting or lovely group never was exhibited on any occasion.'

W. D. FELLOWES, 1821

THE DRAINS OF TUDOR PALACES gave off foul gases, which did little to make James I feel at home when he arrived from Holyrood in 1603. It was one of the principal shortcomings in life up until the nineteenth century that no one quite understood how to deal with sewerage and, while the Court demanded ever more grandeur, nothing could be done to rid this rarified world of unpleasant smells. Nothing, that is, other than try to disguise them with other, more fragrant, aromas such as strewn herbs.

Since the Restoration, Herb Strewers were employed to wander the royal apartments, distributing rue, mint, sage and camomile, along with roses and lavender. Theirs was a vital role; a popular relief to all. Herb Strewers spread their wares whenever the monarch processed, and especially on the rare occasions when that route led among their less hygienic subjects for obligatory religious ceremonies such as the Royal Maundy or touching for scrofula, which was known as the 'King's Evil'.

The first recorded Herb Strewer was Bridget Rumny, who served from 1660 until 1671, receiving £24 per annum, as did all her successors, until the appointment fell into abeyance the year before Victoria came to the throne. To this small sum was added an annual grant of two yards of superfine scarlet cloth for livery. Many served for considerable periods, while successors waited in the wings; one such hopeful, Anne Edwards, died waiting for Elizabeth Jux to expire. She was described instead in the papers of Queen Anne as 'Strewer of Herbs in our Privy Lodgings'. The herbs were probably gathered from the King's Herb House, in the old Palace of Whitehall's grounds. The longest serving full time Herb Strewer was the last, Mary Rayner, who served forty-three years in the post and strewed for George III and two of his sons.

When George IV finally inherited the throne from his tragic father, he celebrated by giving free vent to his flamboyance and planned the most spectacular coronation Britain has ever witnessed. In 1821 there was no longer an imperative to keep the air sweet: improved hygiene had seen to that. Instead, this was a chance to inject yet another note of fashion and display into the proceedings. He had already promised the post to an old friend, Miss Anne Fellowes, who had supported his brother, the Duke of Sussex, by witnessing that Prince's secret (and illegal) marriage to Lady Augusta Murray in Rome. Some thought Miss Fellowes, at fifty-six, rather too old to add lustre to the show, but the king kept his word, providing her with a gleaming badge of office.

Perhaps to offset Anne's fading charms, it was decided that six maidens of genetic birth would attend her. This excited much competition and we are told that 'the Princesses concerned themselves in the appointment of some'. Anne had the final say and, unsurprisingly, two of her nieces were chosen. They carried silver-gilt baskets and scattered flowers along the rich, blue carpet from Westminster Hall to the Abbey, and we are told that 'a more interesting or lovely group never was exhibited on any occasion'. Anne was reported to have 'scattered exotic flowers and aromatic herbs, from time to time filling a small hand basket from the large baskets of her attendants, who always made a profound obeisance as they presented their fragrant burthen [stet] to the mistress.'

Anne Fellowes applied again for William IV's coronation and was granted the job; however, cutbacks in the ceremony abolished the role. Queen Victoria eschewed George IV's splendour and, by Edward VII's crowning, the reduced ritual was established, though this did not deter the Fellowes from petitioning for the position as of right. They still defend the claim in the name of the senior unmarried daughter of the family, who waits for the chance to sweeten the air at Westminster Abbey once again.

Joint Master and Huntsman of the Duke of Beaufort's Foxhounds

THE PERENNIAL DEBATE upon the future of fox-hunting proves the words of Charles Dickens right: even those dedicated to its abolition are 'hunting something'. Since records began, hunting animals has been an instinct, driven by the need for food and a desire for the chase's thrill; something which is implanted in man, the animal, but which is increasingly questioned by evolving arguments of civilization.

The fox was probably hunted even before the ancient Egyptians pursued them, along with animals like oryx, ibex, wild ox, hare and porcupine. Xenophon wrote, as did Homer, upon the hunting proclivities of the ancient Greeks. His geographer, Strabo, writing in the century before Christ, referred to dogs bred in Celtic Briton expressly for hunting. Alfred the Great's biographer, Asser, tells us that at not even twelve years old he 'was a most expert and active hunter, and excelled in all the branches of that noble art, to which he applied with incessant labour and amazing success'. And King Athelstan forced the vanquished ruler of Wales to supply him annually with 'sharp-scented dogs fit for hunting wild beasts'.

The fox, cunning, solitary and a hunter by nature, presented a foe to rural husbandmen from the beginning of organized agriculture in England. Originally it was regarded as quarry for those of lesser rank, while nobility preferred to pursue the stag, which was jealously guarded. Under William I the penalty for poaching a deer was the loss of both eyes. William Twici, Hunter-in-Chief to Edward II, wrote that the fox was a beast of venery but obviously an inferior sport.

Since the fourteenth century the title Hereditary Master of the Royal Buckhounds was vested in the Brocas family, one of whom used his privilege to attempt Henry IV's assassination at Windsor in 1400. This title of Master set the form for leaders of all subsequent packs. In 1528, Henry VIII appointed George Boleyn, Viscount Rochfort, as First Master of the Privy Pack of Royal Buckhounds at Swinley. George III frantically followed staghounds, and many subsequently referred to the fox as 'Charlie' because Charles James Fox was then the Leader of His Majesty's Opposition. George Prince of Wales confirmed the popular move from stag- to fox-hunting in 1793, when he exchanged his staghounds for a pack of foxhounds.

A century or so before, the fox had emerged as the favoured 'higher chase' and, in so doing, united all rural classes together in one sport. The hunt was led by the Master and consisted of huntsmen and followers; it was organized by the hunt servants, including the Huntsman who cared for the pack. Lord Willoughby de Broke wrote that 'the man who hunts the hounds should always feed them.'

Hunting at Badminton began around 1640. The Somerset family became dukes of Beaufort and, being Tory, were something quite rare among the great ducal families. They took little part in politics during the period of Whig supremacy; for them it was much

Dismounted, the **Master** is with Beaufort's foxhounds. These go back some fifty-three generations to 1743 and descend from the Talbot hound brought over by William the Conqueror: they are selectively bred to hunt a specific quarry by the nose. The pack usually consists of seventeen-and-a-half couples (thirty-five foxhounds).

'There is a passion for hunting something deeply implanted in the human breast.'

CHARLES DICKENS, OLIVER TWIST

more consistent with their country-bred Jacobite origins to indulge in the chase. Most became Masters of their own packs and sometimes the Huntsmen too. After chasing a fox from Silk Wood in 1762 the 5th Duke instructed that the pack be retrained as foxhounds. The 10th Duke, probably the greatest huntsman of the twentieth century, was also Master of the Duke of Beaufort's Foxhounds and was known by everyone, even Queen Mary, as 'Master'. He resisted abolition and, speaking in Parliament declaimed that, 'If these Bills are passed and the sound of the horn and the cry of the hounds are not again to be heard, it will be the worst thing ever to happen in this country.'

The countryside is less rurally minded now and its interests are increasingly directed by leisure pursuits that conflict ideologically with those of the hunt. Yet hunting is more popular, and followed by a larger number of people, than at any time in its history. Maintaining packs for the chase in what many perceive to be an anachronistic and inhumane sport remains every Master's primary task; the Master of the Beaufort has traditionally kept one of the best packs in the country; the hounds have no other purpose.

Grand Bard and Cornish Gorsedd (Gorseth Byrth Kernow)

Among more than two hundred ancient stone circles and monuments in Cornwall, which are older than the pyramids, is the spiritual monument of Carn Brae, above Redruth. The Gorsedd's regalia is made from beaten copper with Celtic designs on a background of knotwork. Cornwall's flag is carried by a Past Grand Bard; the **Grand Bard** leads her followers as they watch the sun set.

MANY PEOPLE IN BRITAIN ARE CELTS to some degree. Irrespective of the number, we are surrounded by a rich Celtic culture and during this last century enthusiasts have revived the Bardic Orders to keep these traditions alive.

Celtic words fill the English language and their place names can be found everywhere. In addition the art work, carving and craft inspired by these ancestors is a great influence on contemporary design. Celts occupied the central and western parts of Europe and, though the facts are difficult to ascertain, evidence suggests that the Celtic migrants arrived from France, first in Ireland and then on mainland Britain, between the sixth and fifth century BC.

Living now in a century of renewed ethnic awareness, it is worth reflecting on how much cultural integration happened in these islands before. In every case there is always a rich cultural seam to mine and evidence suggests a good mix occurs where art, literature and ideas are shared. Along with the ancient Britons, the Celts formed one of the founder races and they mixed over a thousand years with Romans, Angles, Jutes and Saxons.

The Celts developed a great artistic identity. Their craftsmanship, ingenuity and adventurousness was matched by their literature, as if different humanities fed from each other. It was a race that celebrated learning and wisdom through a ritual celebration of both. The Bards, who were poets, led this process and they versed everything, including the legends of history. Unfortunately the Anglo Saxon and Norse invasions pushed the Celts to the far west of Britain, particularly to Wales: a country named by the invaders from a word which means 'foreign'.

In 926 King Athelstan fixed the boundary of the 'West Welsh' as the River Tamar, and this remains the boundary of Cornwall. Use of Brythonic Cornish gradually dwindled and, while there is evidence that in Elizabeth I's reign it was still quite widely spoken, the Reformation struck a heavy blow because no effort was made to translate the new prayer book into the language.

There had been no Bardic Order in Cornwall since the twelfth century but, with support from the 'Mother Gorsedd' of Wales, the Gorsedd of the Bards of Cornwall was revived at the traditional site of Boscawen in Un, near Land's End, in 1928. It meets annually on the first Saturday in September, on sites throughout Cornwall, and is opened by the blowing of the 'Corn Gwlas' (Horn of the Nation). The Bards wear simple blue robes with the Grand Bard adorned in a crown and plastron. Specially invited guests then compete in rhyme and performance for awards of both literary and musical merit. Their intention is to 'maintain the national Celtic spirit of Cornwall; to encourage the study of literature, art, music and history in Cornwall; to encourage the study and use of the Cornish language; to link Cornwall with the other Celtic countries; and to promote co-operation amongst those who work for the honour of Cornwall'.

Ceremonies begin with the sounding of the symbolic horn, which calls to the four points of the compass. A specially selected Lady of Cornwall makes an offering of Fruits of the Earth and children dance to harp music before the Grand Bard receives new Bards into the Gorsedd. It is a pastiche which seeks to rediscover lost culture, and its system of customs has evolved to meet this need.

Custos of Harrow

THE FIRST VANDALISTIC GRAFFITI on the panelling of John Lyon's Fourth Form room at Harrow-on-the-Hill was perpetrated in the year the room was added to the 1615 building, by 'WO 1660'. Its founder was a philanthropist who granted his wealth for the support of a school to educate thirty local children. Elizabeth I gave a charter in 1572 that formally began Harrow's life as a school, and arrangements were made later for fee-paying boys to supplement the numbers, as foreigners; an immigration that quickly displaced local attendance completely.

Among a chaos of inscribed names that are still added to boards all over the school, although carving is now regulated by Custos, are eight boys who went on to serve as Prime Ministers. They include Spencer Percival, Sir Robert Peel, Lords Goderich, Aberdeen and Palmerston, Stanley Baldwin, Pandit Nehru and Sir Winston Churchill: men who forged Britain's imperial identity, guided reform, set India on her path to freedom and led the nation to victory against Adolf Hitler. For most of them, the school's head porter, or Custos, was an influential and important character who guided their lives and maintained the environment that provided their home. The name Custos has been used since 1817, when a man called Hope filled the post. Sam Hoare, who followed his father into the post of Custos later that century, served the Headmaster, Dr Vaughan. It was said: 'His softness of manner, at first almost startling, never left any illusion with boys or masters as to either his penetrating insight or his resolute will.' Sam, who was evidently well-regarded, maintained peace in the School Yard, or 'milling ground'.

Winston Churchill arrived at Harrow in April 1888. He was ill-prepared for the place academically and later said that he 'had only enjoyed a few gleams of success'. He visited the Fourth Form room twice

for punishment; an ordeal before breakfast, which was generally preceeded by a short wait beneath with Custos, in his den. Despite selecting the Headmaster's cane, Custos juxtaposed this with stoic reassurance, while pacing feet and whizzing birch rushed judiciously overhead. In a letter to his father, Winston wrote, 'There was rather a row about some broken windows not long ago. I, young Millbank and three others... discovered the ruins of a large factory, into which we climbed. Everything was in ruin and decay but some windows yet remained unbroken; we facilitated the progress of time... the watchman complained to Welldon, who having made enquiries, "swished" us.' But as both a political and military leader, this Old Harrovian surpassed himself: he was also an artist and an historian of the English-speaking peoples. Whilst he vehemently opposed the 1945 Labour Government's rush to give India its independence, it must have amused him to see another Old Harrovian lead the world's largest democracy across the threshold of freedom.

The spire of St Mary's Church stands at the summit of the steep hill that dominates the area, with views across London. It may occupy the site where Norsemen worshipped Tiw, Woden and Thor, gods who gave us the names of three of the days in the week. (Harrow derives from the Norse word *hearg*, meaning a shrine.) Below it, the school hugs one slope, clustered round the founder's first building in which Custos keeps the keys and is available to help administer the Bill, a regular roll-call, for the Bill Master. He also takes a small fee to carve boys' names, for which task the skill of wood-engraving is a requirement for appointment. However, he is no longer expected to make 'one of those lithe and compact birchrods', which for centuries administered justice in the ancient form room overhead.

Dressed in their school uniform, a Shell student (first year) sits on a well-worn desk, and a Monitor looks on as **Custos**, standing in the Headmaster's seat, carves the names of boys into the oak panelling of the Fourth Form room. Custos's keys, the practical symbols of his office, lie at his side, while behind in a small cupboard in the wall the Headmaster's cane was kept. Old Harrovians whose names appear in this room include Byron, Sheridan and Winston Churchill.

'When two boys had agreed to settle their differences in
single combat, Custos would, after a short skirmish,
dissipate the pugilistic gathering by means of a kindly
chaff which rendered his pacific efforts palatable alike
to principals, seconds and onlookers.'

PERCY THORNTON, HARROW SCHOOL, 1885

6
CHANGE OF EMPHASIS
The Twentieth Century

HE REFORM ACTS of the nineteenth century precipitated fundamental changes in the shape of British society and the structures that had been unquestioned for so long. Queen Victoria's relations ruled the great European empires that divided the world. Britain's government was increasingly democratic, and the Queen Empress was more of a figurehead. Victoria's death was marked with gun salutes throughout an empire that could not imagine life without her: it heralded a new century, and different voices made the case for change.

The British Empire began the century facing defeat against Boers in South Africa, and in 1909 the Chancellor of the Exchequer delivered a Finance Bill that included a 'super tax' on wealth and land to pay for the modest social measures expected by voters. The House of Lords threw it out. The Liberal Government reacted with outrage, threatening to flood the Lords with new Liberal appointments if the 'People's Budget' was not passed, and the Bill returned to the Lords to be accepted. The Lords' rebellion precipitated the Parliament Bill, which began the steady erosion of powers vested in the landed Peerage of Dukes, Marquesses, Earls, Viscounts and Barons since the beginnings of feudalism.

The Great War claimed a generation. The hideous bloodshed involved in trench warfare raised questions in the minds of the led, as it did in the stream of youthful commanders that Sandhurst trained to lead from the front. Many of those who fought were willing to sacrifice all for King and Country, but those who survived looked for a better standard of living after victory. The selection of one Unknown Warrior from the millions who had died caught the imagination of a grieving nation. He would keep a lonely vigil against war and surely see a better world develop for the living.

Survivors returned home to the working conditions they had left behind but, despite expectation, change was slow. Socialist movements formed, challenging the interests of both commerce and the establishment: Communism erupted in Russia as the Trade Union movement and the Labour Party embodied the aspirations of Britain's working class. Depression and then the Second World War left the Empire bankrupt, but the electoral success of the Labour Party in 1945 led to the creation of a Welfare State. Their manifesto promised healthcare and education for all.

Belief in Britain survived the Second World War, and with it remained an affection for shared history; the Coronation in 1953, watched by millions on television, demonstrated a nation celebrating itself. However, many objected to a service which exluded the Speaker and concentrated on the landed hereditary peerage. The imperatives that originally united the kingdom – fear of Roman Catholicism, economic advantage and the benefits of colonial trade – lost relevance one by one. First, the internecine tensions between two denominations seemed irrelevant in a society where churchgoing dropped and multi-culturalism, permissiveness and post-deferential self-empowerment were the new icons: the irony of a Vatican bishop becoming the senior diplomat in Britain was largely lost. Second, economic advantages were challenged by nationalists in Scotland who claimed that London was squandering North Sea oil resources: tragedies on the rigs saw the introduction of a new chaplaincy to the oil industry. Third, following the 1945 Labour landslide, imperial philosophy died: independence was granted or coerced, beginning with India in 1948 when George VI stopped signing himself Emperor. Instead he set the foundations of the Commonwealth, of which he became Head.

From the turn of the century executive decisions were almost exclusively a matter for the monarch's Cabinet, led by the Prime Minister, whose name has existed for nearly 200 years, although it only became a formal title in 1905. It is an evolving appointment that shows much of the changing emphasis both of this century and of the story since 1066. The Prime Minister is also First Lord of the Treasury, a post that has given overall responsibility for money since William I conquered England and appointed his half-brother, Odo Bishop of Bayeux, as Lord Treasurer. Odo provided ships for the invasion and fought valiantly in the Battle of Hastings, so he got one of the top jobs after the conquest. The privileges turned his head to embezzlement, and he supported the wrong son after the Conqueror's death, so he fell from power and died with crusaders on the way to Palestine.

The Treasurer's power grew within the medieval court and he became the third Great Officer of State, after the Steward and the Chancellor, and Charles II included him in his small core of advisers called the Cabinet. Parliamentary supremacy was established by the revolution of 1688, although the monarch still governed through ministers he appointed. Under George I the office of Lord High Treasurer, which by then had considerable patronage within its gift, was placed in commission (vested in a committee); the principal commissioner was the First Lord of the Treasury. The king's language difficulties enabled the Cabinet to assume greater power within the court and the political assiduity of Robert Walpole (arguably the first Prime Minister) developed this, by using patronage to secure a working majority in the Commons. Cabinet executive power continued to grow, and in the twentieth century the monarch's constitutional right to choose a Prime Minister was simplified because individual political parties elected their own leaders. But the role continues to gain stature with the advantage of media; Prime Ministers are virtually presidential in their appearance. Recently the Cabinet's power has sometimes been subsumed by individual Prime Ministers, who have been autocratic. Just as Robert Walpole enjoyed the power that plentiful patronage provides, so the Prime Minister and First Lord of the Treasury still has a vast amount of power, and therefore patronage, in his gift.

New appointments are still created to meet utilitarian needs, such as the new First Minister of Scotland's Parliament. After a century of attempted reform of the House of Lords, a new structure will soon appear, with the status of its members enshrined in titles, however egalitarian. The hereditary peerage, with its roots in the land, will then no longer have legislative powers, but the titles will survive. They will remain as more living clues alongside others in this book – clues that enable Britain to trace its history and the development of its freedoms. Each clue and story will serve to remind citizens of the struggle from which constitutional freedoms have evolved and of the need for their vigilant protection.

There are five ranks in the hereditary peerage. Other than Dukes (see page 72), who are the most senior, they appear from left to right in reverse order of seniority as **Baron**, **Viscount**, **Countess** and **Marquess**. Parliamentary robes define their rank through ermine and gold bars. Legislative power, derived from the land that was vested in the hereditary peerage, will soon end but the titles will survive to convey their stories to future generations.

The Unknown Warrior

O{\scriptsize N} 11 N{\scriptsize OVEMBER} 1920 at 11 o'clock in the morning, exactly two years after the Armistice had silenced the ferocious guns of the Great War, George V led the national observance of two minutes' silence and unveiled Lutyens's new Portland stone cenotaph: the 'empty tomb', in Whitehall. He was surrounded by princes, political and military leaders and the thoughts of an Empire, all anxious for symbols adequate to meet the grief at such dreadful loss of life. Beside him, six caparisoned horses drawing a gun carriage stood and fidgeted: the rattling of their bridles the only sound to disturb the respectful hush. Many stared their thoughts towards the simple oak coffin the carriage conveyed. Draped with a Union Flag, it contained the remains of a single unidentified victim, the Unknown Warrior.

Later that day, the coffin was laid to rest inside the door of Westminster Abbey. It was a State Funeral. Ever since, this nameless representative of selfless sacrifice has been a focus for all who seek to gauge the price of war. The grave is frozen in time, while its contents 'grow not old'. Of the millions of visitors to this royal mausoleum, few fail to stop and read the brassy words of imperial confidence that illuminate the black marble and spell out righteous gratitude for the victory this unknown martyr and his millions of comrades won.

Few symbolic inventions have been more magnificently suitable to the utilitarian needs of their time than this. It was a symbolism of such logic and universal acceptance that Westminster's Unknown Warrior was soon joined in his eternal duty by other comrades, each elevated to represent their fallen countrymen and women. Their graves, which are spread among national capitals like Brussels, Washington and Paris, all form a unique Valhalla, designed to provide a focus for innumerable grieving thoughts. The idea of selecting and elevating such a humble representative of the 680,000 slain came from a military Padre, the Reverend David Railton,

during the early stages of 1916: 'It came to me, it was somehow sent to me.'

The idea finally received official sanction from a cautious Government, Church and Sovereign in October 1920, each anxious not to upset public opinion. There was less than a month to go before the Armistice parade. So to a small temporary chapel at the military headquarters in St Pol-sur-Ternoise were brought four bodies, each exhumed from different places on the Western Front. They came from the Somme, Ypres, Aisne and Arras. Each had died in the early years of war, which ensured that nature's work would further hide their identity. At midnight a few days prior to the burial, General Wyatt entered the chapel and found four stretchers, each carrying human remains and covered in Union Flags. He made his random selection by touching one stretcher and the remains were placed into a simple oak coffin.

A military progress of sublime dignity began across France to Calais. HMS *Verdun* conveyed the Unknown Warrior to Dover and a train completed the journey to Victoria Station's platform 8 in London, where two Guardsmen kept sentry overnight until the gun carriage arrived. The Last Post was sounded at every stage and bowed heads saluted the passing coffin.

One-and-a-half million people paid their respects within the first weeks: they were led by 100 holders of the Victoria Cross, who provided a guard of honour at the ceremony. It would be impossible to count the incredible number who have paused since and contemplated the words, 'The most that man can give, life itself... for loved ones... the Lord knoweth them that are his...Unknown and yet well known.' But nearly a century on, lives lost in war are still being added to the the Unknown Warrior's roll. This is an appointment of unique and lasting significance. In a world which questions most things, no logic has yet been found to displace the powerful testimony of a single life given: it is an all-encompassing sacrifice.

Chosen to represent unfathomable sacrifice, **The Unknown Warrior** lies in Westminster Abbey surrounded by poppies under earth brought from Flanders. The inscription reads 'Beneath this stone rests the body of a British Warrior, unknown by name or rank, brought from France to lie among the most illustrious of the land…They buried him among kings because he had done good toward God and toward his house.'

'You have prepared yourself for service to God and other people, and have shown
yourself a worthy member of the Worldwide Scout Movement. I wish you God-speed
on your journey through life; may it prove for you a joyous adventure.'

ELIZABETH II ON QUEEN'S SCOUT CERTIFICATE

Chief Scout

The **Chief Scout** gathers Scouts around a camp fire at Gilwell Park, the headquarters of World Scouting, to relax after a hard day. There are few experiences which can match the feeling of individual success available to Scouts.

THE AUTHOR OF *SCOUTING FOR BOYS* found himself in command of a small town in British Bechuanaland, called Mafeking. Built on the open veld of South Africa, it was close to the Transvaal and was attacked soon after the outbreak of hostilities between Britain and the Boer government of President Kruger. The young officer who faced the assault on 12 October 1899 was the forty-two-year-old Colonel Robert Stephenson Smyth Baden-Powell. The Boers swept onto his position and, for 217 days, he held them off. By the time Colonel Plumer arrived from the north, with a relief column of Rhodesian levies, to rout the Boer commandos into the veld, the British public not only knew of the gallant resistance at Mafeking, they had fed on a stream of heroic reports about Baden-Powell and his men. The Relief of Mafeking, in the first phase of what was to be a bloody and miserable South African War, was a glorious episode designed for the warmongers to stoke imperial jingoism. Baden-Powell returned to England a hero; every boy held him in awe and his book on scouting, published during the siege, kept the printing presses at full speed to meet demand.

Baden-Powell's military service had been imperial by any standard. Starting in India, he went to Afghanistan, Malta and South Africa. The experience of these countries fascinated him, especially the way indigenous people used their land to survive. In action, in both Ashanti and Zululand, he learnt to rely upon vital information gathered from good reconnaissance scouting. A military scout is one who goes ahead and observes the enemy's location, numbers and strength. The word comes from old French *escouter*, to listen; and this is exactly what he did. Finally, his military training and Christian upbringing instilled a philosophy for life. All of these influences poured into the books he wrote and, when he returned to England in 1903, having organized the South African Constabulary, Baden-Powell discovered that youth leaders all over the country were using his book. The founder of the Boys' Brigade asked him to develop a scheme which would captivate boys and develop their citizenship. After an experimental camp at Brownsea Island, in Poole Harbour, he wrote a book called *Scouting For Boys* and, spontaneously, Scout troops formed around the country and across the empire.

The distinguished general retired from the army and ten years later, in 1920, attended the first World Scout Jamboree in London. To the acclamation of all, Sir Robert was made Chief Scout of the World. He had already made his wife, Lady Baden-Powell, Chief Guide, leading a similar but separate organization for girls.

By the outbreak of the Second World War, uniform was worn by everyone. Lord Somers, who became Chief Scout in 1941, led by example and wore his Scout uniform in the House of Lords. The Chief of the Clan Maclean wore his kilt as Chief Scout, until he was summoned to serve as Lord Chamberlain to the Queen in 1971, when Sir William Gladstone, great-grandson of Queen Victoria's disfavoured Prime Minister, led the Movement into Scoutreach, which took the advantages of Scouting life to inner cities.

Following the leadership of its Chiefs, the Scouts welcome everyone to their life of challenge and adventure. No longer a male bastion, it embraces boys and girls, taking them out of their lives into an different environment where they can learn more about themselves, how to succeed and the benefits of respecting fellow team-mates. The appeal of such qualities must work hard to compete with an increasing source of easy and readily available entertainment. The heroism of Mafeking is more questioned than venerated in a post-imperial and politically correct society where uniform is given scant respect by schoolmates. They are increasingly an alien community of leaders.

Adjutant of the Royal Military Academy, Sandhurst

At the conclusion of their training, Officer Cadets parade in front of Old College's impressive building at Sandhurst's Royal Military Academy. Moved here by the Duke of York two years before Wellington achieved his victory over Napoleon in 1814, it has gained a reputation for developing leadership skills in young men and women, which the armies of the world cultivate into command. The climax of this Passing Out parade comes when the graduates turn to march slowly up the ten steps and into the Grand Entrance of Old College. They are followed by the Adjutant on his grey charger. It is symbolic: cadets are passing from training into an active commission of responsibility. Those watching do not miss the significance, and this was particularly true in time of war when the far-off guns pounded out their insatiable hunger for young lives.

The first set of colours was presented to the Royal Military College (as it was then called) in 1813 by Queen Charlotte. Her husband, George III, had finally lost his sense of reason two years before, insanity from which he never recovered. His Queen's life then existed on the whim of their distrusted eldest son, Prince George, who was now Regent. The parade took place as it still does, in front of the Grand Entrance, with its eight large Doric columns supporting a pediment, showing the flanking figures of Mars and Minerva around her husband's crowned cipher.

Amongst the college's officers looking on would have been the Adjutant. It is an appointment which derives its name from the Latin *adjutare*, to aid, and every military formation has one. Their duties are to support a superior officer, to see to general administration and to oversee the training of recruits. At Sandhurst this came to include the disciplined drill of parade manoeuvres, the basis of all military philosophy and teamwork.

Major Frederick Browning, the urbane future commander of the Allied Airborne Corps in 1944, was Adjutant at Sandhurst between the wars. He is credited with giving the Academy's Passing Out parade its ceremonial climax, when the Adjutant follows cadets up the steps on his charger.

Whilst references exist to earlier occasions when it was done, the story goes that during the Sovereign's Parade of 1927, having held off throughout the ceremony, a storm cloud burst overhead. 'Boy' Browning, some say fearing for the cut of his best uniform and others that he sensed the opportunity to display some impressive horsemanship, trotted through the Grand Entrance behind the cadets. Whether or not he was responsible, the tradition has stuck. One reason is clearly symbolic: the Adjutant, who was responsible for the training, should shepherd them from Sandhurst to their new careers.

'Hard pounding this, gentlemen; let's see who will pound longest.'

Duke of Wellington at Waterloo, 1815

Passing in through this door marks the start of an officer's career and generations of commanders began this way. Recently the symbolism has been made complete by the **Adjutant**'s charger shepherding them up the steps at the climax of a ritual that occasionally precedes immediate despatch for service on the front line.

Major General Commanding the Household Division and General Officer Commanding London District

Despite declining numbers, the British Army has managed to retain many traditions enshrined in its regimental system of 1881. This system was designed to foster territorial loyalty and to formalize regiments into administrative, rather than fighting, divisions. One such division was specifically made up of the monarch's Household troops; regiments of cavalry and infantry which, through history, gained close affinity with the Sovereign's protection as the nation's Head of State. Today it is commanded by the Major General Commanding the Household Division.

Originally, after the Restoration in 1660, there were just two regiments, which are now called the Life Guards and the Grenadier Guards. Both acted as close protection for Charles II while he was in exile, loyalty which monarchs have never failed to acknowledge. These regiments are first in precedence for the cavalry and infantry respectively.

One regiment which served Cromwell loyally in the New Model Army changed allegiance a year after his death and, on New Year's Day in Restoration year, were marched by General Monck to London from their headquarters in Coldstream. Taking their name from that border town, the Coldstream Guards became the second regiment of infantry specifically responsible for Charles II's protection. It joined a group that had grown to four, with another regiment, now called the Blues and Royals, which re-formed in 1661, the year of Charles II's coronation.

In 1642 Charles I commissioned the formation of a regiment of foot guards from Scotland. In 1685 this was re-formed and came to England as the third regiment of foot guards: these guardsmen earned the nickname 'kiddies' despite predating all four others. The twentieth century's military needs boosted the Division. Irish Guards were recruited during 1900 and Welsh Guards in 1915 to meet the demands of the Great War. This completed what was to become *septem juncta in uno*, or seven joined in one.

Royal livery derived from the arms born by monarchs. As a result, scarlet, being the heraldic field colour for England's leopards and the tincture of Scotland's lion rampant, became the principal colour worn by royal servants in the courtly surroundings of palace life. So, when Charles I marked the establishment of Britain's first standing army in Windsor Great Park, on 15 February 1645, scarlet was worn for the first time. The famous red tunics which subsequently produced the squares of Waterloo and then fought for and policed the Empire, date from this day. And the ceremonial uniforms still worn for Royal Duties by most of Her Majesty the Queen's Household Division maintain the royal livery, which has long since been replaced by khaki when these soldiers fulfil their tactical role.

The close proximity between troops of all regiments and their Sovereign has always been maintained in the United Kingdom. This helped to enshrine loyalty in the personification of the State, rather than in fluctuating political leadership. Whilst fighting and dying for 'King and Country' catches in the throat of many today, the call served well in the difficult years of two world wars. For this same reason, the appointment of Commander-in-Chief, which no longer exists, provided a direct link between troops and their monarch. He commanded from the gateway of the king's palace, namely Horse Guards. From the office directly above the arch, the Duke of Wellington held the titular sway over an imperial and victorious army spread throughout the world. When the room was vacated by the Commander-in-Chief in the late nineteenth century, he was replaced by the General Commanding the Household Division, who was then called the General Officer Commanding Home District. His window looks out across Horse Guards' Parade where, in most years since 1805, the Household Troops have celebrated their close bond with the monarch by Trooping the Colour in a Birthday Parade.

The Duke of Wellington sat at this desk considering this view as Commander-in-Chief, when the statue of the Grand Old Duke of York provided contemplation for one military commander of another. The window looks out over Horse Guards' Parade where the Household Division stages Trooping the Colour. This is the **Major General**'s responsibility. Until she chose to take the salute from a carriage the Queen attended on horseback – as she is portrayed riding her horse, Burmese.

Commander-in-Chief Naval Home Command

Many cannon which now rest on the Quarter Deck of Nelson's warship, HMS *Victory*, where he died, are imitations. The originals became too heavy for the ageing timbers. The ropes that keep alive the function of this Napoleonic warship are regularly replaced. This veteran lady of Trafalgar still 'wears' the Union Jack and White Ensign: she is both the spiritual symbol of the Royal Navy and a suitable flagship for today's **Commander-in-Chief**.

IN THE DAYS PRIOR TO THE BATTLE that would cost Nelson his life, but earn him immortality in the annals of naval history, he gathered the admirals and captains on board his flagship, HMS *Victory*, to give them their orders. He spoke of 'The business of an English Commander-in-Chief being first to bring an Enemy's Fleet to Battle, on the most advantageous terms to himself… and secondly to continue them there, without separating, until the business is decided.'

Deploying what he himself called the 'Nelson touch', he held his audience throughout, writing afterwards to Lady Hamilton that 'some wept' and 'all approved'. High on *Victory*'s main mast flew Nelson's flag as Flag Officer and Commander-in-Chief. *Victory*, the longest-serving commissioned ship in the world (commissioned 1778), has worn the flag of the senior Flag Officer based at the Royal Navy's principal dockyard ever since Nelson's flagship was berthed there.

Distinctive flags were used to divide the fleet into three squadrons in 1625: each formation was given the colour red or blue or white. They flew distinguishing flags and ensigns of that colour and were commanded by a Flag Officer, or 'Flag man', called Admiral of the Red, Vice Admiral of the Blue and Rear Admiral of the White. However, in 1653 this order of seniority was altered to Red, White and then Blue, which remained in force until the squadron colours were abolished in 1864. These squadrons grew so large during the Dutch wars that they were each subdivided into Centre, Van and Rear Divisions, needing three Flag Officers for command: the senior division was commanded by the Admiral of the Red, while the Van and Rear Divisions had the Vice Admiral and Rear Admiral of the Red.

The Admiral of the Red, as senior officer of the senior squadron, was the Admiral of the Fleet: a post that became the most senior rank in the Royal Navy. There was a total of nine Flag Officer appointments, but as ageing commanders stayed in the service for life, they were known as 'Admirals of the Yellow'; an unkind reference to the yellow flag of quarantine.

Nelson achieved Captain's rank when he was just twenty years old, but it was another eighteen-and-a-half-years before he was further promoted, taking the lowest of 'flag-rungs', Rear Admiral of the Blue, in which he won the Battle of the Nile. By the time he was forty-two he had become Vice Admiral of the Blue. This rank hardly reflected the importance of the command he was then given as Commander-in-Chief Mediterranean.

The navy's role had grown. It no longer merely protected domestic shores (*see* Admiralty Judge of the Cinque Ports, p. 150) but it maintained growing imperial interests across the globe. The admirals who commanded these fleets needed status, and this was provided by appointment as Commanders-in-Chief.

As the Royal Navy's power and influence grew with that of the British Empire, Commanders-in-Chief were established as shore-based appointments as well as sea-going. During the Second World War there were three sea-going Commanders-in-Chief: they commanded the Home Fleet, Far East Fleet and Mediterranean Fleet. These were strategic formations in no way descended from the coloured squadrons but continued a triumvirate structure, each commanded by an Admiral.

From the start of the century the Commanders-in-Chief at Portsmouth have surveyed a dockyard that was once packed with naval power. Gradually masts gave way to funnel and Dreadnoughts were replaced by nuclear-powered submarines. Now there are many empty berths, but despite there being fewer ships, their strategic power considerably exceeds the great battleships of the past. In naval reorganizations of the 1980s *Victory* became the flagship of a new appointment, the Commander-in-Chief Naval Home Command, who is also Second Sea Lord.

Chief of the Air Staff

THE MADNESS OF THE WESTERN FRONT, which was endured by millions during the Great War of 1914–18, was an engine of slaughter. Stalemate forced soldiers to fight inch by inch across lifeless land, while enduring the pungent decay of their comrades, whose cadavers watched as the seasons exchanged the misery of sticky heat for bitter cold. The Prussian strategist Clausewitz had written a century before about the importance of maintaining strategic momentum, and commanders of the opposing armies struggled to find it in order to mount the vital breakthrough. Every advantage was exploited, including offensive operations in the air.

The aeroplane was in its infancy at the outbreak of war; the Wright brothers flew over North Carolina during 1903, and in 1909 the Frenchman Louis Blériot was the first to cross the English Channel. War always concentrates national resources and the aeroplane was a beneficiary of increased investment. Both the army and the navy recognized that the aeroplane offered an advantage, principally in reconnaissance. The first military aeroplanes were unarmed, with the pilots battling it out, keeping one hand on the controls while the other was free to wield a pistol.

The Royal Flying Corps was formed in 1912 as a naval and military air wing but, just before the war, the navy created its own separate formation, the Royal Naval Air Service, and they inevitably competed for resources. Germany developed the revolutionary Fokker monoplane, which was faster and had a fitted machine gun synchronized to fire through the propeller's blades. These challenges faced commanders of air operations and were picked up in London by committees, set up by Asquith's government, who tried to ensure that General Haig had the planes he needed and that they were efficiently administered.

In June 1916 and July 1917 German planes made two bombing runs on London. Public opinion demanded what the Board was coming to accept that Britain needed a coherent air force run by its own ministry in order to defend national interests and mount offensive operations. Thus the Air Ministry was born in July 1917, with a Bill before parliament which became the Air Force (Constitution) Act later that year. General Jan Smuts and the committee he chaired played a crucial role in this decision. Under this legislation, power rested with the Air Council. Gradually, the naval and military air components were brought together and the Royal Air Force was created on 1 April 1918.

A wounded soldier from the Boer War, who subsequently served in South Africa and Nigeria, became the first Chief of the Air Staff. Brigadier General Hugh Trenchard discovered that air operations provided a new outlet for his energies. During the Fokker offensive he pressed for retaliation when losses were heavy: a costly strategy that ultimately proved successful. As its first chief he was known as 'The Father of the Royal Air Force' and remained until 1930. During this time, he built the infrastructure for the Royal Air Force which grew despite strong pressure to dissolve the service back into the navy and army. Trenchard's successors inherited the Royal Air Force, which defended the country through the dark hours of the Battle of Britain. The young pilots who gave their lives in the skies against Goering's Luftwaffe did more than earn their hallowed memorial in Westminster Abbey; they ensured Britain's freedom to defeat Hitler.

The Chief now commands a flexible force for immediate deployment. Today's precision weaponry is a far cry from the pistols of 1914, and enables Britain to wield strategic clout throughout the world. As the first Chief would have wished, this power, which works in concert with the navy and army, enables the country to protect its interests while also contributing to the growing peace-keeping agenda of the United Nations.

The Tornado F3 provides an efficient asset in air operations but for protection it is stored in a hardened aircraft shelter (HAS) at RAF Coningsby. Fighter planes are organized for deployment in Squadrons within Wings within Groups. The **Chief** wears a flying suit with the stripes of an Air Chief Marshal on his shoulder.

Four-and-Twenty Unions in the days of yore
Played a silly sort of game and all were very poor;
Amalgamation came along,
The men began to sing,
'We've been divided long enough,
Unity's the Thing!'

HOLLAND (POLITICAL CARTOONIST)

General Secretary of the Transport and General Workers Union

The **General Secretary** can rest on philosophies established by his predecessor, Ernest Bevin, and the Socialist innovator Keir Hardie, as he marches forward in the changing political scenarios which Unions have accustomed themselves to fight. This struggle is enshrined in the banners which have led marches and which symbolize the rights that workers, since the Industrial Revolution, have gained for their successors.

In 1919 ERNEST BEVIN WON A MINIMUM WAGE of sixteen shillings a day for dock workers, many of whom had served five years in the trenches of northern France. These veterans felt undervalued and exploited, and with a war won at terrible cost, they were now ready to fight for themselves. A few years later, with Bevin's help, a group of unions amalgamated their resources and workers together into the Transport and General Workers' Union. It was democratic and led by an Executive, Chairman and Secretary. Through the depression and the Age of Modernization, this union has defended millions of workers against exploitation.

The origins of this exploitation went back to the eighteenth century. Firstly, from 1720 to 1770, there had been a phenomenal increase in the number of turnpike roads linking England's towns. At the same time, canals opened up communication to inland cities, facilitating the easy transport of goods. Colonies provided trade, European markets opened up and the advent of mechanization and mass-production brought about the Industrial Revolution which lasted for nearly a hundred years from the 1760s.

The infrastructure, factories and mines were built by poorly paid workers. Age-old human values that had operated in rural communities, based on centuries of mutual dependence between lord and servant, failed to keep up with the change. Nor did the Guilds of skilled men manage to adapt. Instead, working men who moved to cities for work found no philanthropic masters to protect them. Hundreds of thousands of families were exposed to hideous exploitation, dreadful living conditions and lack of political power.

Britain became the first industrialized society, an achievement which ill-rewarded those whose backs were broken to bring it about. Workers' Movements were formed but their power was worthless. Robert Owen, one of the few philanthropic industrialists, did his best to set up a general Trades Union in the 1830s; and the 1833 Factory Act, which protected children from some of the worst excesses of exploitation, was

a constructive result. That year George Loveless, a Methodist preacher, organized six agricultural workers in Dorset into a Trades Union. Known as the Tolpuddle Martyrs, they were convicted under a law forbidding 'unlawful oaths' and transported to Australia. However, the opposition of workers to their unfair treatment was sufficiently successful that they were eventually pardoned.

Here was the key: power existed in organizing a united response to bad management. Ironically, for it to work effectively this needed to be managed well and the growing union movement relied on persuasive orators with skills in advocacy; not just to take on the boardroom but also to encourage workers bred instinctively to obey and respect the boss.

The union movement fights on behalf of the weakest members in society. Principally it ensures that working conditions, like safety and pay, are protected. It campaigns for fair employment conditions, pursues prompt review in cases of unfair dismissal, focuses attention on inequity and has taken up socialist issues around the world (although General Secretary Arthur Deakin banned communists for a temporary period). In this vigil against maltreatment and prejudice, the General Secretary is the spokesperson. The appointment takes its legitimacy from the workers, whose membership make the union a potent force. Their interests are represented up to Branch, Region and Executive by the Shop Stewards.

Following legislation passed during the last twenty years it is now more difficult to deploy the strategic power of the Transport and General Workers' Union, both on its own and as part of the greater union movement. The nature of politics has also changed, as have the expectations and conditions of the workforce. Many improvements have been achieved since the union movement began, but the General Secretary vigourously maintains the vigil, aware that the office has an honourable history and with the current membership, a potent present.

Hereditary Keeper and Captain of Dunconnel in the Isles of the Sea

IN THE 1980s, A ROMANTIC HISTORIAN revived an appointment which was granted to his ambitious ancestor under duress by the Lord of the Isles. It carries with it echoes of the ancient kingdom of Dalriada, the monarchy established by the Scots. They were a people who claimed descent from Pharoah's daughter, Scota, who invaded Alba from Ireland and ultimately gave the unified country its name and identity. It also holds echoes of the earliest religious history of north Britain.

From the Sound of Lorne's ferocious waves rises the outline of the islands. They look like the peaks of a mountain range glimpsed above the clouds and are known as the Isles of the Sea. The northernmost one is called Dunconnel (Dun Chonnuil): a stark rock with sheer cliffs which once held a strategic importance to Dalriada, as it protected the open western flank. Named after King Conall, it still has the crumbling fortress he built high atop its bare rock, which proved an impregnable stronghold.

In 563, King Conall invited his kinsman, Saint Columba, to cross the Irish Sea with twelve disciples and to establish a monastery on the outpost island of Iona, at the south-west corner of Mull. From here, Columba converted the king of the Picts and the Pictish people to Christianity and went on to convert much of north Britain as well. It was a mission of remarkable success, built on the example of prayer and discipline set by Columba and his monks.

At the southern end of the Isles of the Sea is Eileach an Naoimh, or Isle of the Saint. Columba and his disciples often travelled here for seclusion. It had an even older religious history, with a ruined chapel used by Saint Brendan of Clonfert in 542. Close by are the old bee-hive cells inhabited by his monks and later by St Columba's. It was here that Columba is supposed to have prayed with such devotion that a refulgent glow came from his cell.

Nearby, supposedly, is the burial place of Columba's mother, Eithne.

Lachlan Lubanach, or Lachlan the Wily, was the son of Black John, an ancestor of the Chiefs of Clan Maclean, and knew all about the Isles of the Sea. In a bid for land and riches, he conspired in 1390 with his brother, Hector the Ferocious, to improve their lot. First they murdered the Chief of Clan Mackinnon, who stood in their way, and then they pursued Good John, the Lord of the Isles. He was the local monarch, who could grant the brothers land, and Lachlan wanted to marry his daughter. Lachlan and Hector planned a 'gentle' kidnap and rowed Good John to the treacherous rock of Dunconnel and took him to its fortress. Here their victim was made comfortable and manipulated into making promises of both land and the hand of his daughter in marriage.

The hapless Lord of the Isles was then rowed to Iona and encouraged to confirm his promises at the sacred Black Stone. As a postscript, and to ensure that the fortuitous meeting at Dunconnel would be remembered, Lachlan asked to be Keeper and Captain of Dunconnel in the Isles of the Sea, so they could always remember the happy meeting which brought about the agreement. After the long list of demands, this was a cheek but a trifle to Good John.

Ironically, Lachlan and his father-in-law came to respect each other greatly. The Macleans held their lands for three centuries, through their loyalty to the Lords of the Isles and then to the Scottish kings who succeeded them. However, they remained loyal to the losing side after the Glorious Revolution and, after the Jacobite Risings, paid for their mistake. The revival of a title which has little but a cheeky story to tell does at least draw our attention to a string of tiny islands, which are clues to the great spiritual and temporal stories of Scotland's formation.

Strachur, on Scotland's west coast, is not far from the ancient Dalriadic fortress of Dunconnel in the Isles of the Sea. The **Hereditary Keeper** wears a symbolic key that echoes the possession of the island which his ancestor tricked from the Lord of the Isles in the fourteenth century.

Doyen of the Court of St James

INTERNATIONAL LAW, with its treaties and protocols, provides the framework within which sovereign states can communicate. The practice by which Heads of State send representatives to other countries facilitates a passage of information and, in times of crisis, a means for formal communication. However, many Heads of State have evolved away from executive power and it is their governments which use these diplomats as a framework through which to advance their policies.

In Great Britain, all ambassadors are accredited to the Court of St James, which means that they arrive with Letters of Credence from their Head of State which they hand to the Queen in person. These documents act as a means of introduction into the monarch's court, and similar letters are prepared and sent with every British High Commissioner and Ambassador posted abroad. Commonwealth countries exchange High Commissioners and the carriage which the Queen sends as a welcoming courtesy is harnessed up to four horses, whereas ambassadors are drawn to their first meeting at Buckingham Palace by only two. The Diplomatic Corps, which comprises all the credential-carrying representatives, is headed by the Doyen. The word comes from old French and means the same as Dean, which in this case refers to his position as the senior member of the Corps, or body.

The Court of St James takes its name from St James's Palace in London which, despite the fact that the Queen lives at Buckingham Palace, remains the monarch's principal residence. It was built by Henry VIII on the foundations of a hospital by the same name and is supposedly surrounded by plague pits where victims of the Black Death were disposed of. In 1531 Henry moved his court here from Whitehall, but no monarchs have lived here since the end of William IV's reign in 1837. Despite their absence St James's remains the traditional home of the court.

In England, as in most countries, the Doyen is the longest-serving diplomat. However, nations with a strong Roman Catholic tradition have maintained the appointment exclusively for their Papal Nuncios – ambassadors from the Vatican State. This tradition reflects the manner in which diplomatic activity began in Europe. In medieval times the feudal system provided little scope for diplomats – disagreements were generally resolved by violence – but the Curia in Rome maintained its power and influence over far-flung Christian kingdoms through legations, embassies headed by a senior priest. Italy, which was until recently a peninsula divided into many independent states, developed this practice further. During the fifteenth century its diplomatic class established a network of representatives, which became the blueprint for diplomacy that subsequently spread through post-Rennaissance Europe.

England's connection with Rome was first cut by Henry VIII and was severed completely when the Pope excommunicated Elizabeth I. Until this point, despite ideological and theological differences, England deemed it pragmatic to maintain its links: Cardinal Reginald Pole represented the Vatican to Mary I and died the same day as his queen. Elizabeth then maintained an agent – ostensibly a spy – at the court of Pope Sixtus V. Since then, centuries of distrust between St James's and the Vatican smouldered. In the nineteenth century, Catholic emancipation and the need to nurture papal disapproval of Irish violence, brought the two courts closer. These differences were symbolically bridged when Elizabeth II sent her carriage to collect Monsignor Bruno Hiem, already acting as Apostolic Delegate, to be the first Papal Nuncio to the Court of St James in 1982. The succeeding Pro-Nuncio served long enough to become Doyen of the Court of St James: the first Papal diplomat to take precedence in England since the last Legate was dismissed in the sixteenth century.

Ambassadors cropped up like hay, Prime Ministers and such as they Grew like asparagus in May, And dukes were three a penny.

WS GILBERT, THE GONDOLIERS, 1899

Roman Catholic archbishops wear purple ferriolas, or robes, over their abatopiano, or piped cassocks. However, when they are Papal Nuncios the robe is made from watered silk. Pectoral crosses are worn by all bishops. The **Doyen** takes precedence over all other diplomats in the Court of St James and operates from his nunciate.

Queen's Swan Marker

IT IS STILL TRUE THAT ALMOST EVERY SWAN which lives upon the open waterways of Britain belongs to the Queen. Recent attempts to revoke this unique status have been overruled and the monarch keeps a post in her Household to maintain an historic tradition that retains a surprising relevance.

Monarchs since the thirteenth century have employed a member of the household to protect these royal birds; known variously as Swan Keeper, Swan Master or Swan Marker, each has been supported by a Swanherd of qualified helpers. Strict medieval laws were backed up with harsh punishments for those who did the 'bird royal' harm. These included imprisonment for a year and a day for stealing a swan's egg and, if anyone was caught killing one, the swan was hung by the beak with its feet just touching the floor, when the criminal had to pour out sufficient wheat to submerge its head until the beak disappeared from sight, costing a small fortune. In 1895, unlicensed killing would get you seven weeks' hard labour. Stealing a tame swan is still larceny and the Malicious Damage Act makes it an offence to either maim or kill one.

The romantic myth that Richard the Lionheart introduced the Mute, or tame, swan to England from Cyprus has been disproved. Six years before the Crusader's return, St Hugh of Lincoln was befriended by a Whooper swan that flew in to kill a herd of Mutes on the day of his enthronement as bishop, in 1186. Royal association with the swan brought a prestige and status among birds which found its way into successive statutes: Edward IV restricted applications for ownership, of which there were many, to men with land exceeding a value of five marks. This did not, however, stem the flow of requests, which made it necessary to develop unique markings on the beak, called Cygninota, to mark one owner's possessions from another.

By Elizabeth I's reign there were over 900 markings recorded, and each July new cygnets were marked according to the nicks and scratches on their parent cobs and pens. Any without markings belonged to the Sovereign. Cygnets were divided according to the parents, any over being given to the monarch or whoever owned the grass where they were found feeding. This was Swan Upping, or Swan Hopping.

When Edward IV was short of money, he applied to the City of London's worshipful Company of Vintners for a loan. In return, a charter of 1473 granted them the right to own some swans on the Thames. A few years later the same privilege was granted to the Dyers Company. Every year the Queen's Swan Marker joins the two Companies' Markers in six rowed skiffs to 'up' the swans between Sunbury and Abingdon. As they pass Windsor Castle, the Queen's Swan Marker gives the toast, 'Her Majesty The Queen, Seigneur of the Swans.' In the seventeenth and eighteenth centuries, when the great barges were still used, this was an excuse for feasting with Swan Banquets of roast cygnet. Times are very different now and this is a hard week's work for the oarsmen, who are all licensed Watermen and Lightermen.

In 1937 a member of Attlee's Labour government wondered, while analyzing the Civil List, why £600 was needed to pay someone for looking after the Queen's swans – surely they could look after themselves? However, the job entails much more than a jolly row up the Thames each year. Swans' need nesting sites of about six feet diameter and with river traffic increasing this needs to be protected. Also, information gathered during Swan Upping in July is passed to Oxford University who survey the health of the birds – something which has improved markedly since they recommended that lead weights used for fishing be banned. The Queen's Swan Marker also has an unending national responsibility to advise on the birds' welfare, with plenty of statutes to back him up.

The Swan Hook is used by the **Queen's Swan Marker** to capture birds on the River Thames when they need to be treated or marked. Scarlet is the colour of the royal livery; the Vintners and Dyers have their own. All help to protect the habitat of birds along a busy waterway.

Chancellor of the Exchequer and Master of the Mint

EACH YEAR, HER MAJESTY'S GOVERNMENT must balance the financial books and one budget, or sometimes more, is delivered on behalf of the Queen's ministers by the Chancellor of the Exchequer, who is responsible for keeping the country solvent, the ministries funded and all debts paid. With the Treasury's advice he is at liberty, subject to approval in the House of Commons, to set whatever rates of taxation and duty he feels are appropriate.

His appointment began in Henry III's reign when the Lord High Chancellor ceased to attend to the business of the Exchequer Court in the Treasury. Hitherto, he had sat with the king and all the Great Officers of State to administer the national finances, issue demands through the Sheriffs and keep records. The Lord High Chancellor and his clerk held the Exchequer seal, issued all writs and maintained the Pipe Roll, which listed every transaction and outstanding account. In his absence, the Lord High Chancellor left his clerk, who acquired the logical title, Chancellor of the Exchequer.

The Pipe Roll was laboriously maintained from 1130 to 1833 when, because the Treasury's role eclipsed the Exchequer, it was rolled up and closed. At the same time, the ancient Exchequer ceased to exist. Its name survived only as the official title of the national bank account, whose statutory name is Her Majesty's Exchequer, or the Consolidated Fund of Great Britain and Northern Ireland.

The same great Officers of State who sat around the chequered cloth of the Court of the Exchequer in medieval times were also present at meetings with the king and his Barons of the Exchequer. Since 1714 the duties of the Lord High Treasurer have been held 'in commission' and these commissioners are members of the Government of the day. For the greater part of the nineteenth century, the Chancellor of the Exchequer's role was seldom of cabinet rank, the Paymaster General and First Lord of the Treasury holding far more power. However, he is now the second name on the Commission for Executing the Office of Lord High Treasurer. During the twentieth century he has gained increasing power within the Cabinet, as the principal minister of finance. He is assisted by the Chief Secretary, who is in the Cabinet but not a Commissioner, and whose title logically stemmed from his role as fixer for the board. The First Lord is the Prime Minister. The other Commissioners are well-placed and hold their appointments *ex officio* to their duties as Government Whips in the Commons. This structure underlines the importance of maintaining parliamentary confidence and support in the financing of Government policy.

As Master of the Mint, the Chancellor takes responsibility for the rightness of the currency. Before 1870 the Master was called the Warden of the Standards. Henry III established the Trial of the Pyx in 1248, in order to find out whether the metals he handed to his many mints were being correctly mixed for the currency. Some took gold and mixed a poor alloy, taking profit from the difference; those who failed to satisfy the Trial were guilty of treason. Whilst the situation is a little different today, the rightness of the currency, its make-up, its output and the measurements of the coins are all checked. When the Verdict is ready the Master of the Mint attends, wearing Chancellor's robes, similar to those worn by the Lord High Chancellor (*see* page 42). Benjamin Disraeli became so enamoured with them that when he ceased to be Chancellor of the Exchequer he was loath to give them up. The Royal Mint has an approximate annual output of £84 million, and the quality must meet the demand.

The budget speech is a brief summary of a copious amount of detailed information, which is digested by parliamentary lawyers into the Finance Bill. Having delivered the speech, the Chancellor of the Exchequer, who has already told his Cabinet

Within hours of delivering the Budget from the Despatch Box in the House of Commons, the **Chancellor** broadcasts his reasons for changing taxation from No. 11 Downing Street.

colleagues how much they can spend, relies upon successful Whipping by his other Treasury Commissioners to get the necessary votes for his Bill to become law. It can be a tense time. Government popularity depends on getting it right. When Lloyd George's 'People's Budget' suffered defeat in the House of Lords, the constitutional crisis which followed led to the Parliament Act of 1911. Now the Lords have no say. But the Chancellor of the Exchequer must still use television to explain petrol increases to the population, whose votes can cast him from the Treasury.

Queen's Remembrancer

SYMBOLICALLY LINKED BY HISTORY to the Chancellor of the Exchequer is the Queen's Remembrancer: both surviving from the medieval Court of the Exchequer, the Remembrancer still receives feudal debts and services on the Sovereign's account. The first Remembrancer, Richard of Ilcester, Bishop of Winchester, was appointed by King Henry in 1154 'to put the Lord Treasurer and the Barons of the Court of Exchequer in remembrance of such things as were to be called upon and dealt with for the benefit of the Crown'. He represents an authority that is impossible to ignore – the Court of the Exchequer, whose power has been evolved into HM Treasury and the Inland Revenue. This power had been enforced since medieval times by the Barons of the Court of the Exchequer, and in particular by the Cursitor Baron, whose duties the Queen's Remembrancer now performs.

Each year the Queen's Remembrancer receives two symbolic debts owed to the Crown from the City of London at the Royal Courts of Justice. The first 'quit rent' is for a scrap of wasteland called the Moors near Bridgenorth in the County of Salop and is paid off by providing one sharp and one blunt knife: the first to cut 'tally' sticks out of hazel rods and the other to mark the debts between two people. These were then split and handed to both parties, to act as unalterable evidence. This strange payment has been made since 1211, a few years before King John was forced to sign Magna Carta. The second was first paid to Henry III's Exchequer in 1235 for 'The Forge', a tenement near St Clement Danes which can no longer be identified. This debt is settled with six horseshoes, of the size worn by war horses that acted as weapons against footsoldiers, and sixty-one nails, each laid out on the chequered cloth.

These quit rents were revived after the Restoration, in order that the City could reassure the Crown of its loyalty, having supported Parliament against Charles I. The merchants fared badly under Cromwell's Puritanism and so the City called for the monarchy's return.

The Remembrancer is custodian of a seal which the Queen gives to the Chancellor of the Exchequer as the symbol of appointment. Without it business in the Treasury and Exchequer Court cannot proceed. At the moment the Queen hands the seal to a politician, he becomes Chancellor until the moment he delivers it back. If there is a resignation or change of government the Queen's Remembrancer must hurry to No. 11 Downing Street so that this exchange can take place.

Queen's Remembrancer is one of the legal hierarchy's most ancient appointments, and has changed a great deal since Henry II appointed the first. Though the title is an honour, it is not just representative of something past. The Office is still responsible for the preparation of the Nomination of High Sheriffs; for suing in the Courts for all fines and sequestrations imposed by the House of Lords, the Court of Appeal and the High Court; for the enrolment of the appointment of Commissioners of Customs and Excise; and it is before the Queen's Remembrancer that the Lord Mayor of London makes his declaration on Lord Mayor's Day.

Since the Queen's Remembrancer Act of 1859 he has also presided over the annual scrutiny of the Coinage of the Realm. But his 'day job' is the onerous one of Senior Master of the Supreme Court, Queen's Bench Division, thereby administering the Central Office of the Supreme Court. The Queen's Bench Division, taking its name from the wooden bench which was once placed in Westminster Hall and used by the judges, is where commercial and maritime law, serious personal injury, breach of contract and professional negligence actions are heard. The Senior Master will hear relevant cases in their interlocutory stages as a judge in that Division. He is also the Prescribed Officer for election disputes and the Registrar of High Court judgements.

The word Exchequer comes from the chequered cloth which covered the table in the twelfth century Court of Exchequer and helped illiterate people understand their accounts visually. The **Remembrancer** gathers a symbolic debt of 6 horseshoes, 61 nails and 2 knives in rent for the Queen. Since 1859 he has presided over the annual scrutiny of the Coinage of the Realm. A Baron's tricorn hat symbolizes that the Court of the Exchequer was filled with barons.

Chaplain to the Oil Industry

TWO TRAGEDIES IN THE OFFSHORE OIL INDUSTRY confirmed the need for a full-time ministry. The first was the Chinook helicopter crash at Sumburgh Airport on Shetland in 1986; the second came two years later when, without warning, an entire oil production platform, known as Piper Alpha, exploded, killing 167 people.

Like every appointment in this book, the Chaplain to the Oil Industry emerged because of a need. As

the oil industry developed it created a community that fell outside the normal parish system provided by the Church's various denominations. During the early months of 1986 the Industrial Chaplaincy at Inverclyde sent the Reverend Andrew Wylie to assess the possibilities of establishing an Industrial Mission among the people involved with oil production. As a result of his work and the support it received from the Church and Industry Committee, the Industrial

Mission Chaplaincy to the Oil Industry and North East was established in September 1986; two months prior to the Chinook disaster at Shetland.

The oil fields demand courage from those who work in the middle of unpredictable seas. Under such conditions, agnosticism can founder as faith pulls quietly beneath the surface. The Chaplaincy now provides sacrament, conversation and a listening ear in this busy alien world.

The high wind-blown flame casts an orange glow over Brent Charlie platform in the middle of the North Sea as night falls on this man-made outpost. As part of the unique new parish formed by the oil Industry the **Chaplain** blesses the work of this remote community.

Boy Bishop of Hereford

A GIFT SERVICE WAS HELD at Hereford Cathedral for the Church of England's Children's Society in December 1973. To mark this event, the cathedral's staff reached back into history and revived the appointment of a Boy Bishop. It was a stroke of genius and turned back the ecclesiastical clock to Henry VIII's reign when the ancient practice, begun in the thirteenth century, was abolished.

The next year, John Eastaugh was appointed Lord Bishop of the diocese and was taken by the idea of symbolically handing over his powers to a child. He encouraged an annual appointment from among the cathedral's choristers, which received support from the Dean and Chapter. Ten years later, ancient ceremonies last exercised in Tudor times were dusted down and the ritual took root. But it was when the Post Office issued its Christmas stamps in 1986, including an illustration of Hereford's Boy Bishop, that the appointment grabbed public attention. It captured the magic which marks Christmas and provided a colourful service brimming with symbolic meaning.

When Christ was asked by his disciples, 'Who is the greatest in the kingdom of Heaven?' he called a child to his side and explained that unless they became like children they could not even enter its gates. Christ's birth was marred by the jealous rage of King Herod, who ordered all children in Bethlehem to be slaughtered. Both stories are symbolic of the supreme sanctity and innocence of childhood which is at the centre of Christian philosophy. Those murdered children became the Church's first martyrs and the Feast of the 'Holy Innocents', as they were called, was celebrated immediately after Christmas.

On Holy Innocents' day, the medieval church did much to elevate children symbolically, drawing precedent from pagan rites established by the ancient Saturnalia of pre-Christian Rome. These festivals permeated popular culture throughout the declining Roman Empire and were known collectively as the Feast of Fools. They were burlesque revelries akin to those indulged in for the Lord of Misrule. Apart from anything else, excitement of this kind raised spirits and attracted adherents to the faith.

In medieval cathedrals it was customary for the choristers to select from their number one to be appointed Episcopus Puerorum, or Boy Bishop. Known as Bishop of the Choristers or Bishop of the Innocents, he was nominated on 6 December, or the Feast of Saint Nicholas. A period of theological preparation took place until the Feast of the Holy Innocents, when the real Bishop handed over his pastoral staff to the child and installed him in the cathedra, or Bishop's throne. The Boy Bishop, assisted by two chorister Deacons, would then preach a sermon and bless the people. He fulfilled all the diocescan bishop's responsibilities except celebrating Mass. He then led all the choristers around the cathedral close singing carols to the priests for the reward of food and money: and it is believed that this established the tradition of visiting carol singers.

When the Reformation burst through the door of ecclesiastical practice, its chill wind froze out many rituals that appeared derisory to the worship of God and his saints, among them the elevation of an innocent over his episcopal master. Henry VIII's daughter, Mary I, thawed many of these restrictions but an Ice Age descended with Elizabeth I. And it is under Elizabeth II that the ice has melted.

Christmas at Hereford is now made more poignant as the evening of St Nicholas's Day begins. At Evensong a procession of candle-carrying choristers leads the Boy Bishop into the cathedral. The Lord Bishop hands over his crozier relinquishing his authority to the child. To the words 'He hath put down the mighty from their seat: and hath exalted the humble and meek,' the Boy Bishop is installed in the Lord Bishop's throne, before blessing the people. It is a lesson in humility for all who witness the occasion and it speaks deep into the soul something of the fragile nobility and wisdom of innocence.

Episcopal trappings of mitre, to represent the tongues of fire on his head, white surplice, pectoral cross and cope, or robe, prepare one chorister for the Cathedra, or bishop's throne. The crozier, or shepherd's crook, completes the vestments that remind Hereford that the **Boy Bishop** has been set symbolically at their head.

'Let a man humble himself till he is like this child, and he will be the greatest in the kingdom of Heaven.'

JESUS CHRIST

Credits

Appointments outlive the men and women who carry them for a generation. Inevitably, many who were photographed for this book no longer hold their appointments; some have moved on, others were removed by the Ballot Box and a few have died. Their names and styles are recorded here as they were on the day that their portrait was taken: the camera has captured an instant both in the lives of each holder and in the evolution of each story.

JC denotes photographs taken by Julian Calder; MC denotes photographs taken by Mark Cator.

President Nelson Mandela addressing both Houses of Parliament in Westminster Hall, London, 11 July 1996 (MC).

Page of Honour to the Queen: Master Thomas Howard, House of Lords, London, 15 November 1995 (MC).

Earl Marshal: The 17th Duke of Norfolk, KG, GCVO, CB, CBE, MC, House of Lords, London, 15 November 1995 (MC).

Knight Brother of the Most Ancient and Most Noble Order of the Thistle: The Lord Younger of Prestwick, KT, in the Thistle Chapel, St Giles Cathedral, Edinburgh, Scotland, 8 July 1998 (JC).

Historiographer Royal: Professor Christopher Smout CBE, Scottish Record Office, Edinburgh, Scotland, 14 November 1998 (MC).

Druids at Stonehenge during the Summer Solstice, Wiltshire, England, June 1982, (MC).

CHAPTER ONE
The Sovereign, Her Majesty Queen Elizabeth II in the House of Lords, London, 16 November 1994 (MC).

High Sheriff of Norfolk: Mr Francis Cator, Ranworth, Norfolk, England, 14 December 1995 (MC).

Archbishop of Canterbury: Most Revd. and Rt. Hon. George Carey in Canterbury Cathedral, Kent, England, 1 April 1996 (MC).

Archbishop of York: Most Revd. and Rt. Hon. John Habgood at Bishopthorpe Palace, York, Yorkshire, England, 8 June 1995 (MC).

Earl Marshal of England: The 17th Duke of Norfolk, KG, GCVO, CB, CBE, MC, in the Court of Chivalry, College of Arms, London, 9 June 1998 (JC).

President of Tynwald: Sir Charles Kerruish OBE in the Legislative Council Chamber, Douglas, Isle of Man, 5 July 1995 (MC).

Bishop of Sodor and Man: Rt. Revd. Noel Jones, CB at St Germain's Cathedral, St Patrick's Isle, Isle of Man, 6 July 1995 (MC).

Master of the Hospital of St Cross: Revd. Outhwaite; **Brother of the Almshouse of Noble Poverty**: Mr Harold Kay; **Brother of the Hospital of St Cross**: Mr Jim Heavens, in the Hospital of St Cross, Winchester, Hampshire, England, 26 November 1996 (JC).

34th Queen's Champion: Lieutenant-Colonel John Dymoke OBE, at Scrivelsby Court, Lincolnshire, England, 10 July 1998 (JC).

Chief Butler of England: Dr Siegfried Youssineau, the Lord of the Manor of Kenninghall, at the entrance of Kenninghall Manor, Norfolk, England, 25 July 1998 (JC).

Grand Carver of England: The 12th Earl of Denbigh and Desmond, at Newnham Paddox, Rugby, Warwickshire, England, 10 August 1998 (JC).

Lord of the Manor of Worksop: Mr John Hunt in Worksop Abbey, Nottinghamshire, England, 11 August 1998 (JC).

31st Hereditary Warden of Savernake Forest: The Earl of Cardigan, Tottenham Court, Wiltshire, England, 14 July 1997 (JC).

Official Verderer of the New Forest: Mr John Burry (standing) in Verderer's Hall, New Forest, Hampshire, England, 19 February 1996 (MC).

Head Agister of the New Forest: Mr Brian Ingram with Agisters Mr Robert Maton and Mr Andrew Napthine, in the New Forest, Hampshire, England, 20 November 1995 (MC).

Order of St John from left to right: **Prelate**: Rt.Revd. Michael Mann KCVO; **Bailiff of Egle**: The 3rd Lord Remnant CVO; **Chancellor**: Professor Mellows TD; **Lord Prior**: The 3rd Lord Vestey, in the Crypt of the Grand Priory Church, Clerkenwell, London, 10 December 1996 (MC).

Archdruid of Anglesey: Mr Robert Griffiths (Bardic name Machraeth), at Parc Caergybi, Anglesey, Wales, 24 June 1998 (MC).

Sergeant at Mace: Mr Patrick Webb; **Hornblower of Ripon**: Mr Alan Oliver, Ripon, Yorkshire, England, 12 June 1998 (JC).

Lord Chancellor of Great Britain: The Lord Mackay of Clashfern PC, QC, on the Woolsack, House of Lords, London, November 1995 (MC).

Lord Great Chamberlain: The 7th Marquess of Cholmondeley in the Stone Hall, Houghton Hall, Norfolk, England. 26 June 1998 (JC).

High Almoner: Rt.Revd. John Taylor, Bishop of St Albans, in front of the Great Reredos, St Alban's Cathedral, Hertfordshire, England, 29 June 1995 (MC).

Lady Marcher of Camaes: Mrs John Hawkesworth; and **Mayor of Newport**: Mr Jeremy George, by Newport Castle, Pembrokeshire, Wales, 22 April 1997 (MC).

CHAPTER TWO
Sword of State: Field Marshal The Lord Carver, GCB, CBE, DSO, MC, Westminster, London, 15 November 1995 (JC).

Knight Grand Cross of the Most Honourable Order of the Bath: Air Chief Marshall Sir Michael Alcock, GCB, KBE, in the Chapel of St John the Evangelist, Tower of London, London, 8 December 1998 (JC).

Knight Companion of the Most Noble Order of the Garter: The 8th Duke of Wellington, KG, LVO, OBE, MC, in Apsley House, London, 14 September 1998 (JC).

Lyon King of Arms: Sir Malcolm Innes of Edingight, KCVO, in the Mercat Cross, Edinburgh, Scotland, 8 July 1998 (JC).

Officers of Arms: from left to right: **Chester Herald**: Mr Timothy Duke; **Bluemantle Pursuivant**: Mr Robert Noel; **Portcullis Pursuivant**: Mr William Hunt TD; **Richmond Herald**: Mr Patric Dickinson; **Maltravers Herald Extraordinary**: Dr John Robinson; **York Herald**: Mr Henry Paston-Bedingfeld; **Norroy and Ulster King of Arms**: Mr Hubert Chesshyre LVO; **Wales Herald Extraordinary**: Dr Michael Siddons; **Howard Pursuivant Extraordinary**: Lt Cdr John Bedells RN; **Garter King of Arms**: Mr Peter Gwynn-Jones LVO; **Norfolk Herald Extraordinary**: Major David Rankin-Hunt MVO, TD; **Somerset Herald**: Mr Thomas Woodcock, at Palace of Westminster, London, 15 November 1995 (JC).

Lord High Constable of Scotland: The 24th Earl of Errol; **Slains Pursuivant:** Peter Drummond-Murray of Mastrick at New Slains Castle, Aberdeenshire, Scotland, 17 May 1998 (JC).

Master of the Horse: The 3rd Lord Somerleyton KCVO, in Windsor Great Park, England, 12 November 1996 (MC).

Master of the Rolls: Sir Thomas Bingham in the Round Room of the Public Records Office, Chancery Lane, London. 28 June 1995 (MC).

Chancellor of the Duchy of Lancaster: Dr David Clark PC, MP, outside the Queen's Chapel of the Savoy, London, 27 July 1998 (MC).

Hungerford office bearers from left to right: **Constable**: Mr Bruce Mayhew; **Tuttiman/Ale Taster**: Mr Barney Wilson; **Bellman and Assistant Bailiff**: Mr Robin Tubb; **Secretary of Commons Committee**: Mr Robert James; **Blacksmith**: Mr Jon Roots; **Honorary Fishery Manager**: Mr Denys Janes, beside River Kennet, Hungerford, Berkshire, England, 13 July 1998 (JC).

Lord Warden of the Stannaries: The 3rd Earl Peel on the cliffs near Botallack, Cornwall, England, 5 December 1996 (MC).

Duke: The 12th Duke of Northumberland at Alnwick Castle, Northumberland, England, 16 November 1997 (MC).

Court Leet and Court Baron of Alcester from left to right: **Bread Weigher**: Mr John Bull; **Fish and Flesh Tasters**: Mr Ian Taylor and Mr Michael Jackson; **Ale Tasters**: Mr William Bowen and Mr Glynn Bromwich; **Marshal to the Court**: Mr Jeremy Howell; **Constable**: Mr Ron Leek; **High Bailiff**: Mr David Young; **Lord of the Manor** (seated) The 9th Marquess of Hertford; **Surveyor of the Highways**: Mr Bob Allard; **Hayward**: Mr Keith Greenaway; **Steward of the Manor** (or **Seneschal**): Mr John Hill; **Immediate Past High Bailiff**: Mr Foster Richardson; **Searcher and Sealer of Leather**: Mr Bernard Hyde; **Brook Looker**: Mr Hamilton Leck; **Chapelayne to the Court**: Revd. David Capron; **Town Crier and Beadle**: Mr Keith Tomlinson; **Low Bailiff**: Mr Rory Duff, Alcester Town Hall, Warwickshire, England, 6 September 1998 (JC).

Lord High Admiral of the Wash: Mr Michael le Strange Meakin on Old Hunstanton Beach, Norfolk, England, 4 June 1997 (JC).

Captain of Dunstffanage: Mr Michael Campbell in the tower of Dunstaffnage Castle, Argyll, Scotland, 4 July 1998 (JC).

Searcher of the Sanctuary and High Bailiff: The Lord Weatherill of Northeast Croydon; **High Steward**: The Lord Blake of Braydeston, in St George's Chapel at Westminster Abbey, London, 30 June 1998 (JC).

Lord Mayor of London: The Rt. Hon. Alderman John Chalstrey, in the Lord Mayor's Coach, Musem of London, 10 June 1996 (MC).

Swordbearer: Colonel John Ansell; **City Marshal**: Colonel Mark Carnegie-Brown (mounted); **Common Cryer and Serjeant-at-Arms**: Colonel Tommy Tucker, City of London, 10 July 1996 (MC).

Tolly-keepers of Winchester College at College Hall, Winchester College, Hampshire, England, 15 June 1998 (MC).

Provost: Sir Antony Acland GCMG, GCVO; **Conduct**: Revd. Charles Mitchell-Innes; **Headmaster**: Mr John Lewis; **Colleger**: Mr Joshua Neicho in Lower School, Eton College, Berkshire, England, March 21 1999 (MC).

Choristers of King's College on the 'backs' of the River Cam, Cambridge, England, 17 October 1988 (MC).

Master of Skinners Company: Mr David Kemp; **Master of Merchant Taylors**: Mr Martin Clarke, Skinners Hall, London, 17 July 1998 (MC).

CHAPTER THREE
Archbishop of Armagh: Most Revd. Shaun Brady (Roman Catholic); and **Archbishop of Armagh**: Most Revd. Dr Robin Eames (Church of Ireland), in St Patrick's Cathedral, Armagh, Northern Ireland, 18 June 1998 (MC).

Gentleman Usher of the Black Rod: General Sir Edward Jones KCB, CBE, at the door of the House of Lords, Westminster, London, 27 June 1996 (JC).

Lord Clerk Register and Keeper of the Signet: The 12th Earl of Wemyss and March KT, JP in Petitions Office, Edinburgh, Scotland, 28 October 1998 (JC).

Washer of the Sovereign's Hands: Mr Peter Houison Craufurd with sons, left: Alexander and right: Simon at Cramond Bridge, Scotland, 14 November 1997 (JC).

Hereditary Falconer: Lord Borthwick, on Borthwick land near Heriot, Midlothian, Scotland, 11 November 1997 (JC).

Lord-Lieutenant of Gloucestershire: Mr Henry Elwes, Colesbourne Park, Cirencester, Gloucester, England, 5 August 1998 (JC).

The Queen's Body Guard of the Yeomen of the Guard in State Apartments, St James's Palace, London. 14 May 1996 (MC).

Standard Bearer of the Honourable Corps of the Gentlemen-at-Arms: Major Sir Fergus Matheson of Matheson Bt., with Major Ivor Ramsden MBE and Colonel David Fanshawe OBE, State Apartments, St James's Palace, London. 14 May 1996 (MC).

Children of the Chapels Royal in the Chapel Royal of St James's Palace, London. 2 May 1996 (MC).

Queen's Guide over Kent Sands: Mr Cedric Robinson, Morecambe Bay, Kent, England, 9 July 1998 (JC).

Abbot of St Benet-at-Holme: Rt.Revd. Peter Nott, Bishop of Norwich at St Benet's Abbey, River Bure, Norfolk, England, November 1995 (MC).

Master Treasurer of the Inner Temple: Mr Edward Nugee, TD, QC in Temple Church, London. 8 July 1996 (MC).

Master Treasurer of the Middle Temple: Mr Michael Sherrard QC; **Master Reader**: Mr Anthony Walton QC, in Middle Temple Hall, London. 28 November 1996 (MC).

Senior Grecian of Christ's Hospital: Miss Lucy Palmer at Christ's Hospital, Sussex, England, November 1996 (MC).

Bailie of the Abbey Court of Holyrood: Mr Patrick Cadel; **Moderator of the High Constables**: Mr David Ross-Stewart, in the Abbey ruins of Holyrood, Edinburgh, Scotland, 10 November 1997 (JC).

Bodley's Librarian: Mr David Vaisey CBE in Duke Humfrey's Library at the Bodleian Library, Oxford, England, 17 December 1996 (MC).

Elder Brethren of Trinity House on the quarterdeck of THV *Patricia* in the Solent, England, 7 August 1996 (MC).

Seigneur de Serk: Mr Michael Beaumont (plus six tenants: Mr Rossford de Carteret, Mr Christopher Rang, Mr Colin Guille, Mr John Brannam, Mr Philip Perree, Mr John Jackson) on the island of Sark, Channel Islands, 28 April 1997 (MC).

CHAPTER FOUR
Red Boxes: Mr John Thorn of Barrow and Hepburn, London. 20 June 1998 (JC).

Lord High Commissioner to the General Assembly: HRH The Princess Royal GCVO; **Pursebearer**: Mr Robin Blair WS; **Macebearer**: Mr James Stewart, Palace of Holyroodhouse, Edinburgh, Scotland, 19 May 1996 (MC).

Lord Justice-General and President of the Court of Sessions, The Lord Rodger of Earlsferry, First Division Courtroom in Old Parliament House, Edinburgh, Scotland, 3 July 1998 (JC).

Clan Chief: Colonel Sir Donald Cameron of Lochiel, KT, 26th Chief of the Clan Cameron, at Achnacarry, Inverness-shire, Scotland, 6 July 1998 (JC).

Captain General of the Queen's Body Guard for Scotland: Sir Hew Hamilton Dalrymple Bt, at Archer's Hall, Edinburgh, Scotland, 28 October 1998 (JC).

Speaker: Miss Betty Boothroyd PC, MP in the House of Commons, Palace of Westminster, London. 10 July 1995 (MC).

Governor of the Royal Hospital: General Sir Brian Kenny, GCB, CBE, at the Royal Hospital, Chelsea, London, 7 June 1996, (JC).

Gentiluomo of the Cardinal Archbishop of Westminster: Mr Anthony Bartlett OBE, in the Throne Room of Archbishop's House, Westminster, London, 3 September 1997 (JC).

Governor of the Apprentice Boys: Mr Alistair Simpson (seated); **Secretary**: Mr Jack Holland (left)**; Committee Member of the Browning Parent Club**:Mr Richard Dallas (right), in the Apprentice Boys Memorial Hall, Londonderry, Northern Ireland, 17 June 1998 (MC).

Privy Counsellor: The Lord Steel PC, KBE, in the National Liberal Club, London. 11 March 1997 (JC).

Admiralty Judge of the Cinque Ports: Mr Justice Clarke on Langdon Cliffs, Dover, Kent, England, 10 September 1998 (MC).

Sisters of the Hospital of the Most Holy and Undivided Trinity from left to right: Mrs Sparkes; Mrs Brice; Mrs Haw; Mrs Mansfield; Mrs Hunter; **Warden**: Mrs Pam Rhoades; **Chairman of the Trustees**: Mr Greville Howard; **Clerk to the Trustees**: Mr Waite; Miss Cooper and Mrs Scott being sworn in at Trinity Hospital, Castle Rising, Norfolk, England, 9 July 1997 (JC).

Woodman of the Ancient Forest of Arden: Mr Robert Hardy CBE, in woods close to his home, 6 November 1996 (MC).

Queen's Bargemaster: Mr Robert Crouch at studios in Clerkenwell, London. 11 December 1996 (MC).

Bargemaster of the Company of Watermen and Lightermen: Mr Robert Prentice and **winners of Doggett's Coat and Badge**: Mr George Saunders and Mr Robbie Colman, under Blackfriar's Bridge, London. 14 October 1997 (MC).

CHAPTER FIVE
Governor of the Falkland Islands: Mr Rex Hunt, Port Stanley, Falkland Islands. July 1982 (JC).

Bearer of the National Flag of Scotland: The Master of Lauderdale, Viscount Maitland, on Salisbury Crags, Edinburgh, Scotland, 16 May 1998 (JC).

Banner Bearer for Scotland: The 12th Earl of Dundee at Bannockburn, Stirlingshire, Scotland, 27 October 1998 (JC).

Cock O' The North: The 13th Marquess of Huntly at Aboyne Castle, Aberdeenshire, Scotland, 18 May 1998 (JC).

Atholl Highlanders: The 11th Duke of Atholl, at Blair Castle, Blair Atholl, Scotland, 23 May 1998 (JC).

Dean of the Arches: Mr Justice Owen in the crypt of St Mary le Bow, London, 30 July 1998 (JC).

First Church Estates Commissioner: Sir Michael Colman, Bt. on the roof of Church Commissioners' building, London. 21 October 1997 (MC).

Field Marshal: The Lord Bramall of Bushfield KG, GCB, OBE, MC, Aldershot, England, 24 July 1998 (JC).

First Sea Lord: Admiral Sir Jock Slater GCB LVO ADC, in the Admiralty Boardroom, Whitehall, London. 12 July 1996 (MC).

Governor and Commander-in-Chief of Gibraltar: Admiral Sir Hugo White, KCB, CBE, The Convent, Gibraltar. 11 January 1997 (JC).

Superintendent of the Corps of Queen's Messengers: Major Iain Bamber on the Grand Staircase of India House, Foreign and Commonwealth Office, London, 20 September 1996 (MC).

Senior Constable of Oxford University: Mr George Davis in front of the Clarendon Building, Oxford, England, 4 June 1998 (MC).

President of the Methodist Conference: Revd. Dr John Taylor in Wesley's Chapel, City Road, London, 10 July 1998 (MC).

Herb Strewer: Miss Jessica Fellowes by West Door of Westminster Abbey, London, 19 June 1998 (MC).

Master of Foxhounds: Captain Ian Farquahar, Badminton Estate, Gloucestershire, England. 5 February 1999 (JC).

Gorseth Kernow Bards from left to right: Mr Richard Jenkin; **Grand Bard**: Mrs Ann Jenkin; Revd. Brian Coombes; Mr Christopher Urew at Carn Brea, Cornwall, England, 19 June 1998 (JC).

Custos of Harrow: Mr Arthur Arnold with a Shell student and monitor, Fourth Form Room, Harrow School, Middlesex, England, 2 June 1998 (MC).

CHAPTER SIX
Baron:The 5th Lord Derwent; **Viscount**: The 1st Viscount Tonypandy; **Earl**: The Countess of Mar (31st in line); **Marquess**: The 7th Marquess of Bath, House of Lords, London, 15 November 1995 (MC).

The Tomb of the Unknown Warrior in Westminster Abbey London, 23 May 1997 (MC).

Chief Scout: Mr George Purdy at Gilwell Park, Essex, England. 5 September 1998, (JC).

Adjutant of the Royal Military Academy, Sandhurst: Major Alexander Matheson, yr. of Matheson inside the Grand Entrance to Old College, Sandhurst, England, 12 March 1996, (MC).

Major General Commanding Household Division: Major General Iain Mackay-Dick, MBE, in Horse Guards' building, London. 20 September 1995. (JC).

Commander-in-Chief Naval Home Command: Admiral Sir John Brigstocke, KCB, ADC, on HMS *Victory*, Portsmouth, Hampshire, England, 3 August 1998 (JC).

Chief of the Air Staff: Air Chief Marshal Sir Michael Graydon GCB CBE ADC in a hardened aircraft shelter (HAS) at RAF Coningsby, Lincolnshire, England, 8 November 1996 (MC).

General Secretary of the Transport and General Workers Union: Mr Bill Morris at Transport House, London. 26 November 1998 (MC).

Hereditary Keeper of Dunconnel in the Isles of the Sea: Sir Fitzroy Maclean of Dunconnel Bt. KT, CBE, Strachur, Argyll, Scotland, 19 September 1995 (MC).

Doyen of the Court of St James: Archbishop Luigi Barbarito in the Apostolic Nunciature, Wimbledon, London, June 1995 (MC).

Queen's Swan Marker: Mr David Barber by the River Thames at Cookham, England, 21 September 1998 (JC).

Chancellor of the Exchequer: Mr Kenneth Clarke, PC, QC, MP in 11 Downing Street, London, 26 November 1996 (MC).

Queen's Remembrancer: Master Robert Turner at studios, Clerkenwell, London, 11 December 1996.

Chaplain to the Oil Industry: Revd. Angus Smith on Brent Charlie Oil Platform, North Sea, 6 November 1997 (MC).

Boy Bishop of Hereford: Master Vaughan Hyett enthroned in the Cathedra of Hereford Cathedral, England, 7 December 1996 (MC)

In Pensioner at the Royal Hospital: Battery Sergeant Nicholas Keating MM, Royal Hospital, London. 7 June 1996 (JC).

Senior Drum Major Household Division: Senior Drum Major Steve Boyd Irish Guards at Wellington Barracks, London. 10 January 1997 (JC).

Index

In Pensioner, Battery Sergeant Nicholas Keating MM, aged 101, sits by his berth in the Long Ward of the Royal Hospital, Chelsea. His scarlet coat is based on the service dress from the Duke of Marlborough's time. He wears from left to right the Military Medal, the First World War medals known as 'Pop, Dick and Harry', the Defence Medal and War Medal from the Second World War and the Long Service and Good Conduct Medal. The black hat is called a Shako.